W9-BRD-833

The **Knowledge Management Fieldbook**

FINANCIAL TIMES
Prentice Hall

In an increasingly competitive world, it is quality
of thinking that gives an edge. An idea that opens new
doors, a technique that solves a problem, or an insight
that simply helps make sense of it all.

We work with leading authors in the fields of
management and finance to bring cutting-edge thinking
and best learning practice to a global market.

Under a range of leading imprints, including
Financial Times Prentice Hall, we create world-class
print publications and electronic products giving readers
knowledge and understanding which can then be
applied, whether studying or at work.

To find out more about our business and professional
products, you can visit us at www.business-minds.com

For other Pearson Education publications, visit
www.pearsoned-ema.com

Pearson
Education

The Knowledge Management Fieldbook

Wendi R. Bukowitz and
Ruth L. Williams

PRICEWATERHOUSE COOPERS

FINANCIAL TIMES
Prentice Hall

An imprint of Pearson Education

London · New York · San Francisco · Toronto · Sydney
Tokyo · Singapore · Hong Kong · Cape Town · Madrid
Paris · Milan · Munich · Amsterdam

PEARSON EDUCATION LIMITED

Head Office:
Edinburgh Gate
Harlow CM20 2JE
Tel: +44 (0)1279 623623
Fax: +44 (0)1279 431059

London Office:
128 Long Acre,
London WC2E 9AN
Tel: +44 (0)20 7447 2000
Fax: +44 (0)20 7240 5771
Website:www.business-minds.com

First published in Great Britain 1999
Revised edition published 2000

© Pearson Education Limited 1999, 2000

The right of Wendi Bukowitz and Ruth Williams to be identified as
authors of this work has been asserted by them in accordance
with the Copyright, Designs, and Patents Act 1988.

ISBN 0 273 63882 3

British Library Cataloguing in Publication Data
A CIP catalogue record for this book can be obtained from the British Library.

All rights reserved; no part of this publication may be reproduced, stored
in a retrieval system, or transmitted in any form or by any means, electronic,
mechanical, photocopying, recording, or otherwise without either the prior
written permission of the Publishers or a licence permitting restricted copying
in the United Kingdom issued by the Copyright Licensing Agency Ltd,
90 Tottenham Court Road, London W1P 0LP. This book may not be lent,
resold, hired out or otherwise disposed of by way of trade in any form
of binding or cover other than that in which it is published, without the
prior consent of the Publishers.

10 9 8 7 6 5 4 3 2

Typeset by Pantek Arts, Maidstone, Kent
Printed and bound in Great Britain by Biddles Ltd, Guildford & King's Lynn

The Publisher's policy is to use paper manufactured from sustainable forests.

Contents

Preface

It was the late spring of 1999, and the manuscript for *The Knowledge Management Fieldbook* was well along in the editorial process. We'd been writing about knowledge management – trading ideas, arguing strenuously, and experiencing occasional epiphanies – for more than a year. We felt pretty confident that we'd got it all hashed out, organized, and articulated, but we knew we were chasing a moving target. We just didn't know how fast everything would change and how soon we were in for another intellectual shakeup. By the end of the summer, we had both joined PricewaterhouseCooper's Intellectual Asset Management practice and we found ourselves in the midst of heated conversations about the terminology we had used to talk about knowledge management. It's been a sobering lesson in just how important language can be.

Intellectual asset management is a subcategory of knowledge management which is concerned with a specific class of organizational knowledge. Not surprisingly, IAM practitioners, many of whom interact regularly with both attorneys and financial professionals, are rather particular about how they define the term "intellectual asset." We realized, in looking back over what we had written in *The Knowledge Management Fieldbook*, that our own treatment of the term was less than rigorous. We are taking this opportunity afforded by the second printing of the *Fieldbook* to set things right.

In the first printing of the *Fieldbook* we used the term "knowledge-based assets" to refer to all those intangibles from which the organization derives value. You will see in this edition that we have very consciously replaced this with the terms "knowledge capital" or "intellectual capital." In the accounting and legal professions – disciplines from which KM practitioners borrowed the term – "asset" refers to something owned by the organization. As we note throughout the book, many of the most important sources of value for organizations – namely people and the knowledge they have in their heads – can never be owned by the organization. In fact, one of the greatest challenges of the KM practitioner is to find ways of deriving value from a resource that is not only not owned, but often ephemeral.

In this revised edition, we reserve the term "intellectual assets," or IAs, for those forms of knowledge that the organization has defined, codified, described, or otherwise articulated. Examples of IAs include computer software, business processes and methodologies, contractual customer or supplier agreements, knowledge bases, data, reports, and presentations, as well as patents, trademarks, copyrights, and trade secrets. IAs are also often referred to as "explicit knowledge" because they have been transformed from individual knowledge into something more concrete, such as a paper or electronic document or a set of rules or code. But there is an additional distinction between IAs and intellectual capital (IC) – organizational ownership. An organization *owns* its IAs, even if it doesn't own the knowledge that produced them. For example, organizations own software code written by employees, but they do not own the brains of those employees. Sometimes, as in the case of patents and other legally protected forms of IAs known as intellectual property (IP), the organization actually does own the underlying knowledge, or at least its application or expression.

This brings us to one of the core differences between KM and IAM, both of which seek to derive value from knowledge. First, KM is concerned with *all forms of knowledge* including knowledge which is unarticulated and uncodified. KM looks at the full spectrum of intellectual capital available to the organization. For example, KM might facilitate communities of practice – informal groups within organizations that are often responsible for the transfer of knowledge through tacit, or at least uncodified, means. Knowledge management requires an enormous cultural change component designed to create an environment in which information is shared freely within the organization.

IAM, on the other hand, deals almost entirely with articulated and codified knowledge and is therefore concerned with the conversion of IC into IA or IP. Not all IC can or should be converted into IA. Tacit knowledge is one example, which is one reason why tacit knowledge is almost impossible to transfer on a broad scale. When knowledge is articulated or codified, it often loses nuances of meaning that rely on individual interpretation and use. Furthermore, from a strategic perspective, some knowledge may not be worth articulating and codifying. Identifying which IC should be converted into IAs is one of the main tasks of intellectual asset management.

Converting IC into IA has several advantages:

◆ It is easier to *transfer* articulated and codified knowledge from one individual to another or from one to many.

◆ The organization is better able to *retain* knowledge in the event that its creator departs.

◆ The organization is able to *trade* or *sell* IAs irrespective of the individuals who originally developed them.

◆ The organization *can claim ownership rights* to articulated and codified knowledge and is in a better position to protect that knowledge legally should it decide that this is desirable.

KM is also concerned with codification of IC into IA, but the rationale for doing so is to achieve the first two objectives – transfer and retention. IAM takes another tack – it homes in on *ownership* and *safeguarding* of knowledge in order to extract value. However, achieving such organizational IAM nirvana often requires broadscale behavioral changes, and this is where KM approaches work hand in glove with those of IAM.

Like the knowledge management process presented in this book, IAM examines the alignment of an organization's entire portfolio of intellectual assets, acquiring, divesting, and leveraging these assets to achieve strategic goals. In fact, IAM is an intriguing place for organizations to begin their KM efforts for several reasons. First, IAM borrows a wide spectrum of tools and techniques from the practice of IP, which deals with the most concrete form of intellectual capital. Patents, trademarks, servicemarks, copyrights, and trade secrets are legally defined assets. As a result, their boundaries have been delineated and value can be placed on them. Even brand and corporate reputation are generally understood among business people as important levers for creating and sustaining value with stakeholders, and techniques for arriving at a financial valuation are in use. IP measurement and valuation approaches suggest a set of tools that help IAM visualize, measure, and manage assets that are currently outside the traditional scope of IP, bringing the same level of methodological rigor and value assessment to these important, but elusive assets.

IAM can also be an easy way to begin "selling" KM to senior management. While KM programs often struggle over how to bring home the bacon, IAM presents the organization with a series of early wins. Donating a languishing patent to an educational institution can yield a significant tax benefit; going after delinquent licensees can add dollars to the bottom line; being able to articulate a portfolio of technology assets can improve competitive position in joint venture or partnership negotiations; preventing employees from walking out the door with know-how that is essential to the business and setting up shop with a competitor fences off desirable markets for a longer period of time.

Finally, attention to ownership of intellectual assets is on the rise as organizations come to grips with the true locus of value creation. Many are seeking ways to legally protect assets, such as business processes and methods, that were once considered outside the realm of IP. Visualizing, organizing, and otherwise articulating this intellectual capital are first steps on the road to legal protection, and IAM provides the tools for moving the process along.

The Knowledge Management Fieldbook is a book about KM, not IAM. It is aimed at helping business people understand the implications of this new world in which we live, where we are required to manage what we cannot see. Throughout the book we ask people to look through a new management lens, one that we hope will encourage them to see their opportunities in an altered light. But KM is a field that is still finding itself – looking for sure footholds in a strange landscape. We believe that IAM is one of those footholds.

Wendi R. Bukowitz
Ruth L. Williams
PricewaterhouseCoopers

About the authors

Wendi Bukowitz and **Ruth Williams** are members of the Intellectual Asset Management group at PricewaterhouseCoopers, where they are using their expertise in knowledge management to further the organizational practice of creating and extracting value from intellectual capital. Bukowitz and Williams continue to break new ground in their work with organizations through projects that explore how previously un- and under-tapped sources of value can be transformed into intellectual assets. Within PricewaterhouseCoopers, Wendi is leading the effort to implement an innovative intellectual asset management (IAM) process that can be directly linked to revenue growth. Ruth is focusing on the development of successful practices and tools that can be used to implement IAM in client organizations. Both continue in their roles as thought leaders by conducting research initiatives that uncover trends in organizational IAM practices.

Wendi has also participated in such landmark initiatives as Arthur Andersen's Global Best Practices KnowledgeSpace, the Knowledge Imperative Symposium, the Brookings Institution Working Group on Understanding Intangible Sources of Value, and the Organization of Economic Cooperation and Development's Symposium on Measuring and Reporting Intellectual Capital.

Ruth has directed multi-client studies in a range of emerging areas including on-line communities, next-generation leadership, and collaboration with such leading organizations as Motorola, Shell Oil, Kaiser-Permanente, Ford Motor Company, and Sun Microsystems. Ruth was previously Co-Director of Arthur Andersen's Next Generation Research Group.

Acknowledgements

We would like to offer a blanket thank you to everyone who has supported our work on this book because there are far too many people to mention each one by name. You know who you are. However, we would be remiss if we did not single out a few of those who have gone above and beyond the call of duty in their support.

We would like to thank our colleagues who read early drafts of the manuscript and provided us with bracing and important criticism – Joe Cothrel, Sharon Oriel, Gordon Petrash, Colleen Burke and Ria David. We would also like to thank those who helped us complete the field test of the Knowledge Management Diagnostic and offered similarly insightful feedback – Lucinda Berlew, Laura Pitts, Drew Bartkiewicz, Kevin Lacroix, Keith Southey and Angela Hornsby. Ruth Schmidt, one of the best graphic designers we know, contributed her talents to the Knowledge Management Process Framework.

Most of the interviewees who helped us create the Profiles and Points of view in the *Fieldbook* are mentioned by name in the text. We would like to recognize those who are not: Henrik Jensen, The Danish Ministry of Business; Anita Schedin, Skandia; Dr Mark Moore and Declan Hayden, Massey-Ferguson; Colin Jones, Rover Group; Tracy Hutcheon and Keith Southey, Canadian Imperial Bank of Commerce; Ron Helgeson, Teltech; Margareta Barchan, Celemi; Henry Gowen, 3M; Kristian Ulrik Eiberg, Oticon; and Lisbet Thyge Frandsen, Ramboll.

The staff at Financial Times Prentice Hall have been enthusiastic boosters of our work and we thank everyone – especially Pradeep Jethi, our editor; Penelope Allport, our project manager; Helen Baxter, our copy editor; and Claudia Orrell, who looked after sales and marketing.

Lastly, we would like to thank our families for supporting our decision to make this *Fieldbook* a reality.

Wendi R. Bukowitz
Ruth L. Williams
PricewaterhouseCoopers

1 How to use The Knowledge Management Fieldbook

Toto, I've a feeling we're not in Kansas anymore.

Dorothy from *The Wizard of Oz*[1]

The concepts and theories of knowledge management have been well documented. Yet, there are few, if any other guidebooks for thinking about how to implement knowledge management within the organization. That is because, to paraphrase Tom Stewart's blunt assertion in his book, *Intellectual Capital*, no one knows how to write a cookbook with knowledge management recipes. We agree with him. Knowledge management is a fast-moving field that has been created by the collision of several others – human resources, organizational development, change management, information technology, brand and reputation management, performance measurement and valuation. New understanding is generated every day as organizations experiment, learn, discard, retain, adapt and move on.

However, while there is not a cookbook solution to implementing and achieving improvements in knowledge management performance, paths have emerged that, in the case of some organizations, have yielded benefits. *The Knowledge Management Fieldbook* charts those paths, using workbook techniques that permit you to make connections between concepts and specific actions. The principle that has guided the creation of *The Knowledge Management Fieldbook* is usefulness. We have designed the *Fieldbook* to encourage scribbling in the margins with ideas, doodles and reactions. This *Fieldbook* is really a work in progress. We have provided you with building blocks from which we hope you will fashion a vision of knowledge management in your organization and construct a concrete set of first steps that can help you move toward it.

The scope of the Fieldbook

You may already have your own definition of knowledge management. Here is ours:

Knowledge management is the process by which the organization generates wealth[2] from its knowledge or intellectual capital.

Wealth results when an organization uses knowledge to create more efficient and effective processes. Like traditional reengineering, this has a bottom-line impact because it lowers cost (you do not reinvent the wheel) or because it reduces cycle time (you get what you need faster, you get it out the door to the customer faster, the customer pays you faster) which improves cash flow. Wealth also results when an organization uses knowledge to create customer value. A top-line impact occurs when intellectual assets are used to boost innovation and promote the development of unique market offerings which command a price premium.

> **Wealth results when an organization uses knowledge to create customer value.**

The definition of knowledge management begs another definition – that of intellectual capital or knowledge:

Intellectual Capital or Knowledge: Anything valued by the organization that is embedded in people or derived from processes, systems, and the organizational culture – individual knowledge and skills, norms and values, databases, methodologies, software, know-how, licenses, brands, and trade secrets, to name a few.

One critical distinction between intellectual capital and what has traditionally been deemed value-generating in organizations – physical "tangible" assets – is that it is not always owned by the organization. This means that deriving benefit from knowledge or intellectual capital is not under the organization's direct control. In fact, some intellectual capital is better thought of as rented, leased or borrowed. Gordon Boronow, the President and COO of American Skandia, an insurance company headquartered in Sweden, goes so far as to suggest that much of an organization's intellectual capital is volunteered on a daily basis. The value generated results from discretionary acts on the part of individuals, thus the process of extracting that value must be managed far differently from the process of extracting value from tangible assets.

Throughout the *Fieldbook* we use the terms knowledge and intellectual capital more or less interchangeably. When we use knowledge to mean organizational knowledge, then it falls within our definition of intellectual capital. But when we use knowledge to mean individual knowledge, some of it falls within the boundaries of our definition and some does not. What individuals know may or may not be of value to the organization. If it is not, we would not consider it a focus of knowledge management. The *Fieldbook* takes the position that a process for generating, building

> **Some intellectual capital is better thought of as rental, leased or borrowed.**

and extracting value from knowledge *does* exist. Some of its elements can be overtly managed in the way that most organizational processes are managed, while other elements must be managed indirectly, by forming hospitable environments in which knowledge can be created and shared. The *Fieldbook* examines both the process and the environmental conditions by which organizations generate wealth from their intellectual capital or knowledge.

> **What individuals know may or may not be an asset to the organization.**

The *Fieldbook* takes the position that a process for generating, building and extracting value from knowledge *does* exist. Some of its elements can be overtly managed in the way that most organizational processes are managed, while other elements must be managed indirectly, by creating hospitable environments in which knowledge can be created and shared. The *Fieldbook* examines both the process and the environmental conditions by which organizations generate wealth from their intellectual capital.

Knowledge management: why now?

Information and communications technologies are one set of major forces that has moved knowledge management front and centre. These technologies have made it possible for people to share enormous amounts of information unconstrained by the boundaries of geography and time. As floods of information course through organizations, people quite naturally begin to ask, 'Does this information really help me?' and 'Is this the best way to get it?' The answers to these questions are typically qualified 'yeses' because while these technologies are changing the way we create, transfer and use knowledge, they cannot wholly replace low-tech, high-touch[3] methods. In fact, some forms of knowledge can only be developed and shared using these more traditional approaches.

> **Information and communications technologies are one set of major forces that has moved knowledge management front and centre.**

The idea of different forms of knowledge was introduced to the business world by two of the most influential thinkers in the knowledge management arena, Ikujiro Nonaka and Hirotaka Takeuchi. In 1991 Nonaka authored an article that appeared in the *Harvard Business Review* and in 1995 along with Takeuchi, the theories presented in it were expanded in *The Knowledge-Creating Company*. While the book is complex and introduces many concepts, one of the most important is the distinction between explicit and tacit knowledge.

'Explicit knowledge' is knowledge that individuals are able to express fairly easily using language or other forms of communication – visuals, sound, movement. In the *Fieldbook*, we treat explicit knowledge as equivalent to information. 'Tacit knowledge' is knowledge that an individual is unable to articulate and thereby convert into information. Tacit knowledge is more useful to an organizational system if it can be transferred to others so they too can use it. Transfer of explicit knowledge is relatively straightforward. Transfer of tacit knowledge can be achieved either by first converting it into explicit knowledge and then sharing it, or by using approaches in which it is never made explicit. Another way to look at forms of knowledge, which may be more helpful to organizations than the tacit versus explicit distinction, is as follows:

1 **known knowledge**: knowledge that the individual *knows* she knows.

2 **unknown knowledge**: knowledge that the individual *does not know* she knows because it has become embedded in the way she works.

Both forms of knowledge are critical to the organization, and knowledge management is concerned with sharing both types:

◆ **Helping knowers share what they know they know.** For example, a person may know a great deal about the pharmaceutical industry, but unless he writes about it, creates a presentation, mentors others, or gives a speech, the knowledge benefits only one person. There are many tools and approaches that organizations can use – both technology- and people-based – to facilitate the process of communicating and sharing known knowledge by converting it into information.

On the whole, knowledge management, especially if it is information technology-based, is concerned with known knowledge. What most companies call 'turning tacit into explicit knowledge' is not really that at all. Companies typically try to get people to share what they know they know, but have not bothered to share. There are often deeper reasons than lack of time that account for the fact that experts do not share knowledge. Identifying and removing these obstacles is an important part of successful knowledge management.

> There are often deeper reasons than lack of time that account for the fact that experts do not share knowledge.

◆ **Helping knowers articulate and share what they do not know they know.** For example, someone may spend several years serving a particular customer. He may be so expert at conducting this type of business that certain key ways of operating become habits, so routine that they are done without thinking in much the same way that automobile commuters can arrive at their destinations with little memory of actually driving there. Bringing this kind of knowledge to a more conscious level so that it can then be shared with others is often an unfamiliar process to the expert. Groups also go through this unfamiliar process when they try to understand what they have learned from a particular work experience.

Getting experts to articulate unknown knowledge requires skilled observation, facilitation and interviewing techniques as well as the ability to codify the knowledge in a form that many people can consume. Nevertheless, converting unknown knowledge into information may not be the best way to transfer it. Some types of knowledge lose something in the translation when an attempt is made to represent them as information. Instead of wasting energy 'making tacit knowledge explicit' organizations may be better served by focusing on tacit-to-tacit forms of transfer. Tacit-to-tacit transfer includes such techniques as mentoring, on-the-job experiences, and apprenticeships. Its major drawback is that it results in a transfer to only a small number of recipients.

> **Some types of knowledge lose something in the translation when an attempt is made to represent them as information.**

Now we come full circle to the impact of information and communications technologies on knowledge management. Standard information technologies such as databases and intranets speed the delivery of known knowledge throughout the organization. Newer technologies that are becoming more widespread support the transfer of unknown knowledge. For example, video conferencing via satellite allows people to observe demonstrations and engage in real-time dialogue that approximates the tacit-to-tacit transfer. These technologies reduce the scope of the trade-off between richness, or depth of knowledge, and reach, or the extent to which knowledge can be diffused by creating an environment that is both high-tech and high-touch. They are moving us towards a both/and rather than either/or world (see Figure 1.1). Evans and Wurster introduced this simple model for understanding the way that technology is changing the economics of information. We have adapted the model to show how technology is gradually blurring the distinction between types of knowledge that at one time required radically different modes for creation, transfer, and use by moving us toward a high-tech, high-touch work environment.

The other set of forces that has pushed knowledge management to the fore is the legacy of reengineering and downsizing which has resulted in a serious brain drain for many organizations. Brain drain takes two basic forms:

1 Experienced people leave under their own steam.

2 Experienced people are cut loose as part of an across-the-board downsizing initiative.

> **A more insidious form of brain drain occurs because reengineering rarely factors knowledge flows and filters into its equation for process efficiency and effectiveness.**

Many people leave their employers through voluntary early retirement or by accepting severance packages. The problem is that often the best people – those confident of finding work elsewhere or of going into business for themselves – are the ones who take advantage of these programmes. When they do, critical knowledge and skills walk out the door.

A more insidious form of brain drain occurs because reengineering rarely factors knowledge flows

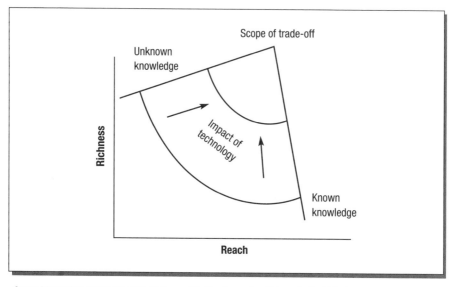

Source: Adapted from chart in the article 'Stategy and the New Economics of Information' by Philip Evans and Tom Wurster of The Boston Consulting Group, Inc. © 1997

Fig 1.1 ◆ How technology is blurring the distinction between types of knowledge

> **A key role of middle managers has been to make meaning or knowledge from the information gathered at the front line.**

and filters into its equation for process efficiency and effectiveness. This means that the less than obvious but equally critical knowledge is forced out the door too, typically in the person of the middle manager. Downsizing has eviscerated the ranks of middle management in most organizations. Middle managers have been widely considered a fatty layer between the front line and senior executives that should be dieted out of existence. However, a key role of middle managers has been to *make meaning* or knowledge from the information gathered at the front line, a task for which the senior executives of the organization generally have neither the time nor the appropriate perspective.

Nonaka and Takeuchi described the dilemma of the vanishing middle manager in *The Knowledge-Creating Company*. They describe middle managers as the strategic 'knot' that binds top management with front-line workers. 'They are a bridge between the visionary ideals of the top and the often chaotic realities of business confronted by front-line workers ... they are the true "knowledge engineers" of the knowledge-creating company'.[4] Henry Mintzberg, a professor of management, also envisions middle managers as important levers for change in organizations. Mintzberg asserts that organizations really function as a set of concentric rings rather than as a pyramidal cascade of reporting relationships.[5] Sandwiched between senior executives and front-line workers, middle managers perform an even more critical role than binding top to bottom or inner to outer core. They tie the company together *horizontally* by looking for opportunities to leverage skills, methodologies and capabilities – in other words, organizational knowledge. Closer to the marketplace than the senior executive and possessing a more strategic perspective than the front-line worker, the middle manager realizes the potential of strategy by binding it to tactics (see Figure 1.2).

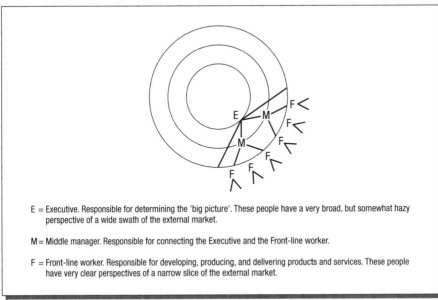

E = Executive. Responsible for determining the 'big picture'. These people have a very broad, but somewhat hazy perspective of a wide swath of the external market.

M = Middle manager. Responsible for connecting the Executive and the Front-line worker.

F = Front-line worker. Responsible for developing, producing, and delivering products and services. These people have very clear perspectives of a narrow slice of the external market.

Source: Adapted from 'Musings on Management: ten ideas designed to rile everyone who cares about management,' Henry Mintzberg, *Harvard Business Review*, July–August, 1996, pp. 61–67

Fig 1.2 ◆ Middle manager as a strategic knot and horizontal link

> **Knowledge management represents an effort to repair damage and an insurance policy against loss of organizational memory in the future.**

Once middle management was 'out' it was not surprising that knowledge management was 'in'. Knowledge management represents an effort to repair past damage and an insurance policy against loss of organizational memory in the future. Knowledge management is about re-establishing a context for connection, much of which was disrupted by reengineering. These connections can be between different types of information, people and information, and people and other people. Knowledge management covers both new and old, familiar and unfamiliar territory. Deciding where to start can be daunting, but it is the challenge that most knowledge management practitioners face.

Who should use this book

The Knowledge Management Fieldbook is a thinking person's guide to the subject for those who:

◆ already understand why knowledge management is important;

◆ have committed themselves to action;

◆ want to know what to do next.

You will not find a detailed argument about the importance of knowledge management or a justification for embarking on knowledge management activities in this book. We assume that you already accept the need to think more closely about and better manage the flows of knowledge through your organization to extract value from them. If you would like to read or refer to a book that extensively traces the emergence of the knowledge management movement and its rationale, we have provided you with a selected bibliography at the end of the *Fieldbook* which lists some excellent sources. What you will find in this book is not THE ANSWER, but a set of answers that are based on the strategies and tactics of pioneering organizations that are using knowledge management to improve business performance.

We also assume that you are beyond the point of wondering whether you should do something about knowledge management and have already decided that some or all of your activities should be devoted to it. Some of you may be adding this new responsibility to an existing job, others of you may have been tapped to focus exclusively on knowledge management for your entire organization or a strategically critical segment of it.

People responsible for constructing an organizational response to the knowledge management challenge come from a wide range of functional and operating groups. The knowledge management movement is still in its early stages of evolution, and even though there are knowledge managers and chief knowledge officers, what the landscape will eventually look like is uncertain. Yet, it seems to us that these many different functional and operating paths all lead to the same organizational intersection – the creation and management of knowledge flows in order to generate organizational wealth. The purpose of *The Knowledge Management Fieldbook* is to offer you a framework for thinking about the knowledge management process and a guide for acting on your insights.

> The knowledge management movement is still in its early stages of evolution, and even though there are knowledge managers and chief knowledge officers, what the landscape will eventually look like is uncertain.

Organization of the Fieldbook: the Knowledge Management Process Framework

The contents of *The Knowledge Management Fieldbook* are organized by the Knowledge Management Process Framework (see Figure 1.3). The Knowledge Management Process Framework follows two streams of activity that occur simultaneously in organizations:

1 the day-to-day use of knowledge to respond to demands or opportunities from the marketplace;

2 the more long-range process of matching intellectual capital to strategic requirements.

The framework is a simplified way of thinking about how organizations generate, maintain and deploy a strategically correct stock of knowledge-based assets to create value. We believe that all elements within the process must be managed in relation to one another in order to achieve the right mix and amount of knowledge and the capability to deploy it.

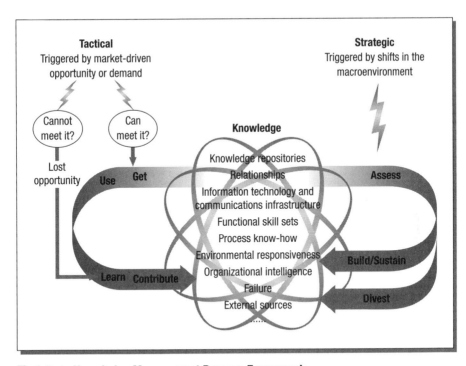

Fig 1.3 ◆ **Knowledge Management Process Framework**

The tactical process

The tactical side of the knowledge management process spans four basic steps as people gather the information they need for their daily work, use knowledge to create value, learn from what they create and, ultimately, feed this new knowledge back into the system for others to use as they tackle problems of their own. Each step requires the participation of everyone in the organization to some degree. The activities that define these process steps are not well-bounded, so we have depicted them on a continuum. However, each process step does have a core set of activities that cohere well enough to distinguish one step from the next. The following sections describe each of these core activities.

Get

The processes 'Get' and 'Use' are the most familiar to organizations. After all, people have always sought out information and then used it to solve problems, make decisions or create new products and services. However, the advent of new technologies that allow an almost unimaginable quantity of information to flow into the organization is changing the face of 'Get'. Now, instead of being forced to take action based on little or no information, people are more likely to find that the challenge is making their way through piles of irrelevant information to get to the one 'nugget' that is critical to their needs. How can this process be made more *efficient*? Mainly through the tools and services that the organization makes available to its members.

Use

When it comes to using information, innovation has become the byword of the day. How can members of the organization combine information in new and interesting ways to create more *innovative* solutions? It becomes critical for people to climb out of their silos and look for ideas under rocks and in nooks and crannies they would not otherwise have considered. The organization can provide many tools to enhance out-of-the box thinking, but even more important is to establish the kind of environment where creativity, experimentation and receptivity to new ideas are encouraged.

> When it comes to using information, innovation has become the byword of the day.

Learn

The processes 'Learn' and 'Contribute' are relatively new to organizations. This is not to suggest that in the past no one learned from their experiences or contributed to the organizational knowledge base. However, the formal recognition of these processes as a means of creating competitive advantage *is* new. The challenge for organizations is

> **The challenge for organizations is to find ways to embed the learning process into the way people work.**

to find ways to embed the learning process into the way people work. This means resisting the crisis mentality that always places short-term needs ahead of engaging in structured reflection that has the potential to pay off in the longer term.

Contribute

Getting employees to contribute what they have learned to the communal knowledge base is one of the toughest nuts organizations have to crack. On the one hand, companies can save time and money by transferring 'best practices' across the organization and by applying knowledge gained from one experience to another. Technology has made it relatively easy to organize, post and transfer certain types of information. On the other hand, contribution is not only time consuming, but is also seen as a threat to individual employee viability. Creating a knowledge management infrastructure can help with some of the onerous requirements of 'packaging' information for organization-wide consumption. The greater challenge is convincing people that contribution will ultimately pay off both for the organization and for themselves.

The strategic process

The right-hand side of the Knowledge Management Process Framework illustrates knowledge management at the strategic level, where the goal is alignment of the organization's knowledge strategy with the overall business strategy. Strategic-level knowledge management calls for a continual assessment of existing intellectual capital and a comparison with future needs. While individuals and groups are clearly involved in providing the information that eventually impacts resource allocation decisions, this part of the knowledge management process is more particularly concerned with the role of specific groups and organizational leadership. Yet looking at the organization through a knowledge management lens calls forth a whole new model of the business – one that requires a new form of management and a new contract with the individuals that comprise the system and determine its success. It is not leadership as usual, but leadership as a partner with middle management and the front line.

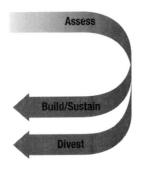

Assess

Organizations have not traditionally considered evaluating intellectual capital to be a part of the strategic planning process but this is precisely what strategic-level knowledge management entails. Assessment requires the organization to define its mission-critical knowledge and map current intellectual capital against future knowledge needs. This process requires pulling in a much more eclectic set of information from

> **Developing metrics that demonstrate whether the organization is growing its knowledge base and profiting from its investment in intellectual capital will be an increasing organizational challenge.**

a wider range of sources than management has considered in the past. Developing metrics that demonstrate whether the organization is growing its knowledge base and profiting from its investment in intellectual capital will be an increasing organizational challenge.

Build and Sustain

This step in the knowledge management process, which ensures that future intellectual capital will keep the organization viable and competitive, requires a fresh look at what it means to manage. Increasingly, organizations will build their intellectual capital through relationships – with employees, suppliers, customers, the communities in which they operate and even competitors. Deriving value from these relationships is what will ultimately force traditional management – which emphasizes direct control of people – to give way to a more facilitative style which emphasizes the management of environments and enablers.

Divest

> **Some knowledge can be *more* valuable if it is transferred outside the organization.**

There is a tendency for organizations to hold on to physical assets that they have developed even if they are no longer creating value; this holds true for knowledge as well. Yet some knowledge can be *more* valuable if it is transferred outside the organization. Organizations that examine their intellectual capital in terms of both opportunity costs – resources spent maintaining that intellectual capital that could be better spent elsewhere – and alternative sources of value are well-positioned to realize the benefits of divestiture.

Chapter structure

To simplify the task of sifting through the *Fieldbook* to pinpoint information that is most valuable to you, each chapter that corresponds to a knowledge management process step has been organized using the same format.

Introduction

- ◆ Provides a look at the chapter's major points at a glance.
- ◆ Places the process step in context with respect to the steps immediately

preceding and following it.

◆ Introduces a set of imperatives – the building blocks that must be in place to perform this process step optimally.

The introduction is intentionally brief so that you can easily skim through it and gauge your interest in devoting the time to a full exploration of the chapter's contents. For example, you might decide that part of a chapter is more germane to your organization's situation than the others and start there, cycling back to other information as it becomes apparent to you that it is pertinent to your needs.

Imperatives

◆ Describe why the imperative is critical to the process step.

◆ Pose a series of challenges with which each imperative confronts the organization.

The imperatives provide an organizing rubric for thinking about the approaches and concepts that are described in detail within the chapter.

Challenges

◆ Provide a general understanding of what is meant by the challenge.

◆ Outline approaches that organizations use to deal with this challenge.

◆ Create an opportunity for structured reflection with a short exercise called Think about it! that asks you to consider the implications of this information for your organization.

◆ Place the challenge in the context of your organization by asking you to complete a *quick prioritization*.

This section is the heart of each chapter. The challenges are the obstacle course around which the organization must learn to manoeuvre. They are the key to achieving performance excellence in knowledge management. As proof that the challenges are not merely theoretical, but grounded in experience, examples are cited that demonstrate how today's organizations are constructively dealing with them. Profiles of organizations that illustrate most of the challenges are presented along with expert points of view. To ensure that a linkage is made between what others are doing and what you can do, a brief exercise called 'Think about it!' and a prioritization drill called 'Quick prioritization of challenge' adjoin most of the challenges. We strongly recommend that you take the time to complete both of these activities. The one activity which gets the shortest shrift in professional life is the pause that is required for learning to take place. These short exercises are designed to provide that pause and move you closer to determining the relevance of each challenge for your organization.

Agenda for action

◆ Pulls together ideas from the chapter in a format that points you to specific next steps that can be taken within your organization.

To help you implement the ideas in this *Fieldbook*, use the 'Agenda for action' that appears at the end of each chapter. To make it easier to get started, the agenda is restricted to a limited set of action steps organized around the challenges presented in the chapter. Completing the agendas for all of the process areas that are important to your organization will help you translate the ideas from the *Fieldbook* into activities that move your organization closer to its knowledge management objectives.

Getting started with the Fieldbook: the Knowledge Management Diagnostic

In our experience, very few people truly have the time to consume an entire book's worth of information, so we have designed this *Fieldbook* to work in a variety of ways. If you can make the investment and work your way through all of the material, you will get a comprehensive and detailed picture of the entire knowledge management process. You will be able to pick and choose among all of the levers that affect organizational outcomes to create an 'Agenda for action' in a highly comprehensive fashion. For those of you who cannot make that kind of time investment, you can also derive value from the *Fieldbook* by reading about those aspects of the knowledge management process that interest you the most.

To help guide your use of the *Fieldbook* – and to help you determine how well you are performing the various aspects of the knowledge management process – we have created a Knowledge Management Diagnostic (KMD) which can be found in the next chapter. The KMD is built around the Knowledge Management Process Framework, and each section corresponds to a step in the knowledge management process. The instrument asks you to rate how closely a specific statement about knowledge management describes your organization's activities. It is a qualitative and subjective assessment tool that is intended to provoke you into thinking about all of the elements that combine to create a successful approach to knowledge management.

In some instances, the KMD should be used to assess an entire organization. If your organization is a large one, however, it is more likely that you will use it to assess a discrete segment. This is because few people possess a sufficiently broad view and detailed enough information to assess the entire knowledge management process of large organizations. Before responding to the KMD questions, you will need to determine at what level, or for what sector, of the organization you feel qualified to make an assessment. If you feel the assessment should include other parts of the organization than the one in which you operate, you will need to get other people involved in the assessment process. Involving other people is also beneficial because it enhances the perspective and validity of the responses, and because it often stimulates both provocative and valuable discussion.

Once you have completed the KMD and scored your results, you can use them to hook into sections of the book that deal with important areas where your organizational performance could benefit from improvement. For example, if upon completing the KMD, you found that your organization's ability to effectively use knowledge was poor, you might decide to review the entire 'Use' section of this *Fieldbook* in detail and skim other areas which are less important. The KMD creates a baseline measure that you can use to track your performance in knowledge management. Go ahead and photocopy it! Then respond to the questions, and save your results. A year from now, once you have had a chance to implement some of the 'Agendas for action', assess your organization again and see how you have progressed.

In the long run, the ability to take a systematic approach to knowledge management is itself a competitive advantage. The Knowledge Management Process Framework is one way of structuring your approach. The *Fieldbook's* chapters and the Knowledge Management Diagnostic are both built on this framework to insure that you 'touch all the bases' as you consider knowledge management in your organization.

Notes

1 *The Wizard of Oz*, screenplay by Noel Langley, Florence Ryerson, Edgar Allan Woolf, adaptation by Noel Langley, from the book by L. Frank Baum.

2 By "wealth" we mean some form of economic, social, political or environmental benefit conferred upon a large number of people. The term "value" is often used to mean the same thing.

3 High-touch refers to situations in which people interact directly with one another in a physical environment rather than within the virtual environment of cyberspace.

4 Ikujiro Nonaka and Hirotaka Takeuchi. *The Knowledge-Creating Company*, p. 28. Oxford: Oxford University Press, 1995.

5 'Musings on management: ten ideas designed to rile everyone who cares about management', Henry Mintzberg, *Harvard Business Review*, July–August 1996, pp. 61–67.

2 Knowledge Management Diagnostic

Introduction and instructions

Target the right knowledge management areas for your organization	Knowledge management is a wide-ranging field. To help you zero in on areas that might benefit most from your attention, we have created the Knowledge Management Diagnostic (KMD). The KMD is based on the contents of *The Knowledge Management Fieldbook*. However, you do not need to read the *Fieldbook* before you use the KMD. In fact, the reverse is true. The KMD has been created to help you better use the *Fieldbook*. Completing the KMD will help you identify knowledge management areas in which your organization is weak and point you to the chapters of the *Fieldbook* that focus on these process steps.
KMD structure	The KMD is divided into seven sections that correspond to the seven working chapters of the *Fieldbook* that discuss each knowledge management process step. Each section of the KMD contains a list of 20 statements that you need to evaluate for your organization or for some part of it. The evaluation criteria are: S – the statement is strongly descriptive of my organization, M – the statement is moderately descriptive of my organization, W – the statement is weakly descriptive of my organization.
Decide what group you will evaluate	You will need to decide whether you are evaluating the entire organization or only some part of it before you start the KMD so that your frame of reference remains consistent throughout. Some people have been given the task of initiating knowledge management at the enterprise level while others are looking at knowledge management within one group or across several groups. The KMD can be used at any of these levels.
Completing the KMD	We recommend that you complete the KMD in one sitting. First, respond to each of the statements. Then, compile your score for each section and for the KMD as a whole. Most people will need 30–45 minutes to complete the KMD.

Interpreting your results	You can score your organization or group for each knowledge management process step as well as for the overall knowledge management process. The scoring is simple to interpret – the higher your percentage score, the better your organization's performance of a particular knowledge management process step. The average score for the overall knowledge management process of organizations that field-tested the KMD was 55%. Scores for each individual knowledge management process step ranged from 30% to 70%.
Other ways to use the KMD	In addition to guiding you through the *Fieldbook*, the KMD can also stimulate discussion about knowledge management in your organization. Copy the diagnostic and ask everyone on your work team to complete it. Compile the results as averages and frequencies (if you have enough people participating). Create graphics that portray these results and present them to the work team as a way to open up discussion about what works and what does not in your organization's current knowledge management process. Varying the groups or individuals who complete the KMD can provide different views of the knowledge management process and uncover strengths upon which you can build and weaknesses that need to be shored up.

Instructions

For each section, read each of the statements. Consider the organization (or unit) that you are evaluating and decide to what degree the statement describes your organization (or unit).

If the statement is *strongly descriptive*, circle S.
If the statement is *moderately descriptive*, circle M.
If the statement is *weakly descriptive*, circle W.

Instructions for computing your section score follow the statements in each section. Instructions for comparing your section scores and computing your overall knowledge management process score appear after Section 7.

Section 1

	Strong	Moderate	Weak
People provide complete explanations when they make information requests.	S	M	W
Groups and individuals routinely document and share information about their expertise.	S	M	W
We have distinguished between knowledge management roles that are primarily administrative in nature, and those that are more content-focused.	S	M	W
People are able to customize their information environment.	S	M	W
The electronic and physical places where we store our knowledge are kept up to date.	S	M	W
The organization allocates resources to communities of specialists that wish to manage their knowledge.	S	M	W
Training on new systems focuses on how these technologies can be used to improve the quality and efficiency of how people work.	S	M	W
People only request information when they really need it.	S	M	W
People distinguish between information they want the organization to send automatically to their desktops and information they want to search for on an as-needed basis.	S	M	W
Communities of specialists are easy to identify, making it clear to others in the organization where to go for specific information.	S	M	W
Requests for information posted to the intranet or discussion forums are generally easy to understand.	S	M	W
Specific individuals identify, collect, classify, summarize and disseminate organizational knowledge.	S	M	W
Experts play a role in identifying important information for other users.	S	M	W
The electronic and physical places where we store our knowledge contain the best information available on a wide range of critical topics.	S	M	W
When people are given the task of searching for information they are able to fulfill the request.	S	M	W

People can search for information across a wide variety of applications and databases.	S	M	W
The organization has created electronic and paper-based tools which direct people to available resources.	S	M	W
Corporate information specialists help people use on-line tools, including the Internet.	S	M	W
We have established ways for people to document and share information.	S	M	W
We distinguish between information that should be centrally controlled and information that anyone should be free to document and share.	S	M	W

Section 1 score

Calculating your score

Number of Ss: ⬜ × 3 = ⬜

Number of Ms: ⬜ × 2 = ⬜

Number of Ws: ⬜ × 1 = ⬜

Your point score ⬜

Total point score possible 60

Your percent score ⬜ **% for Section 1**
(Your point score
divided by 60)

Section 2

	Strong	Moderate	Weak
Our reporting relationships do not interfere with people getting the information they need.	S	M	W
Office space is not used as a symbol of status or seniority in our organization.	S	M	W
People would say that changes in our workspace are based as much on a need to collaborate as on a need to cut costs.	S	M	W
Everyone can describe how their decisions can affect overall organizational performance.	S	M	W
Everyone speaks up if they have an opinion or idea to offer.	S	M	W
We seriously consider what others might call crazy or outrageous ideas as part of our problem-solving process.	S	M	W
We view collaborating with competitors to grow the industry as a good thing to do.	S	M	W
We give all promising ideas thorough consideration, no matter who they come from.	S	M	W
We make a point of not structuring some of our meetings because it helps us think more creatively about problem solving.	S	M	W
Involving our customers in the process of creating and developing new products and services is a well-established practice in our organization.	S	M	W
Our workspace provides us with the flexibility to take our work where we need to with very little effort.	S	M	W
Anyone who has a good idea can get support to follow up on it.	S	M	W
People would describe our organization as flexible rather than rigid.	S	M	W
We have just the right level of security protocols for our sensitive information.	S	M	W
Everyone in our organization can explain the basics about our financials.	S	M	W
We frequently partner with suppliers to improve the value we deliver to the customer.	S	M	W
Our workspace is designed to promote the flow of ideas between work groups.	S	M	W

People in our organization can use the information they get to improve their work.	S	M	W
We adjust our reporting relationships based on the work that people need to do.	S	M	W
We use approaches that people would call playful as part of our problem-solving process.	S	M	W

Section 2 score

Calculating your score

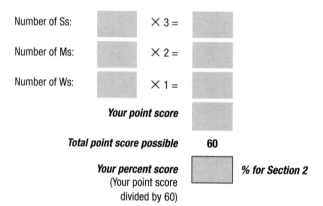

Number of Ss: × 3 =

Number of Ms: × 2 =

Number of Ws: × 1 =

Your point score

Total point score possible   **60**

Your percent score   **% for Section 2**
(Your point score
divided by 60)

Section 3

	Strong	Moderate	Weak
Before people fix problems, they consider the overall context in which the problem occurred.	S	M	W
We build models of our decision-making systems to better understand why things happen the way they do.	S	M	W
Teams engage in off-site learning experiences to find better ways of working together.	S	M	W
We use work-related games and simulations to think more clearly about our business situations.	S	M	W
Reflecting on lessons learned from work experiences is an established practice in our organization.	S	M	W
People apply what they learn outside the organization to their work.	S	M	W
When people finish projects, they generally take the time to meet with their team and analyze what went wrong and what could have been done better.	S	M	W
Our planning process includes looking at a number of scenarios so that we can think through how to respond in different situations.	S	M	W
Our learning process often includes gathering feedback from customers.	S	M	W
When a failure occurs, our first response is *not* to assign blame.	S	M	W
People in our organization exhibit a natural curiosity.	S	M	W
People admit when they fail.	S	M	W
People apply the ideas they developed in past work situations to new ones.	S	M	W
When we have a big success, we talk together about what we did right.	S	M	W
In our organization failure is considered an opportunity to learn.	S	M	W
Our organization supports group activities that promote mutual learning.	S	M	W
At some time or another, everyone in our organization does 'hands-on' work to get first-hand experience of the consequences of their decisions.	S	M	W

Learning from failure is incorporated into how we conduct subsequent work.	S	M	W
We try to ensure that people have some overlapping responsibilities, so that it is easier to learn from one another.	S	M	W
We treat disagreement as an opportunity to learn from one another.	S	M	W

Section 3 score

Calculating your score

Number of Ss: $\times 3 =$

Number of Ms: $\times 2 =$

Number of Ws: $\times 1 =$

Your point score

Total point score possible   **60**

Your percent score   *% for Section 3*
(Your point score
divided by 60)

Section 4

	Strong	Moderate	Weak
Dedicated roles, such as knowledge manager or knowledge coordinator, support the knowledge-sharing process.	S	M	W
The organization has determined where knowledge sharing across groups will yield the highest mutual benefits.	S	M	W
We acknowledge individual contribution to our groupware systems by linking it to the name of the original author.	S	M	W
Face-to-face interactions are used to strengthen electronic communications.	S	M	W
People would say that sharing knowledge does not diminish the individual's value to the organization.	S	M	W
People are members of multiple communities, making it easier to transfer knowledge across the entire organization.	S	M	W
People who refuse to share knowledge do not get certain organizational benefits.	S	M	W
We link people across traditional organizational units and functional groups to promote knowledge sharing.	S	M	W
Professional moderators and facilitators help people better express what they know so that others can understand it.	S	M	W
Electronic and physical spaces where we store our knowledge have an intuitive structure that helps people direct their contributions.	S	M	W
People have a say in what happens to the ideas and expertise they share with others.	S	M	W
Knowledge-sharing behaviour is built into the performance appraisal system.	S	M	W
Face-to-face interactions are used to transfer difficult to articulate 'tacit' knowledge.	S	M	W
Our organization looks for ways to remove barriers to knowledge sharing.	S	M	W
Processes for contributing knowledge to the organization's repositories are seamlessly integrated into work activities.	S	M	W
People can identify others in the organization who might benefit from their knowledge.	S	M	W

	S	M	W
Knowledge sharing is publicly recognized.	S	M	W
The organization has legitimized sharing knowledge by giving people the time to do it.	S	M	W
People focus their knowledge sharing activities on mission-critical information.	S	M	W
People operate under the assumption that when they use knowledge contributed by others in the organization, they are obligated to contribute their own knowledge at some point.	S	M	W

Section 4 score

Calculating your score

Number of Ss: [ ]   × 3 = [ ]

Number of Ms: [ ]   × 2 = [ ]

Number of Ws: [ ]   × 1 = [ ]

Your point score [ ]

Total point score possible 60

Your percent score [ ] ***% for Section 4***
(Your point score
divided by 60)

Section 5

	Strong	Moderate	Weak
We recognize that knowledge is part of the resource base from which our organization generates value.	S	M	W
Members of the senior management team frequently talk about knowledge management when reporting on the state of the organization.	S	M	W
The process of measuring knowledge helps us better understand what it is we are trying to manage.	S	M	W
We measure our knowledge management process and its results.	S	M	W
We issue an *external* document that reports on how well we manage knowledge.	S	M	W
We can link knowledge management activities to measurable results.	S	M	W
People know what metrics are used to monitor the knowledge management process and its results.	S	M	W
We talk about measuring knowledge in ways that people can readily understand.	S	M	W
We have developed a framework that links knowledge management activities to strategic outcomes.	S	M	W
We have a framework that describes how our organization's different forms of knowledge interact with one another to create value.	S	M	W
We experiment with different ways of measuring how well we manage knowledge.	S	M	W
We issue an *internal* document that reports on how well we manage knowledge.	S	M	W
We rely on a blend of hard facts, numbers, rules of thumb and non-metric information to make knowledge management decisions.	S	M	W
Senior management assesses what knowledge needs to be developed when it allocates resources.	S	M	W
Assessment of intellectual capital is part of our overall organizational performance measurement process.	S	M	W
We have been practicing knowledge management for some time without calling it that.	S	M	W

	S	M	W
We rely on a team whose members have valuation, measurement and operating expertise to assess our knowledge management process and its results.	S	M	W
We have mapped the process flow of knowledge management activities.	S	M	W
People can explain the difference between valuation and performance measurement.	S	M	W
We use qualitative as well as quantitative metrics to gauge the effectiveness of our knowledge management process and its results.	S	M	W

Section 5 score

Calculating your score

Number of Ss:		× 3 =	
Number of Ms:		× 2 =	
Number of Ws:		× 1 =	
	Your point score		

Total point score possible   **60**

Your percent score   % for Section 5
(Your point score
divided by 60)

Section 6

	Strong	Moderate	Weak
We routinely ask ourselves how we can leverage our knowledge into other areas.	S	M	W
It does not matter which group came up with an idea or technology, anyone in the company can use it.	S	M	W
We believe that knowledge management is everybody's business.	S	M	W
We encourage people to think about how their non-work-related activities could benefit the organization.	S	M	W
Our IT systems connect us to information sources we need to do our work.	S	M	W
Our formal and informal values are aligned.	S	M	W
Our IT systems promote the formation of different networks of people.	S	M	W
Our top executives ask all managers to include knowledge management in their business plans.	S	M	W
Our product development process explicitly includes our customers.	S	M	W
Our organization treats people like sources of value rather than costs.	S	M	W
We have launched a group or appointed a person to lead our knowledge management effort.	S	M	W
People generally trust the information they find in our IT systems.	S	M	W
We find ourselves increasingly teaming up with other organizations in strategic networks or partnerships to bring innovative products to market.	S	M	W
We view information technology as a tool to help us get our work done.	S	M	W
We have had successful new product ideas come from employees' non-work interests.	S	M	W
Our products (or services) deliver much higher value as a result of the knowledge they contain.	S	M	W
We strive to retain people who have mission-critical skills.	S	M	W

We have a formal policy that ensures we share technology and ideas across unit or group borders.	S	M	W
People know when it is not appropriate to share knowledge externally.	S	M	W
We see our products and services as having both a tangible and intangible (or knowledge-based) dimension.	S	M	W

Section 6 score

Calculating your score

Number of Ss: $\times\ 3 =$

Number of Ms: $\times\ 2 =$

Number of Ws: $\times\ 1 =$

Your point score

Total point score possible   **60**

Your percent score   *% for Section 6*
(Your point score
divided by 60)

Section 7

	Strong	Moderate	Weak
Our decision to acquire knowledge is based on how much we can leverage it.	S	M	W
When a new opportunity arises, we first try to retool our existing skills before we hire a lot of new people.	S	M	W
We make divestment decisions based on *both* the strategic importance of intellectual capital and financial projections.	S	M	W
We try to understand the impact of relationships on productivity before we automate tasks and replace person-to-*person* contact with person-to-*computer* contact.	S	M	W
Before we accept new projects or orders, we think about whether the knowledge we will build for our organization can be used in other ways.	S	M	W
We participate in industry-based research groups to help us decide whether we need to acquire new knowledge.	S	M	W
When groups find ways to work with fewer people, they figure out how to pursue higher value activities rather than terminate people.	S	M	W
We may refuse to work for a customer if doing the work does not build knowledge that we can use in other ways.	S	M	W
We divest knowledge in a planned, deliberate way.	S	M	W
When we get rid of businesses or groups of people, we treat the people who are affected with dignity and respect.	S	M	W
We regularly review our promotion practices to make sure that we are not losing people with strategically important knowledge.	S	M	W
We apprentice our people to other organizations to determine if we need to acquire new skills or expertise.	S	M	W
We form alliances with organizations that complement our skill sets as an alternative to doing everything ourselves.	S	M	W
When we divest tangible assets, we are aware of the knowledge components they carry.	S	M	W

We outsource skills and expertise that do not support our core competencies.	S	M	W
We routinely examine whether we are supporting non-strategic knowledge at the expense of strategically critical knowledge.	S	M	W
Before we terminate people, we try to determine if their skills and expertise can be used elsewhere.	S	M	W
We prefer to use the resources and skills we have in place when testing a new business idea.	S	M	W
We make use of informal relationships with related businesses in our local area to keep our knowledge pool up to date.	S	M	W
Our organization considers the impact that letting people go will have on loyalty, contribution and commitment.	S	M	W

Section 7 score

Calculating your score

Number of Ss: ⬚ × 3 = ⬚

Number of Ms: ⬚ × 2 = ⬚

Number of Ws: ⬚ × 1 = ⬚

Your point score ⬚

Total point score possible **60**

Your percent score ⬚ *% for Section 7*
(Your point score
divided by 60)

Knowledge Management Diagnostic scoring sheet

Compare your section scores

Each section of the KMD corresponds to a chapter of the *Fieldbook*. Transfer your percentage scores for each section to this page and compare them. If you score lower in some sections than others, you might consider focusing your use of the *Fieldbook* on these process steps. Scores for organizations that field-tested the KMD ranged from 30% to 70% for each section.

Section	Percentage score	Corresponds to ...
Section 1	%	Get
Section 2	%	Use
Section 3	%	Learn
Section 4	%	Contribute
Section 5	%	Assess
Section 6	%	Build/Sustain
Section 7	%	Divest

Compute your overall knowledge management process score

Transfer your *point scores* for each section to this page and use them to compute an overall score for the knowledge management process in your organization. We do not expect any organization to achieve 100% on the KMD. Organizations that field-tested the instrument averaged 55%.

Section	Point score
Section 1	
Section 2	

Section 3

Section 4

Section 5

Section 6

Section 7

Your total

Total possible　　　**420**

Overall percent score   % for knowledge management
(Your total divided by 420)

3 Get

> Water, water everywhere, nor any drop to drink.
>
> **Samuel Taylor Coleridge,** *The Ancient Mariner*

Today, instead of being forced to take action based on little or no information, people are more likely to find that the challenge confronting them is weeding through piles of irrelevant information to get to the one 'nugget' that is critical to their needs. Information technology is both the culprit and the traffic cop for this knowledge management process step. On the one hand, IT has opened the floodgates of information and sent it coursing through organizations. On the other hand, IT systems become smarter every day, capable of directing people through a maze of irrelevance to the information they need.

At a glance ...

What is new?	Technology has enabled huge strides in providing access to information.
What is the problem?	Growing availability of information has created overload.
What is the individual or team objective?	Finding the right information at the point of need.
What is the organization's responsibility?	Providing tools to access and manage information.

Introduction

Data, information and knowledge – whether it is the raw numbers needed to compute a department budget or the sophisticated skills necessary to build a new software product – are what enable members of the organization to solve problems, meet customer requests or respond to changes in the marketplace. Getting information is nothing new to organizations. What *has* changed is that we have moved from an era of not enough information to an embarrassment of inforiches. People are under tremendous pressure to wade through it all, deftly navigating their way to the precise piece they need at the precise time that they need it. Getting this 'stuff'[1] – whether it is the design specifications for the wing of a 747 or the company expert in environmental contracts – is generally the first step in the knowledge management process, and it depends on the following *imperatives* and *challenges*.

Imperatives and challenges

Articulation	People can describe their information needs:
	◆ *Understand and communicate intended use of information.*
	◆ *Direct information requests appropriately.*
Awareness	People know where to find knowledge resources:
	◆ *Provide signposts: directories, Yellow Pages, and maps.*
	◆ *Use communities of practice to cast a spotlight on organizational knowledge.*
Access	People have the tools they need to find and capture information:
	◆ *Balance push and pull technologies.*
	◆ *Involve the user in tailoring navigation and capture tools.*
Guidance	New organizational roles support information seekers:
	◆ *Convert librarians into cybrarians.*
	◆ *Create a new role: the knowledge manager.*
	◆ *Use experts as information filters.*
Completeness	The knowledge infrastructure is comprehensive and well-organized:
	◆ *Provide access to both centrally managed and self-published information.*
	◆ *Create frameworks and processes that promote knowledge reuse.*

1 Articulation

People can describe their information needs

There are two basic approaches people use to locate the information they need to do their jobs. The first is an *active search* in which people look for a specific set of information either directly or indirectly – for example, by assigning the task to someone else, such as a research librarian. The second approach is a *passive search*, which usually consists of a department-wide, community-wide or organization-wide announcement of an information need. Responses to the request then flow back to the requestor. The advent of groupware systems has made the latter approach increasingly popular. However, its success is predicated on the willingness of other members of the enterprise to respond to such requests.

In the case of both active and passive information searches, the ability to articulate information needs is essential. Yet many searches for information founder at this early stage. Meeting the following *challenges* can get information seekers off to a good start.

Challenges

◆ *Understand and communicate intended use of information.*
◆ *Direct information requests appropriately.*

Understand and communicate intended use of information

Any search for information must begin with a clear sense of what the seeker plans to *do* with the information. Understanding the objectives of the search will also help determine what combination of active and passive approaches is appropriate and provide a good indicator of when enough information has been assembled.

If information users assign the task of finding information to someone else, articulation is even more critical. This is particularly true when the information gatherer – often a junior member of a team – is not intimately involved with the work itself. When search goals are poorly communicated to the person performing the search, the scenario goes something like this: the individual locates an information source, makes a call and at the first question from the source attempting to clarify the purpose of the search, hits a wall. The searcher either has to go back to the team for clarification, or instead requests 'everything you've got' and receives an enormous pile of unfiltered information. In both cases, time is lost articulating the problem further downstream in the project. Even junior members of teams need to grasp sufficient detail to understand what they are looking for, know it when they find it and know when they have found enough.

Often, people searching for resource material will enlist the services of a corporate librarian. Many librarians have repositioned themselves as 'information needs consultants'. Rather than going off and looking for disjointed pieces of information, they interview their clients to understand how the information will be used. At consulting firm Booz Allen & Hamilton, for example, a corporate information specialist is part of each client team, ensuring that information requests are well directed. At McKinsey & Company corporate information specialists have taken on the role, previously held by field-based consultants, of 'intelligent interrogators'. In addition to searching for information, both internally and externally, they help searchers understand what it is they need and how to request it (see Profile).

PROFILE *McKinsey & Company*

When organizations increase rapidly in size, personal networks cease to be the key to finding critical organizational knowledge. Companies often find it necessary to bring in people whose mandate is to keep tabs on who knows what and to help others find their way to the appropriate internal resource. At McKinsey, experienced professionals assist people looking for information to better articulate what they really need.

During the 1980s McKinsey & Company, one of the world's most prestigious consulting firms, experienced exponential growth. Not surprisingly, the firm's increased size accelerated the rapid diffusion of expertise. After decades of being a relatively intimate network of professionals, McKinsey was suddenly a truly global firm, where partners did not know one another, and picking up the telephone was no longer the quickest way to get an answer to a pressing client problem.

McKinsey's Organization Practice was one of the first to recognize that what the firm now needed was an effective way for client teams to tap into firmwide expertise rapidly. In 1989 McKinsey launched the Rapid Response Network (RRN), a distributed team of four to six professionals knowledgeable in the field of organizational consulting. The team members were stationed in time zones ranging from London to San Francisco. McKinsey's decision to staff the RRN with professionals who had solid consulting experience was significant. It meant that when an individual called into the Network's Atlanta-based hotline he or she would be able to have a conversation with an 'intelligent interrogator' – someone who understood how to help the caller articulate his or her question in ways that would facilitate the search for answers. The RRN had software support in the form of both a request tracking database and a resources database which included the best thinking – both inside and outside McKinsey – on organizational issues, as well as information on who in the firm were leading thinkers in these areas.

'The RRN constituted a real shift for McKinsey,' says Phil Terry, Manager of New Media and Knowledge Systems. 'Our culture has always placed a heavy premium on what people know. The flip side is that people are sensitive to acknowledging what they don't know. The message that establishing the RRN sent was, "It's OK if you can't do it alone".' The RRN team exemplified this philosophy. Although virtual, it was a close-knit unit of people who supported one another. Members maintained contact through biweekly conference calls and biannual face-to-face meetings. Information exchange within the group was seen as a key factor in developing an understanding of organizational design and the strategy work going on across McKinsey.

Today, with the growth of networking technologies, much of the RRN's work now focuses on maintaining a web site of information and thinking on organizational issues. 'Our shift to increased use of technology has never blinded us to the need for a human interface,' notes Lynn Heilig, one of the original RNN members, now a knowledge manager. The group still runs a hotline, but it is staffed by senior information specialists who were trained by the professionals who originally managed the initiative. Like their predecessors, these information specialists help consultants articulate their questions and then give those who need it assistance in navigating a web site that is becoming increasingly rich and detailed.

The original RRN positions held by senior consultants have been transformed into a knowledge manager function. Within the Organization Practice – a functional specialty that crosses all industries – there are nine or ten sub-areas (for example, human resources, culture, change management, leadership), and each of these sub-areas has a knowledge manager. Knowledge managers sit at the vortex of McKinsey's various communities of practice, not only overseeing web site content, but also interacting with a network of consultants and practice leaders to create the links that define the community.

The knowledge manager also serves as an 'informed layer' that sits between the information specialist, whose primary function is to find information, and expert consultants who directly serve clients on organizational issues and are held in reserve to help with highly specialized or complex questions. The result is a kind of 'query triage' in which questions that cannot be answered from web-based information get routed to the knowledge manager who has considerable content knowledge. Only questions that cannot be handled by knowledge managers are passed on to experts who have been pre-selected based on their willingness to provide assistance.

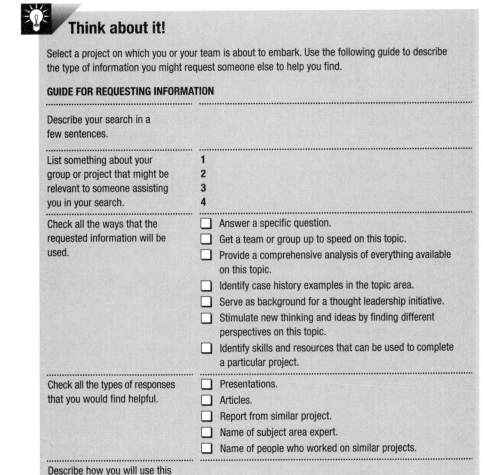

Think about it!

Select a project on which you or your team is about to embark. Use the following guide to describe the type of information you might request someone else to help you find.

GUIDE FOR REQUESTING INFORMATION

Describe your search in a few sentences.	
List something about your group or project that might be relevant to someone assisting you in your search.	1 2 3 4
Check all the ways that the requested information will be used.	☐ Answer a specific question. ☐ Get a team or group up to speed on this topic. ☐ Provide a comprehensive analysis of everything available on this topic. ☐ Identify case history examples in the topic area. ☐ Serve as background for a thought leadership initiative. ☐ Stimulate new thinking and ideas by finding different perspectives on this topic. ☐ Identify skills and resources that can be used to complete a particular project.
Check all the types of responses that you would find helpful.	☐ Presentations. ☐ Articles. ☐ Report from similar project. ☐ Name of subject area expert. ☐ Name of people who worked on similar projects.
Describe how you will use this information.	
Describe how getting this information could benefit the person who completes the task and/or the organization as a whole.	

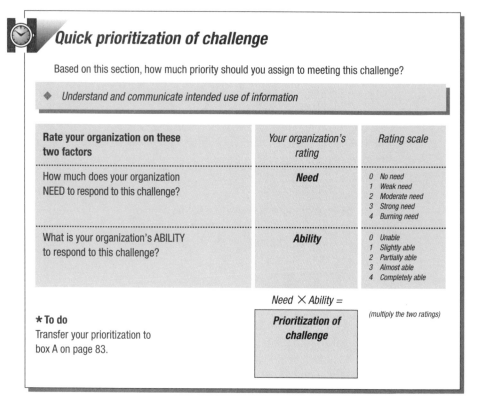

Quick prioritization of challenge

Based on this section, how much priority should you assign to meeting this challenge?

◆ *Understand and communicate intended use of information*

Rate your organization on these two factors	Your organization's rating	Rating scale
How much does your organization NEED to respond to this challenge?	**Need**	0 No need 1 Weak need 2 Moderate need 3 Strong need 4 Burning need
What is your organization's ABILITY to respond to this challenge?	**Ability**	0 Unable 1 Slightly able 2 Partially able 3 Almost able 4 Completely able

Need × *Ability* =

★ To do
Transfer your prioritization to box A on page 83.

Prioritization of challenge

(multiply the two ratings)

Direct information requests appropriately

The existence of corporate intranets or other company-wide electronic communications systems has created the potential for anyone in the organization to request information from anyone else with the click of a mouse – the quintessential passive approach. Passive information requests can easily be abused, clogging electronic highways with postings that begin 'Does anyone know ...' In large organizations such universally directed requests are both inappropriate and inefficient. There are usually specific individuals or groups who are best equipped to respond to particular information requests. For example, groups may have their own intranet web sites which include a venue for posting questions. Knowledge managers for these groups can pass questions on to appropriate experts. Experts are far more likely to respond to requests for information if they receive only those that are matched to their specific expertise. Blanket requests for information should be used sparingly if at all.

Many organizations have implicit rules about the use of individualized E-mail versus E-mail distribution lists. For example, Hewlett-Packard's mechanical engineers make extensive use of both forms of communication. If an E-mail message or phone call is placed to one or two individuals, a response is expected. Mass E-mails or voice mails are reserved for the dissemination of information. They are not considered appropriate if the sender expects a response. A possible exception is distribution lists which are specific to a group of individuals who are used to providing one another with assistance.

Organizations that have no implicit or explicit guidelines about designing passive information requests might want to consider ways of creating some. Here is a starting point:

✓ Make a concerted effort to find the information via an active search before requesting that someone else supplies the information. Company intranets are information-rich, and a call to the help desk may be in order before placing a call to the expert.

✓ Always let others know who else has been contacted for the same information. If, instead, someone sends identical individual E-mail messages to five different people, he or she may: (a) find themselves in a round robin of referrals or (b) end up with five angry people who have all gone to a lot of trouble only to find out that they have duplicated one another's efforts.

✓ Let others know what basic information has already been gathered so that they do not point requestors to something that has already been secured.

✓ Be sure the information is truly needed. People who consistently make information requests 'just in case' may find others soon stop responding.

✓ Give a little something back. Offer to post findings or final work in a place where others can view it.

Think about it!

Consider three types of information that you frequently need. List them in the first column of the following space. Fill in the second column using the options for directing requests.

Types of information we need most often	*Best ways to direct information request*
1	
2	
3	

Options for directing information requests:
◆ Contact a corporate information specialist.
◆ Send an E-mail or voice mail to a distribution list.
◆ Send E-mails or voice mails to a few individuals.
◆ Post a general request where all members of the organization will see it.
◆ Post a request where a specific group will see it.
◆ Other:_____(specify).

Quick prioritization of challenge

Based on this section, how much priority should you assign to meeting this challenge?

◆ *Direct information requests appropriately*

Rate your organization on these two factors	Your organization's rating	Rating scale
How much does your organization NEED to respond to this challenge?	*Need*	0 No need 1 Weak need 2 Moderate need 3 Strong need 4 Burning need
What is your organization's ABILITY to respond to this challenge?	*Ability*	0 Unable 1 Slightly able 2 Partially able 3 Almost able 4 Completely able

Need × *Ability* =

★ To do

Transfer your prioritization to box B on page 84.

Prioritization of challenge

(multiply the two ratings)

2 Awareness

People know where to find knowledge resources

Anyone who has ever worked in a large organization has heard the lament, 'We're always reinventing the wheel!' One of the most obvious reasons this happens is that even when people know *what* they are looking for, they do not know *where* to look. Often, it is difficult for members in one part of the organization to know what information exists elsewhere. A large number of 'does anyone know?' postings on the corporate intranet can be a red flag that people in the organization are confused about where information resides.

Even in highly centralized organizations, information tends to be dispersed, and members of one group rarely communicate with those in other groups unless they happen to be thrown together on a project. When an initiative begins from 'the bottom up', the benefit is that it tends to be closely linked to how people work. But the disadvantage is that individuals in different parts of the organization, who might conceivably profit from sharing ideas and expertise, tend to be unaware of one another's efforts. In fact, it is not infrequent for companies to go outside their own organizations to seek expertise, when, unknown to them, the skills and knowledge reside in some other part of the organization. Organizations can make members aware of enterprise-wide knowledge by meeting these *challenges*.

Challenges

◆ *Provide signposts: directories, Yellow Pages and maps.*
◆ *Use communities of practice to cast a spotlight on organizational knowledge.*

Provide signposts: directories, Yellow Pages and maps

Both paper-based and electronic 'knowledge pointers' – known variously as directories, Yellow Pages or maps – not only let people know what expertise and resources are available to them, but also describe where to find them. Resources need not be confined to those within the organization, but can also include external databases or publications; experts, such as consultants or academics with whom the organization has relationships; or professional associations. Knowledge maps should not be confused with knowledge repositories, which actually contain the information itself.

While it is not critical that these directories utilize the latest technology, electronic distribution has clear advantages in terms of both timeliness and reach. For example Chevron Corporation, an early proponent of identifying and transferring internal best practices, created a widely acclaimed 'Best Practices Resource Map' of expertise and information organized around internal business processes. Realizing that the hard copy version would be quickly outdated, plans to offer the map on the organization's best practices web site were soon underway (see Profile).

PROFILE ◆ *Chevron*

Finding expertise in large organizations can be a bewildering experience, full of blind alleys and wrong turns. Chevron responded by creating a map so that people could literally see where to go.

In 1994, global oil giant Chevron formalized its effort to share best practices across its business units by introducing new tools to the organization on a worldwide basis. Among these tools was a best practices database, which took a process approach to organizing best practices content. At the same time, many different units, including the corporate group and both upstream and downstream business entities, had launched their own initiatives for sharing best practices ideas. Their approaches ranged from networks and best practice teams to databases, workshops and conferences. The challenge was bringing all these activities together.

Rather than mandate that individual initiatives be centralized, the company hit on another solution – a Best Practice Resource Map that could point people interested in finding out more about best practices in a certain area to existing resources and groups that already had initiatives in place. At first glance, the Best Practices Resource Map is reminiscent of a guide to the London Underground. Its colour-coded main categories comprise the seven criteria from the Baldrige Award, which are also used for Chevron's quality review process. A subsequent breakdown follows that of the International Benchmarking Clearinghouse's Process Classification Scheme, a nod to Chevron's strong focus on a process-based approach to knowledge sharing. Within each process category is a list of resources with a brief description of the resource, a reference to the pertinent organization within Chevron, and the name of a person to contact for further information.

The map was designed to provide pointers to solutions, not the solutions themselves. The underlying idea was to promote cross-fertilization of ideas by putting teams of people working on similar issues in touch with one another. The map was enormously popular, and the first 7,000 copies were soon gone. It also became obvious that at the rate best practices initiatives were springing up, it would be difficult to keep the map current.

During the time the Best Practices Resources Map was being compiled, Chevron was also busy developing its intranet. Numerous best practice web sites started to spring up, organized by individual best practices teams. Soon the intranet began to catch on as a critical information resource, and today usage is doubling every 100 days. Given this trend, as well as the other benefits of intranet-based information resources – including key word searching, ease of updating and instant accessibility for all employees – the Best Practices Map was transferred to an electronic format almost as soon as the paper version came off the presses. Now the map is only one of the best practices resources available on the web site, known as the Knowledge Connection. Pertinent sections of the electronic map can be easily hotlinked to individual team web sites. The site continues to be maintained by Chevron's corporate quality staff.

'The Best Practices Map is a great pointer to team-based initiatives,' says Quality Consultant Patricia Wagner. 'Going forward our vision is to better identify both team and individual expertise.' Chevron's best practices database allows teams and individuals to contribute best practices immediately by filling out a standardized form. Submissions are helping to make the organization's expertise more visible and more accessible. Ultimately the database will offer pointers to people with specific knowledge. 'We're moving closer to an organizational understanding of expertise at Chevron,' adds Wagner. 'And the closer we get, the more people, teams, and communities of practice are coming forward of their own accord.'

Think about it!

Create your own mini-directory. Consider the last project you worked on. List the types of information you needed to gather in the first column. Use the second column to list the sources you used to obtain that information. Ask several other members of your team to go through the same process and compare your results.

Type of information	Source(s) of information
1	a
	b
2	a
	b
3	a
	b

Quick prioritization of challenge

Based on this section, how much priority should you assign to meeting this challenge?

◆ *Provide signposts: directories, Yellow Pages and maps*

Rate your organization on these two factors	Your organization's rating	Rating scale
How much does your organization NEED to respond to this challenge?	**Need**	0 No need 1 Weak need 2 Moderate need 3 Strong need 4 Burning need
What is your organization's ABILITY to respond to this challenge?	**Ability**	0 Unable 1 Slightly able 2 Partially able 3 Almost able 4 Completely able

Need $\times$ *Ability* =

★ To do	**Prioritization of challenge**	*(multiply the two ratings)*
Transfer your prioritization to box C on page 84.		

Use communities of practice to cast a spotlight on organizational knowledge

Redundant work often goes on in organizations, unknown to those performing it. With the assistance of new technologies, however, individuals who have common professional goals and interests are now able to extend across boundaries of time and space to connect with others in the organization with whom they have previously had little contact. These groups are often called communities of practice or communities of interest. They provide a natural focal point for organizing and promoting knowledge in a particular area. While overbureaucratizing these communities can force them underground, assigning a knowledge manager to oversee on-line content, post resources and monitor discussions is a good way for organizations to demonstrate support for their activities.

Buckman Laboratories, a specialty chemicals manufacturer in Memphis, Tennessee, has organized electronic forums around its core product lines. The forums are a resource for professionals in each of these areas – not only a place to pose questions, but also a source of the latest information. The organization fully supports each forum community by providing 'sys ops' to manage them and section leaders to review material. Discussion threads are automatically stored after 30 days in a separate section of the system. Sys ops and section leaders also know where the expertise resides in the organization, and can direct those with questions to the appropriate information sources.

Research and knowledge services firm Teltech, which has created a methodology for helping clients build the kind of corporate Yellow Pages or expert directory outlined in previous challenge, defines community of practice as the basic unit for which knowledge sharing is critical (see Point of View). Professional communities possess specific 'competencies' – clusters of skills and expertise that make them competitive. Building knowledge repositories and directories around communities makes the search for expertise within large organizations both easier and more intuitive.

POINT OF VIEW ▸ *Creating Corporate Yellow Pages at Teltech*

'We need to make our expertise available to everyone in the organization.' It's a goal that is on a lot of executive wish lists these days. One of the most straightforward ways to accomplish this is to create an electronic directory or Yellow Pages that points members of the organization to people who can help them with specific problems or issues. 'Before embarking on one,' says Andy Michuda, CEO of Teltech, a research and knowledge management services firm, 'organizations had better ask themselves a very simple question: Why?'

There are many compelling reasons for an organization to develop a directory of experts. Michuda points to an example of a European pharmaceutical company that surveyed ongoing research and found that 70% of its current research had already been conducted elsewhere in the organization. The potential benefits to this organization of knowing in advance what it had already accomplished are obvious. But even a strong business case does not guarantee that people will use a directory to find resources elsewhere in the organization. This is one reason why Teltech conducts 'readiness surveys' of its clients. The surveys use an interview approach to dig beneath the rhetoric, policies and procedures to understand how the organization really works. 'If we find a culture that is totally antithetical to sharing expertise across silos, we walk away from the project,' says Michuda.

If a client is considered ready to move forward, Teltech follows a set of basic guidelines:

1 **Look for communities in need**: You do not have to create a corporate-wide directory – usually it makes the most sense to share expertise within a specific community. Look for communities within the organization where the greatest knowledge gaps exist and where the potential benefits of sharing expert information can be achieved. The work of the community must also be strategically critical to the organization.

2 **Lay the groundwork**: This means asking basic, but very important questions:

    ◆ What type of knowledge does the community need to be successful?

    ◆ What are the key decisions that will impact success?

    ◆ What information is needed to support these decisions?

    ◆ What are the knowledge sources in the organization (people, documents, databases)?

    ◆ What are the key competencies (combination of skills and expertise) that will lead to success?

    Answering these questions ensures that the information that goes in is not just the 'nice to know'. It's the 'need to know'.

3 **Think the way the organization thinks**: Teltech typically includes a thesaurus in its expert directories. The thesaurus is customized for each organization, reflecting the jargon, acronyms and terminology that are part of its daily lexicon. People who are looking for a particular form of expertise can type in the term they use. Up pops a range of related words. The field of related words can be narrowed or broadened according to the searcher's needs. This user-friendly approach means people are not forced to think like the application; instead, it 'thinks' like them.

4 **Make it as easy as possible for people to comply**: Gathering information on people's expertise calls for the individuals themselves to cooperate by supplying a lot of personal data. Teltech has developed a range of tools, both paper-based and electronic, that guide people through the information collection process. Some organizations provide training so that everyone can move through the process together. This also saves on a lot of back-and-forth communication if people have questions. It is important not to start with a blank slate asking people 'what are you an expert in?' or 'what to you do well?' Instead, Teltech provides lists of terms and concepts from its own expert database and asks people to rate themselves in these areas. Finally, cautions Michuda, 'Always make it clear to people what's in it for them – that they will benefit from knowing where to find expertise when they need it. They're a lot more likely to cooperate if they're clear on this point.'

5 **Use multiple information sources**: You cannot always rely on people to accurately report what they are good at. For example, Michuda points out that cultural differences need to be accounted for: North Americans tend to overstate their expertise, while Europeans understate it. One solution is to ask

people who they go to for specific types of information. These responses can be cross-checked with self-reported responses.

6 **Integrate updating with other work processes**: Once an expert directory is up and running, one more big headache waits in the wings – maintaining it. Some organizations take on this task themselves, while others outsource the responsibility to Teltech. Regardless of who does it, the less burdensome the process, the more likely the directory will be kept up to date. For example, many organizations conduct debriefs at the end of projects. Teltech editors take these debriefs and extract key points to incorporate into the expert database biographies of the team members who participated in the projects. There are also ways to link into the human resources review process, which exists in almost every organization. By adding just a few additional steps to this process, updated competencies can be captured and added to the expert directory.

'Organizational expertise is a fluid state of affairs,' says Michuda. 'But a well-developed directory can provide a fairly accurate snapshot.' The more accurate the snapshot, the more likely that members of the organization will find the directory useful and help keep it up to date.

 Think about it!

Most people in organizations belong to some kind of community of practice by virtue of the kind of work they do. It might be a community of mechanical engineers, office managers or human resource professionals. Think about a community of practice to which you belong. Use the following space which reprises the questions posed in the Teltech Point of view to structure how you might approach organizing your community's knowledge.

Community of practice: ....

Questions from Teltech profile	*Thoughts*
What type of knowledge does the community need to be successful?	
What are the key decisions that will impact success?	
What information is needed to support these decisions?	
What are the knowledge sources in the organization (people, documents, databases)?	
What are the key competencies (combination of skills and expertise) that will lead to success?	

Quick prioritization of challenge

Based on this section, how much priority should you assign to meeting this challenge?

◆ *Use communities of practice to cast a spotlight on organizational knowledge*

Rate your organization on these two factors	Your organization's rating	Rating scale
How much does your organization NEED to respond to this challenge?	**Need**	0 No need 1 Weak need 2 Moderate need 3 Strong need 4 Burning need
What is your organization's ABILITY to respond to this challenge?	**Ability**	0 Unable 1 Slightly able 2 Partially able 3 Almost able 4 Completely able

Need ✕ *Ability* =

★ To do
Transfer your prioritization to box D on page 85.

Prioritization of challenge

(multiply the two ratings)

3 Access

People have the tools they need to find and capture information

In the first imperative, *Articulation*, we talked about using two different approaches to searching: active and passive. In the parlance of information technology, these approaches are known respectively as 'pull' and 'push'. Technically, pull involves the user actively searching through a large repository of information, for example, the Internet, and then selecting a relevant sub-set. However, we use the term in a very general sense, to include anything from browsing an intranet to making a series of phone calls to identify an expert. Push, in its strictest sense, refers to the unsolicited distribution of information to a user's desktop by an information source. However, of more interest for the purposes of information gathering is 'push with permission,' in which people define their information needs and then wait for information matching this description to flow back to them. This type of push can range from the use of filters or tailored news feeds to posting a 'does anyone know?' question on a specific web site and waiting for an expert to respond.

The organizational challenge for the pull approach is to find better ways for users to *navigate* their way to what they need. The challenge for the push approach is to find better ways to *capture* what users need in the first place. Push and pull are two poles of a continuum. Organizations that come up with the best solutions will have to face the following *challenges*.

Challenges

◆ *Balance push and pull technologies.*
◆ *Involve the user in tailoring navigation and capture tools.*

Balance push and pull technologies

Technology-induced information overload has resulted in a new danger for organizations: user tuneout. People stop paying attention to information and make decisions without it, much as they did before it became so universally available. Fortunately, information technology has also spawned a number of tools that may at least partially solve the problem it helped to create. Evaluating and testing these tools has become a key responsibility of many IT departments. Furthermore, as corporate intranets become increasingly crowded with information, adapting Internet navigation and information capture tools for use internally will be critical. In fact, it is not surprising that developers of tools originally built for the Internet – from search engines and intelligent agents to filters and chat applications – are finding lucrative business opportunities selling their wares to technology-savvy organizations.

The sheer plethora of products currently on the market presents a problem that is nearly as overwhelming as the information glut itself. It is not our intent to review these 'knowledge management' products – the field of players changes far too rapidly. Instead we will consider how to combine push and pull strategies optimally so that information reaches the right person in the right place at the right time.

Pull: tools for navigation

The simplest pull technology is the one we use the most often: the web browser. When a user types a universal resource locator (URL) into a browser, it pulls a file from a web server and displays it on the user's desktop. But when we think of pull, we usually think of another common tool: the search engine. Without these search technologies, intranets and the Internet would be nothing more than unexplored frontiers. Search engines review, accept or reject and deliver information with amazing rapidity. The user enters one or more keywords, and the search engine returns a list of links of everything in the system containing those words (if the search is of the Internet or an intranet, the links are to web pages). Often the result is more information than is either necessary or relevant. However, with practice, it is possible to use various 'advanced search' functions to refine searches to obtain more focused results.

Search technologies have increased in importance as organizations migrate their information systems to intranets. Sun Microsystems launched one of the first corporate intranets, SunWeb, in March 1994. Users can navigate SunWeb by browsing an alphabetical directory of all sites or by searching the entire network, but neither method is very practical for such a large volume of information.

Instead, users can perform narrower searches across domain, functional organization or geographic location using the company's powerful search engine.[2]

Another pull tool is the directory, which allows users to scroll through a set of topics and then drill down to the one that best fits their needs. Yahoo!, one of the most profitable Internet portals, began as a directory categorizing web sites by topic area. Most web sites, as well as corporate intranets, have some form of organizing framework that allows users to navigate to the information they need. The navigational framework provides an alternative to locating information through a key word search.

Customized search engines and directories can support highly targeted searches when they make use of metadata. Metadata is information about information. For example, the name of a document's author is a piece of metadata. If all documents within a repository contain consistent information such as author, date of creation and subject or key words, then searching or browsing can be done according to these categories. Effective use of metadata requires agreeing on each category and what it means. For instance, does 'author' mean the person who wrote the document, or the person who is responsible for updating it?

A set of 15 basic 'metatags' called the Dublin Core (after the Dublin, Ohio-based Online Computer Library Center) was developed in 1995 to facilitate location of information on the Internet. The Dublin Core established a standard that has been adopted by many developers of corporate intranets. While most corporate intranets today use some form of metadata, they vary in the degree to which they are successful at capturing it for every document. Ford Motor Company has rigorously pursued the use of metadata, both for the information published on its intranet and that which is housed in its enormous knowledge base, the Enterprise Information System (see Profile).

PROFILE ➤ *Ford Motor Company*

People in mega-corporations face the same challenges finding information on their organizations' intranets as they do finding it on the Internet: there is too much, and searches can yield as much nonsense as helpful material. Ford has combined aggressive use of metadata with an educational approach that helps users incorporate information management into their daily work processes.

In 1994, when the Internet was finally beginning to make its presence known in the corporate world, Ford realized it had a potential solution to an enormous information management problem. With 360,000 employees who mainly exchanged information via paper, E-mail or face-to-face meetings, the world's second-largest automaker was relying heavily on the information management habits of individuals to ensure that product development teams – called programme teams – had access to current information. Surveys showed the current system was not as effective as it might be. Respondents said that, on average, they could only find 50% of the information they needed to do their jobs. Interestingly, this was a figure that conformed to national averages in external studies that Ford had gathered.

'We knew we had a terrific opportunity to improve the situation,' says Stevie Cote, Manager of the Enterprise Information Management (EIM) group. Cote's team partnered with one of Ford's reengineering initiatives to survey programme teams about the type of information they needed to do their work. Responses were prioritized into a list of 82 items, which in turn directed the order in which the intranet was populated with product development content. Cote's team was also given the task of developing standards for the management and authoring of content on Ford's intranet, which was launched in July 1996.

Ford realized from the beginning that it had to create an intranet that could be centrally managed, otherwise it would soon find itself with a hodge-podge of sites as difficult to navigate and search as the Internet itself. The EIM group developed a customized solution for category searching similar to Yahoo!, called InfoNet. For a site to be searchable via InfoNet, site owners must provide a minimum level of metadata, including author, organization name, key words and topic (from a pre-selected list), as well as a brief abstract. This ensures far more targeted searches than would result with a traditional Internet search engine. Today, most of Ford's 800 sites are officially registered in this fashion. To further encourage central management, Ford has set up a 'Web Farm' which offers low hosting charges as well as development space so that teams can easily set up and maintain their sites.

At the time Ford launched its intranet, it was simultaneously centralizing a wealth of technical and other valuable information into a repository called the Enterprise Knowledge Base (EKB). The EKB can be viewed through a web browser and is searchable by the same set of metadata used to organize and search sites on the intranet.

Ford's efforts have yielded some impressive results. With all of the programme teams making use of the intranet, people say they can now find 90% of the information they need to do their jobs. But the key has not just been in the central management of information. Says Cote, 'One of our biggest challenges has been to get people to realize the value of managing their own information.' The organization of the EKB gave Ford a universal template for categorizing information on everyone's desktops. In addition, the EIM has provided both group and one-on-one training to assist people with information management. Cote points out that part of the process consists of asking the question, 'What do I have on my desktop that could be leveraged out to others through shared drives, the EKB, or the intranet?' The next step for Ford is to help people create their own customized templates that request and pull information automatically to their desktops – a Ford version of 'My Yahoo!', the customization service offered by Internet portal Yahoo!

But that is still only half the story. According to Bud Mathaisel, Ford's CIO, 'There's a tremendous amount of knowledge embedded into the *way* we work.' For example, Ford's rigorous product development process requires programme teams to go through a series of check points in which managers review the product development process status. Now, instead of their having to search for documentation at each stage, the system automatically hyperlinks reviewers to the relevant information in the EKB. Says Mathaisel, 'Where we've really seen savings and reduced cycle time is when we've been able to build information access into the work process itself.'

Push: tools for information capture

Pull is the hunter's approach to getting information. The user is on the prowl, looking for something in particular. But only looking for information in places with which they are familiar cuts users off from what they don't know they don't know. This is where push comes into play. Push alerts us to information and information sources that we never knew existed.

Information is sometimes pushed to us whether we want it or not – two good examples are E-mail and voice mail. But as a business tool, push is of limited use unless people can specify what they *want* pushed to them. While this kind of customization has long been a feature of clipping and research services, it was a labour-intensive effort. This changed in 1996 when a company called PointCast introduced a technology that was able to automatically deliver highly customized, web-based news to a user's desktop. For the first time, push was viewed as a viable form of information retrieval. Although push technologies have not had the impact once predicted for them, largely because of bandwidth issues, elements of push are now part of many standard intranet and groupware applications. Push tools do not always deliver actual information to people. They may alert a user, generally via an E-mail message, that certain information is available or that a particular web site has been updated. These 'notifications' are an invitation to pull.

Determining which form of information retrieval – push or pull – will 'win' in organizations is not a particularly fruitful line of inquiry. Clearly both are here to stay. What organizations have to grapple with is deciding which information should be pushed to people, and which information people should discover on their own. Another issue is how much information should be allowed to flow into the organization from the outside through use of push applications.

In many ways the push versus pull decision is specific to each person, depending on what work that individual is involved in at a particular point in time. Consider the case of a research pharmacologist working for a biotechnology firm. She may wish to be alerted when *any* information is posted on the corporate intranet concerning transdermal drug delivery, or even to have the material delivered directly to her desktop. On the other hand, she may want to go out and gather information on the chemical side effects of a certain drug only when she happens to be looking at how the drug interacts with use of a transdermal patch. As her research evolves, so do her knowledge needs, and she may want entirely different information pushed to her. Decisions about information access and delivery are a challenge because they are so dependent on individual users at a particular point in time. Table 3.1 outlines some of the differences between push and pull information retrieval.

Data mining is a very specific form of information retrieval that has become increasingly sophisticated since enterprise resource planning (ERP) software has made it possible for data to flow into data warehouses from a wide range of formerly incompatible systems and outside sources. The term data mining is used both to describe the generic process of analyzing the information in a data warehouse, and a specific set of techniques – including artificial intelligence tools,

Table 3.1 ◆ **Some differences between push and pull technologies**

	Push	Pull
Objective	Information capture	Navigation
User	Passive: Someone or something other than user *sends* the information	Active: User *seeks* the information
Technology	Always active	Active only when used
Best for	◆ Continuing knowledge needs ◆ Urgent or time-dependent information ◆ Creating awareness of what can be pulled (notification)	◆ One-time knowledge needs ◆ Conducting research ◆ Detailed information
Main advantage	Brings important material to user's attention	Allows user to access information at point of need
Main disadvantage	Can overload users since they don't control it	Requires time on the part of the user (both to master the technology and to deploy it)
Examples	◆ Search agents ◆ E-mail	◆ Search engines ◆ Browsers ◆ Directories, frameworks

neural networks and fuzzy logic – in which data is automatically explored to identify complex trends and relationships that may be far from obvious. Data mining represents the impressive strides we have made toward creating meaning from masses of data using pure technology. To date the information analyzed by these tools is largely transactional. It comprises only a small slice of the knowledge people need in the course of their daily work. Nevertheless, as data mining develops and becomes accessible to more members of the organization, it is becoming an increasingly important knowledge management tool.

Think about it!

Look at the examples of types of information listed in the following space. Add three more types of information that are specific to your work team. Use Table 3.1 to help you decide whether it is preferable to access this information when needed (pull) or to have it delivered regularly to the desktop (push).

		Push	Pull
1	Staff changes in your group	☐	☐
2	News or articles about customers	☐	☐
3	Changes to employee benefits	☐	☐
4	Employment policies	☐	☐
5	Job descriptions	☐	☐
6	Project status reports	☐	☐
7	News or articles about your company	☐	☐
8		☐	☐
9		☐	☐
10		☐	☐

Quick prioritization of challenge

Based on this section, how much priority should you assign to meeting this challenge?

◆ Balance push and pull technologies

Rate your organization on these two factors	Your organization's rating	Rating scale	
How much does your organization NEED to respond to this challenge?	**Need**	0	No need
		1	Weak need
		2	Moderate need
		3	Strong need
		4	Burning need
What is your organization's ABILITY to respond to this challenge?	**Ability**	0	Unable
		1	Slightly able
		2	Partially able
		3	Almost able
		4	Completely able

$Need \times Ability =$

Prioritization of challenge	*(multiply the two ratings)*

★ To do

Transfer your prioritization to box E on page 86.

Involve the user in tailoring navigation and capture tools

Organizations have been quick to realize the drawbacks of both push and pull technologies, particularly when it comes to using the Internet. Internet search engines, unless used by an experienced professional, yield too many hits. Furthermore, web site developers have learned how to game the system using a practice called spamdexing in which they manipulate search engines to ensure that their sites show up high on a search list, even if they are not particularly relevant. Push technologies have also received some bad press. Unless customization is highly sophisticated, the amount of information that is pushed to people when the entire Internet is the source is overwhelming. Multiply that by the number of workers in a large organization and the result is a major bandwidth headache.

Making information retrieval both faster and more accurate is the goal of both push and pull tools. The key is user involvement in customizing available tools. One way to customize pull tools is to learn the fine points of conducting advanced searches for the various Internet and intranet-based search engines. Advanced searches are typically one-off approaches to customized pull. Two of the more permanent approaches are bookmarking and creating customized or 'personalized' views. Bookmarks (also called 'Favorites' by those using Microsoft Internet Explorer) allow users to save and organize the URLs (or electronic addresses) of web pages as well as to navigate to them instantly without having to conduct searches or plug lengthy addresses into their browsers.

Personalized views are a way of organizing access to material on the Internet or an intranet. 'My Yahoo!' is one of the most well-known examples. A personalized view can include links to web pages, a list of key topics that a user wants to be searched regularly (for example the name of a client, or industry news), events, relevant training, etc. Views actually combine features of both push and pull. They can be visualized as a large set of labelled filing cabinets. The files are regularly and automatically refilled with different contents (push), but users need to open them in order to look inside. The better the user can tailor a view to meet his or her specific needs, the more useful the content inside the files will be.

Push tools are almost by definition customized by the user. In some cases, it is a simple matter of choosing what mailing list to subscribe to, or what news sources to receive. In most cases, however, customization involves filtering. Filters are a way of screening out unwanted items from large flows of incoming information. The user describes his or her interests, using key words, and information that matches the description is delivered accordingly. Some vendors offer software that stores profiles for everyone in the organization and then matches these to a wide range of information sources. More advanced or 'intelligent' filters are programmed to perform filtering operations even when the user is not present. These operations can include searching databases for information that matches a profile, generating abstracts of large documents, or extracting specific data. Intelligent filter technologies are summarized in Table 3.2.

All of the tailored push approaches have one thing in common: The more users become involved in personalizing their information retrieval strategy, the

Table 3.2 ◆ Intelligent filter technologies

Intelligent filters

◆ *Collaborative* or *social filtering*: The software compares the user's preferences to those of other users to predict which information will be of interest. Collaborative filtering makes use of agents which learn from other agents. It offers the tantalizing potential for community-building: the software's ability to match up like-minded individuals has important implications for eliminating work redundancies and creating communities of practice across functional areas or within geographically dispersed organizations.

◆ *Psychographic filtering*: Uses a psychographic profile to perform the same function as the collaborative filter.

◆ *Adaptive filtering*: This is the most sophisticated of the filters. By asking the user to rate material that has been delivered, the software is able to 'learn' the user's preferences, changing course (along with her.)[3]

---

better the application will work. Generally user involvement will fall into one of the following categories:

◆ create profile of interest areas using key words or descriptors;

◆ create an 'information hierarchy' which rates the importance of types of information and information sources (sources could even be specific individuals);

◆ rate the value of information once it is received;

◆ provide commentary on a specific piece of information for the benefit of others.

In the short term, all of this involvement can be time consuming. In the long run, it saves time and vastly enhances the quality of information delivered to individual users. But people often need a boost to get started. Organizations that assist users in maximizing these unfamiliar technologies will reap the benefits. One approach is to assemble a knowledge customization team made up of technologists, information specialists and knowledge managers, as well as representatives from the technology vendor organizations. These teams can work with individual users or teams of users to develop interest profiles, select appropriate databases for their desktops and customize available information retrieval technologies (see Think about it! exercise which follows).

Think about it!

The major hurdle in introducing information retrieval tools to an organization is convincing people that it is worthwhile to:

◆ make the initial time investment to customize them;

◆ continue to tweak them to maintain their viability.

This is clear role for a knowledge customization team.

Think about your organization or a team in which you participate. Write down the names of people whom you believe could assist others in customizing their information environment. Then rate the following tasks according to how much you believe you or your team could benefit from this type of assistance by placing a checkmark in the appropriate column.

This rating is for: .... Self .... Team

Names of potential knowledge customization team members   *Current role on team*

....

....

....

....

Task	*Low benefit*	*Moderate benefit*	*High benefit*
Creating personalized views	☐	☐	☐
Using filtering tools	☐	☐	☐
Organizing different types of content	☐	☐	☐
Establishing information delivery priorities	☐	☐	☐
Using advanced searches	☐	☐	☐

Quick prioritization of challenge

Based on this section, how much priority should you assign to meeting this challenge?

◆ *Involve the user in tailoring navigation and capture tools*

Rate your organization on these two factors	Your organization's rating	Rating scale
How much does your organization NEED to respond to this challenge?	**Need**	0 No need 1 Weak need 2 Moderate need 3 Strong need 4 Burning need
What is your organization's ABILITY to respond to this challenge?	**Ability**	0 Unable 1 Slightly able 2 Partially able 3 Almost able 4 Completely able

Need ✕ *Ability* =

★ To do
Transfer your prioritization to box F on page 87.

Prioritization of challenge

(multiply the two ratings)

4 Guidance

New organizational roles support information seekers

So far we have discussed information delivery via technology and information delivery via human beings as separate approaches. But increasingly, developers of cutting-edge knowledge management technologies recognize that people are a critical link between databases and the individuals trying to get something out of them. Powerful search engines aside, there is nothing like the human mind for detecting nuance and filtering the essential from the merely interesting. The more information is available, the more important human intermediaries become.

Disintermediation, the removal of the middleman in the mad charge to bond with customers, has been the topic of much excited discussion in the business literature. The Internet, in particular, is a significant force that allows companies to market their products directly to consumers without going through wholesalers, distributors, or even stores. Consumers' all-powerful access to information (assisted by a range of intelligent filters and agents) could soon allow them to describe what they need, post the description, and have sellers come to them. While this bright future may turn us all into computer-bound shoppers, when it comes to information, direct access can be both a blessing and a curse. As a result, we see a trend toward reintermediation, the growing use of people as filters for information. Reintermediation puts people in the middle, directing information traffic, ensuring that information seekers get what they want.

Why professional information filters make sense comes down to an issue of time and efficiency. Easy access to the Internet created an initial euphoria over the availability of 'free' information. But people have begun to realize that even with powerful search engines and filtering systems, looking for information in this vast sea is a waste of their time. In fact, this is the reason some organizations have resisted giving employees Internet access. Not so much because they believe people will spend their days trolling for dream vacations, dates or Dilbert jokes, but because they fear people might lose themselves in the ever-spiralling search for the perfect piece of information.

Taking the opposite position, other organizations have embraced the Internet wholeheartedly, dispensed with their corporate information departments and made research everybody's job. We believe that this approach is even more misguided than attempting to control information access. The result has generally been either that people spend an inordinate amount of time researching or they 'wing it'. Smart organizations look for ways that individuals with certain skills and knowledge can stand at the information floodgates and direct the flow so that it enhances rather than overwhelms.

These organizations have been able to meet the following *challenges.*

Challenges

- ◆ *Convert librarians into cybrarians.*
- ◆ *Create a new role: the knowledge manager.*
- ◆ *Use experts as information filters.*

Convert librarians into cybrarians

Organizations focused on knowledge management should pause before replacing their corporate information departments with an enterprise-wide Internet browser licence. A far more practical approach is to repurpose former librarians as Internet and electronic information intermediaries: cybrarians. Teamed up with knowledge managers and subject matter experts, cybrarians can guide employees to Internet sites that contain useful information. Cybrarians add Internet expertise to their already considerable skills in deftly searching on-line databases. For example, within the Global Best Practices initiative of professional services firm Arthur Andersen, corporate information specialists help content developers locate highly specific information on business processes even when research requests begin as nebulous. Content developers are then able to populate the firm's intranet with important resources used by its business professionals.

'A straightforward word search would never turn up the kind of information my clients require,' says Abbe Leffel, Manager of Customized Research at Arthur Andersen. 'I know exactly what I am looking for, so I can skim and discard irrelevant material very rapidly and toggle back and forth between different types of databases.' Leffel also knows her community and can anticipate many of their requests. In fact, she not only *pulls* information in response to specific client needs, she also *pushes* it, scanning more than 50 periodicals a month and flagging those that are pertinent to her customers' current or ongoing areas of interest.

Corporate information specialists are well aware that the opportunity now exists for them to dust off their image as mousy introverts and become key players in the brazen digital age. They can become part of 'knowledge teams' as cybrarians or take on the new role of knowledge manager. At Heller Financial, a Chicago-based financial services firm, information professionals are the force behind the company's intranet (see Profile).

◆ PROFILE ▶ *Heller Financial*

In recent years, companies have been closing their corporate libraries right and left, and many traditional librarians have found themselves on the unemployment lines. But the skills of the corporate information specialist are actually more critical than ever. It's just a matter of figuring out how to apply them in the transformed world of on-line technologies.

Heller Financial is a global financial services company based in Chicago. It provides small and medium-sized businesses with financing and leasing options ranging from working capital loans to collateral-based financing and equipment leasing. About 60% of Heller's 2,500 employees are based in the USA, 30% of them at corporate headquarters, including those in Corporate Finance.

Heller never had a formal information services function, but in the mid-1990s the Corporate Finance Group began to feel that they needed a library with a trained group of information specialists to handle their increasingly complex resource requirements. In addition, they needed professionals who could help them evaluate and navigate the burgeoning number of on-line information sources. The Corporate Finance Group's Business Information Center started small with two individuals whose responsibilities focused primarily on administrative tasks such as contracting with on-line tools providers. Michelle Madigan, Manager of Information Services, who came on board in 1994 as Head Librarian, says that plans for the Center were basic. 'The idea was that we would perform limited research and help people understand the kinds of on-line information available to them on their desktops. But it was clear that we could do much more.' The Internet turned that conviction into reality.

At Heller, as at many organizations, the librarians were one of the first groups to become aware of the Internet because of their role as on-line researchers. Says Madigan, 'Librarians are power users. Unlike most people, they probably make use of almost 100% of the power on their desktops.' The Business Information Center decided to be aggressive with their new-found knowledge. They launched Heller's first external web site in January 1996, when 'Internet' was just a high-tech buzzword to most marketing people. That was only the beginning. Madigan and her team knew the Internet would soon become part of everyone's work life at Heller, not just those at the Business Information Center. They decided to do everything they could to help their clients help themselves. In short, they became a training centre that introduced Heller to the power of the Internet.

'The idea was not to achieve complete disintermediation,' explains Madigan. 'On the contrary, at Heller people need to spend about 80% of their time generating revenue, and doing research is not part of this picture. Nevertheless, there are tools we can put on people's desktops which allow them instant access to the information they need to stay competitive – with very little effort on their part.' The only problem was getting people to use the tools. So the Business Information Center staff launched a company-wide training programme to teach people how to use the Internet and various information applications being deployed across the organization. In fact, the team has travelled to all of Heller's regional offices to introduce people to the expanding set of Business Information Center services.

It quickly became clear that the Business Information Center could benefit the entire organization, and the group was reorganized into a shared service available to all business units. This has made it one of the few groups within Heller that can look across the entire organization from a knowledge perspective with a good understanding of both information needs and information resources.

By 1997 the Business Information Center had been rechristened the Knowledge Center and its role had grown to fit the new name. Providing Heller professionals with direct access to most of the information that they had previously needed an information specialist to secure gave Knowledge Center staff time to pursue more value-added activities. In addition, the Knowledge Center played a critical role in cataloguing the voluminous information available over the Internet.

The Knowledge Center's view across the organization combined with its understanding of the emerging information environment made it a perfect candidate for developing Heller's intranet. This was exactly the challenge the Knowledge Center took on as it looked for ways to transfer its skill in gathering external knowledge to the internal environment. The Knowledge Center worked with other groups in the organization to design an intranet which was launched in October 1997. The information resource was so popular that several business units began clamouring for individual sites. A second iteration, launched in June 1998, included links to each business. The Knowledge Center continues to serve as the publisher of the intranet, providing support and training to content authors and quality assurance for all sites.

The Knowledge Center remains small – seven people – and it is so well-integrated into the organization that downsizing or outsourcing is not a major concern. The Knowledge Center plans to develop a corporate Yellow Pages, moderate on-line discussion groups and identify and nurture communities of practice. 'People used to not know what to make of us,' smiles Madigan. 'But now senior executives include us on company tours. We've even been proclaimed a "best practice".'

Think about it!

Listed in the following space are activities that information professionals perform in many knowledge-based organizations. Consider the value of activities that information professionals in your organization currently perform (put a checkmark in the appropriate column) as well as whether they should add those activities to their jobs if they do not perform them today.

Activity	Currently perform		Should add to job
	High value	Low value	✔
Conduct Internet searches	☐	☐	☐
Train people on Internet use	☐	☐	☐
Maintain intranet	☐	☐	☐
Push information to people on topics of interest	☐	☐	☐
Provide summaries of recent articles of interest on various topics	☐	☐	☐
Help people find information on intranet and corporate databases	☐	☐	☐
Help people use and customize information retrieval tools	☐	☐	☐

Other:

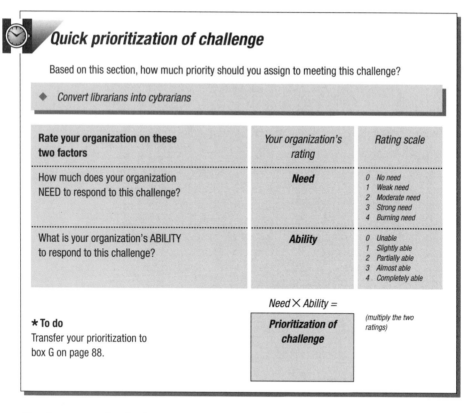

Quick prioritization of challenge

Based on this section, how much priority should you assign to meeting this challenge?

◆ *Convert librarians into cybrarians*

Rate your organization on these two factors	Your organization's rating	Rating scale
How much does your organization NEED to respond to this challenge?	**Need**	0 No need 1 Weak need 2 Moderate need 3 Strong need 4 Burning need
What is your organization's ABILITY to respond to this challenge?	**Ability**	0 Unable 1 Slightly able 2 Partially able 3 Almost able 4 Completely able

Need × Ability =

★ **To do**
Transfer your prioritization to box G on page 88.

Prioritization of challenge

(multiply the two ratings)

Create a new role: the knowledge manager

The term 'knowledge manager' has become something of a catch-all. Many organizations testing the knowledge management waters seem certain they need knowledge managers, although they are not quite sure what knowledge managers do. As a result, the role has become rather amorphous, encompassing anything from secretary to chief knowledge officer. To structure the role of the knowledge managers, we suggest, first, that a large part of their responsibility should be the management of on-line systems – intranets and other information repositories. Second, knowledge managers should serve a group of individuals who share common professional goals, also known as communities of practice.

Knowledge manager responsibilities can be roughly divided into two levels – those which are more administrative in nature and those which are more content-specific. The knowledge and skill levels required for these two sets of responsibilities are quite different and it makes sense to assign them to different individuals. We use the term knowledge coordinator for those who perform administrative functions, reserving knowledge manager for those who are more concerned with managing the content of the on-line systems. The following are guidelines for establishing these roles.

Guidelines for establishing the knowledge coordinator

Information management requires a great deal of administration. The more information there is in the organizational knowledge base, the more critical administration becomes. These administrative tasks, which are the responsibility of the knowledge coordinator, include:

✓ **Cataloguing content**: In larger communities of practice a great deal of information may be housed in an on-line system. Active communities tend to post material on a daily basis. Categorizing this material quickly becomes a critical function. The knowledge coordinator works with the knowledge manager or a content expert to determine which categories meet the needs of the community.

✓ **Maintaining timeliness**: On-line systems are used to post time-dependent information. However, individuals who post material rarely take responsibility for removing it at a later date. This task generally falls to the knowledge coordinator.

✓ **Confirming accuracy of member profiles**: It is important that members of the virtual community provide updated information about themselves, including phone numbers, addresses, E-mail addresses, areas of expertise and on-the-job experience. However, knowledge coordinators will often do a lot of the legwork required to keep member information up to date.

✓ **Providing access**: Frequently on-line communities require special passwords for participation. Knowledge coordinators can distribute routine passwords and process requests for admission into the on-line community.

✓ **Assisting new users with technology**: New users to an on-line system may have trouble with navigation. The knowledge coordinator should be able to walk them through the basics. A talented knowledge coordinator might even lead user training sessions or create tutorials.

✓ **Responding to member queries**: The knowledge coordinator serves as a human focal point for questions from the community regarding knowledge resources (e.g. sales aids, presentations, product specifications, customer information) that are (or could be) housed in an on-line system. Individuals who cannot locate resources should be able to call someone. These information requests also provide a window into the needs of the community.

Guidelines for establishing the knowledge manager

The knowledge manager does more than organize content within an on-line system. He or she must understand and even anticipate the community's needs. While the knowledge manager is not necessarily a content expert, he or she must be familiar and comfortable with areas that are of importance to the community. The following are responsibilities of the knowledge manager:

✓ **Answering on-line questions**: The on-line environment is frequently the only venue in which a geographically dispersed community can communicate. A large percentage of community postings are in the form of questions. The knowledge manager is responsible for seeing that such questions are answered, preferably in the on-line setting, but through one-to-one communication if necessary. The knowledge manager must liaise with experts – often by telephone – to make sure they assist other members of the community.

✓ **Facilitating on-line discussions**: In communities which are comfortable in the on-line environment, on-line conversations will take place. Members of the community will debate a particular issue, creating a lengthy 'thread' of ideas. The knowledge manager can not only moderate this discussion by interjecting questions and new lines of inquiry, but can also summarize the discussion and post the summary for future reference if the conversation is especially pertinent.

✓ **Scouting out useful material**: Knowledge managers should always be on the lookout for information – either elsewhere in the organization or outside the organization altogether – which would be helpful to the community. Pertinent information includes an events calendar, articles from news feeds, competitor data, etc. Knowledge managers may work with corporate information specialists to scan numerous sources – including the Internet – for information and post an analysis to the on-line system.

✓ **Guiding members of the community to other useful sources**: Not every-thing can be housed within a single on-line system. Part of the knowledge manager's responsibility is to direct members of the community to information that lies outside the boundaries of the system. For example, a very useful tool that the knowledge manager can provide is a map or directory to 'who knows what' within the community and the organization as a whole, as well as key sources outside the organization (such as academic institutions or associations). The Knowledge Manager can also set up links ('doc links' or 'hyperlinks', depending on the platform) to other on-line sources.

✓ **Networking within the community**: Finally, the knowledge manager's activities are by no means confined to the on-line setting. In order to understand the needs of the community, the knowledge manager must know the community. In particular, he or she must develop relationships with experts, because the knowledge manager will often wish to involve them in on-line discussions or encourage them to contribute resources to the on-line system. Networking requires face-to face meetings with key individuals and involvement in professional activities.

Many organizations struggle with the question of whether the duties of a knowledge manager constitute a full-time position or whether they can be tacked onto an existing job. Naturally, the answer will depend on the size of the community and its information needs. However, it is our general observation that the 'tacking on' approach rarely works. There is always an inherent conflict between the knowledge manager's responsibilities – many of which are concerned with building and maintaining an infrastructure – and 'fire-fighting' tasks which may be tied to other responsibilities. The result is inevitable: 'Fire fighting' takes precedence over building and maintenance. Content available to the community begins to lose currency and it ceases to be considered a resource. The on-line system is abandoned and the knowledge manager is reassigned. Of course, not all organizations can afford a full-time knowledge manager. An alternative solution is to assign the role to an individual who already has 'knowledge-brokering' responsibilities, such as a corporate information specialist. At the very least, organizations opting for part-time knowledge managers need to remain on the lookout for signs of 'crisis creep' which can sabotage the best-laid plans for providing ongoing support.

Think about it!

Consider the activities typically performed by knowledge coordinators or knowledge managers that are listed. Rate their importance to your organization and how well they are currently executed by placing an 'X' on the scales that are displayed beside each activity. Examine gaps between importance and performance to determine how to develop job descriptions for individuals performing these knowledge roles within your organization.

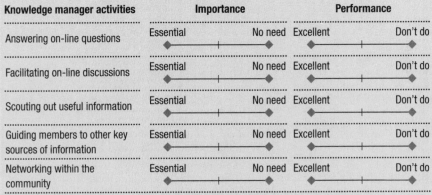

Knowledge manager activities	Importance	Performance
Answering on-line questions	Essential ◆——+——◆ No need	Excellent ◆——+——◆ Don't do
Facilitating on-line discussions	Essential ◆——+——◆ No need	Excellent ◆——+——◆ Don't do
Scouting out useful information	Essential ◆——+——◆ No need	Excellent ◆——+——◆ Don't do
Guiding members to other key sources of information	Essential ◆——+——◆ No need	Excellent ◆——+——◆ Don't do
Networking within the community	Essential ◆——+——◆ No need	Excellent ◆——+——◆ Don't do

Knowledge coordinator activities	Importance	Performance
Cataloguing content	Essential ◆——+——◆ No need	Excellent ◆——+——◆ Don't do
Maintaining timeliness of information	Essential ◆——+——◆ No need	Excellent ◆——+——◆ Don't do
Confirming accuracy of user profiles	Essential ◆——+——◆ No need	Excellent ◆——+——◆ Don't do
Providing timely access to password-protected areas	Essential ◆——+——◆ No need	Excellent ◆——+——◆ Don't do
Helping users understand information technology basics	Essential ◆——+——◆ No need	Excellent ◆——+——◆ Don't do
Responding to user queries	Essential ◆——+——◆ No need	Excellent ◆——+——◆ Don't do

Quick prioritization of challenge

Based on this section, how much priority should you assign to meeting this challenge?

◆ Create a new role: the knowledge manager

Rate your organization on these two factors	Your organization's rating	Rating scale
How much does your organization NEED to respond to this challenge?	*Need*	0 No need 1 Weak need 2 Moderate need 3 Strong need 4 Burning need
What is your organization's ABILITY to respond to this challenge?	*Ability*	0 Unable 1 Slightly able 2 Partially able 3 Almost able 4 Completely able

Need × Ability =

★ To do
Transfer your prioritization to box H on page 88.

Prioritization of challenge

(multiply the two ratings)

Use experts as information filters

Experts are nothing new. But with the surge of knowledge-based businesses, true expertise is at a premium. Amid a morass of information, who better than an expert to say what is truly valuable? If an expert can pass judgment on a particular piece of information, it becomes *de facto* more valuable because a credible source has validated it. Using experts as human filters who can narrow down information options to the best of the best is the premise that launched a company called The Mining Co. (since renamed About.com) which uses expert 'guides' to trawl through the sea of information on the Internet and assemble links to the most useful sites on their own web site. The company has created a platform for more than 600 subject-specific sites. 'Pre-screening' the Internet was also the idea behind Dow Jones Interactive's Web Center, which leverages the expertise of subject-area editors who regularly use the Internet for research (see Profile).

Many knowledge management technologies also make use of experts to determine the value of, or even add value to, information before it is passed on to a community. Some of these systems allow experts to publish material which is automatically routed to individuals whose interest profiles match the expert's contribution. The advantages of these 'expert contribution' models include:

◆ Important information is brought to the attention of individuals who might otherwise not know of its existence.

◆ The system takes care of notifying people who most need the information.

◆ Search time for critical information is minimized since it is automatically pushed to users.

◆ Experts are able to raise their visibility in the organization.

◆ Communities of practice are automatically formed as people with similar interests find one another and the experts they can use as resources.

Despite these advantages, using experts as information filters is not a silver bullet. The organization must grapple with the issue of whether employing experts for this purpose is the best use of their time. Not surprisingly, many organizations dodge the issue by saying they want experts to perform these tasks yet continue to reward them for doing whatever they were doing before. For this reason, experts themselves may be reluctant to take on the filtering/publishing role. Ultimately the benefits of using experts as filters depend on how well the organization can leverage the expert's ability to sift through and pass judgment on information without subverting the other ways they add value to the organization.

▶ PROFILE ▶ *Dow Jones Interactive Publishing*

Today, with more employees accessing the Internet from work, research has become an increasing part of many people's jobs. But access to the Internet creates its own problems: staying abreast of which web sites contain the best information can be time consuming. At Dow Jones Interactive, where editors sift through mounds of information and then make sense of it for others, an internal tool ultimately became an external service.

Dow Jones Interactive Publishing is a division of Dow Jones & Company that provides web-based business news and information tailored to corporate and consumer audiences. The division has two core products, The Wall Street Journal Interactive Edition and Dow Jones Interactive (DJI), the division's business intelligence service.

One of the tasks of the 40 editors responsible for DJI is to scan Dow Jones' various news wires, which are targeted to financial professionals such as analysts and traders, and to 'repurpose' this information for its broader corporate clientele. The job often calls for editors to conduct research in order to flesh out stories and provide both context and background.

Early users of the Web, the DJI editors – who generally specialize in particular industries – developed a grasp of which sites on the Internet offered the most useful content for their areas of professional interest. Each editor soon had a list of bookmarks which he or she often shared with others who covered the same industry segments. Sometimes editors even reviewed sites for the benefit of their co-workers. Ultimately the entire collection of editors' bookmarks and reviews was organized into a directory of web sites. Almost as soon as the initiative began, the group realized that this valuable research tool could be offered externally to enhance the usefulness of DJI's core news service. The team began looking at ways that editors' knowledge of the Web could be leveraged into plans that were already underway for a broader web-based service.

The result was the Dow Jones Business Directory. In late 1998 the service was expanded into the Dow Jones Web Center, which offers indexing and searching capability across several thousand pre-selected sites. Sites are crawled at least once, and sometimes four times a day to check for new material and broken links. Reviews of specific sites include ratings of design, ease of navigation and speed, as well as content.

'The Web Center is an ongoing initiative,' says Timothy M. Andrews, Vice President and Editor at DJI Publishing. 'We keep adding sites – often based on customer recommendations – but we also prune those that no longer offer top-quality content. The idea is to serve as an "infomediary" so that users don't have to do their own filtering.'

 Think about it!

The following is a list of activities performed by experts who serve as information filters for others in the organization. All of these activities are time consuming, which means that experts will spend less time on other activities, such as conducting research, serving customers or managing businesses.
Think about how critical these activities are in light of the trade-offs they require, then rank them in order of importance, with 1 being the most important for your organization or group.

Rank order these activities with 1 being most important

☐ Experts spend time reviewing information for accuracy and quality before it is sent out to others in the organization.

☐ Experts add commentary to information to enhance its value before it is sent to others.

☐ Experts help select the best of the best information to be archived for future use.

☐ Experts are 'on call' to help others with problems or issues requiring a high level of subject knowledge.

☐ Experts contribute their own information (papers, code, presentations, proposals, designs, etc.) to the organization's information systems.

☐ Other: ....

Quick prioritization of challenge

Based on this section, how much priority should you assign to meeting this challenge?

◆ *Use experts as information filters*

Rate your organization on these two factors	Your organization's rating	Rating scale
How much does your organization NEED to respond to this challenge?	*Need*	0 No need 1 Weak need 2 Moderate need 3 Strong need 4 Burning need
What is your organization's ABILITY to respond to this challenge?	*Ability*	0 Unable 1 Slightly able 2 Partially able 3 Almost able 4 Completely able

Need × *Ability* =

★ To do	Prioritization of challenge	(multiply the two ratings)
Transfer your prioritization to box I on page 89.		

5 Completeness

The knowledge infrastructure is comprehensive and well-organized

Almost every knowledge management initiative includes plans for some kind of digital source of information – a knowledge base of best practices, a network of linked web pages on a corporate intranet or a database of skills and experience. The logic behind creating these elegant electronic houses is the irrefutable convenience of supermarket shopping: if I could only get it all in *one place*, I would be able to spend more time doing the things that really count. Useful as these knowledge containers can be, organizations run the risk of being mesmerized into thinking that a technology solution can be used to address what is primarily a people issue. To make these repositories truly useful sources of information, organizations need to address the following *challenges*.

Challenges

◆ *Provide access to both centrally managed and self-published information.*

◆ *Create frameworks and processes that promote knowledge reuse.*

Provide access to both centrally managed and self-published information

The explicit knowledge that is housed in information systems can be divided into two broad categories, both of which are aimed at expanding the individual's access to organizational knowledge:

1 **Centrally managed information**: Centrally managed systems, also called 'convergent', contain codified or packaged information, organized within a specific framework. The information can range from the mundane, such as policies and procedures, to the more thought-based, including effective approaches to business processes, ideas about how to serve customers or even archives of past thinking that might prove useful in the future. While the information may come from a variety of sources and individuals, it generally goes through a quality control or sanctioning process before it is published and made available to others. A central publishing group serves as a gatekeeper for this information. Experts affiliated with the publishing group perform quality control. On the downside, centralized processing takes time, so information does not immediately become available to users. In addition, the packaging process removes information one or more steps from those who created it. On the upside, users know that the information they access has the organization's official seal of approval as being the 'best of the best'.

2 **Self-published information**: Self-publishing or 'divergent' systems allow anyone in the organization to make their information available. Self-published content may take the form of information artifacts, such as documents, presentations, lines of code or graphics, but it can also include discussion threads or electronic conversations and E-mail. These systems are particularly useful in pulling together people with common interests to form an on-line community where information can be freely exchanged. Often the best of self-published information makes its way into centrally managed systems. Self-publishing models greatly expand the amount of knowledge that is available to searchers. There is also no time lag between the moment an individual decides to contribute a piece of information and the moment it becomes available to others. However, *caveat emptor* applies with this model: there is always a danger of the uninformed informing the uninformed.

Dividing all organizational systems into these two categories is overly simplistic. In reality, they exist on a continuum. At one end of the spectrum are the centrally managed knowledge bases and information repositories that are run by departments for which this is a sole responsibility. At the other end are personal web sites on which individuals advertise their knowledge wares. In between are individual groups or communities of practice within organizations which publish content on their own web sites. The publishing process may be centrally determined, but these groups are responsible for quality control of their material.

Centrally managed and self-publishing systems take very different approaches to the collection and dissemination of information, some of which are outlined in Table 3.3.

Table 3.3 ◆ Types of knowledge systems

Centrally managed	Self-publishing
Content has been 'scrubbed'/expert sanctioned: best of the best	Credibility is variable; runs the risk of the uninformed informing the uniformed
Content must stand the test of time	Content can accommodate time-dependent information
Strategically important or 'mission-critical' content – quality over quantity	Content concerned with solving problems in the here and now – more tactical in emphasis
Misses informal, collaborative knowledge	Allows informal exchange, question and answer format, dialogue
Connects people to information	Connects people to information, but more importantly to other people
Labour intensive – content 'packaged' by dedicated staff	Content generated by the community
Content may not be immediately available to users	Content can be made available to users as soon as it is created

Organizations need to understand how centrally managed and self-publishing systems balance each other, and what type of information is appropriate for each. From the perspective of users, it is not necessary to separate these two types of systems. In fact, the more seamlessly users can navigate between the two, the better. For example, the ability to add commentary (a self-publishing feature) to material housed in a centrally managed repository can enhance its value. Nevertheless, users should be able to distinguish between sanctioned knowledge and that which has been contributed by fellow members.

Think about it!

Using the descriptions from Table 3.3, create a chart which lays out the rationale for centrally managing or self-publishing the five major types of information that are most important for your work group. (Choose one using a checkmark.) For example, consider such questions as:

◆ Is it critical for me to know that this information has passed some kind of organizational standard? If yes, the information should be centrally managed.

◆ Is the goal to generate as many ideas as possible around this topic regardless of whether they have been finely tuned or not? If yes, a self-publishing model is preferable.

Our group's major information types	Centrally managed	Self-published	Rationale
1			
2			
3			
4			
5			

Quick prioritization of challenge

Based on this section, how much priority should you assign to meeting this challenge?

◆ *Provide access to both centrally managed and self-published information*

Rate your organization on these two factors	Your organization's rating	Rating scale
How much does your organization NEED to respond to this challenge?	**Need**	0 No need 1 Weak need 2 Moderate need 3 Strong need 4 Burning need
What is your organization's ABILITY to respond to this challenge?	**Ability**	0 Unable 1 Slightly able 2 Partially able 3 Almost able 4 Completely able

Need × Ability =

★ To do

Transfer your prioritization to box J on page 90.

Prioritization of challenge

(multiply the two ratings)

Create frameworks and processes that promote knowledge reuse

No matter how many resources an organization pours into creating highly sophisticated knowledge systems, the question looms: will people use them? For any knowledge base or intranet to draw users, it has got to be *better* at helping them find information than the systems and networks with which they are already comfortable and familiar. Having a solid framework and processes for making organizational knowledge available will ultimately ensure that people will use the information.

When creating knowledge repositories or intranets, keep in mind the following principles.

Start with the work

Before considering any information technology solution, managers first need to address some very basic questions:

◆ How do we think about information?

◆ If someone in this company were looking for a piece of information, how would they frame their search?

◆ What categories of information are important to us?

◆ In short, how do we work in this organization?

The prime directive of a knowledge management system is to integrate it with how people think about the information they need to do their work and how they get their work done. A consulting firm may think about critical information in terms of industry groups, methodologies and client proposals. A high-tech company may think in terms of product categories and alliances. A bank may organize itself around customer information and product offerings. Sub-groups within an organization may approach work differently. For example, factory workers may think about the information they need to perform discrete tasks, whereas the sales force needs to access information by customer group.

Those responsible for building knowledge management systems must understand how different work groups approach information, because this 'embedded template' defines how the information should be organized. An intuitive framework is as important to making a knowledge base or intranet navigable and accessible as the most user-friendly software. For instance, professional services firm PricewaterhouseCoopers organizes much of its information around the client engagement process (see Profile). NatWest Markets, the investment banking arm of UK-based NatWest Group, began piloting knowledge management initiatives across its 7,000 employees, they created a series of knowledge-sharing databases organized around the needs of a small cross-functional community of individuals who were focused on pharmaceutical clients. The databases, which were highly specific to the work of this community included:

◆ experience: employee credentials and work history;

◆ product innovations: new products and background on deals, including how they were structured;

◆ opportunities: inside details on potential deals.

It is important to involve users in developing a framework which makes sense to them. This is not the same as expecting users to provide the content for a knowledge base or intranet. But it does help ensure that if users have something to contribute, they will know where to put it, and if someone needs to find something fast, they will know where to look.

Avoid clutter: quality over quantity

Knowledge repositories and intranets are not dumping grounds for every thought anyone in the organization has ever had. They should be containers for knowledge that the organization – or a particular group within the organization – considers important and potentially useful to others. But if a knowledge base contains fourteen documents on the same topic, users are forced to wade through all of them before choosing the best.

In the previous challenge we talked about centrally managed knowledge systems. These systems have an advantage over self-publishing systems in that it is easier to control the amount of information that gets fed into them. Filtering for the best of the best can be done before information enters the system. For self-publishing systems the issue of clutter has to be addressed after the fact. Nevertheless, having a process for regular spring cleaning led by knowledge managers and subject matter experts helps eliminate duplicative material.

Update, update, update

Nothing drives users away faster than outdated information. Even the perception of staleness should be avoided. Unless the presentation from 1993 is the best that the organization has to offer, use the one from the current year. If pages have been deleted from the intranet, make sure links to the page have been deleted as well. If a discussion thread is no longer relevant, get rid of it or archive it elsewhere. When users encounter obsolete material in a knowledge base, it undermines trust in the entire system.

The more a knowledge repository or intranet grows, the more difficult it is to keep it up to date, and the larger the staff needed to manage and maintain it. This brings us back to the previous point – less is more. The constant need to update may mean that a minimalist approach is preferable. Offering pointers to information rather than the information itself is one way to achieve this. In the case of centrally managed systems, it is always a good idea to maintain accurate and current records of where information comes from so that original contributors can assume some of the responsibility for updating or excising outdated information.

Train one-on-one

In the final analysis, no one will be able to find anything in an organizational knowledge base if they do not know how to use it. A problem that besets many cutting-edge technology solutions is underutilization. The root cause is 50% inertia and 50% terror. Even though knowledge-sharing tools might make their lives easier in the long run, people are often reluctant to change their habits. The assumption that people will use knowledge-sharing tools because they are available is an erroneous one.

Are in-depth, place-based training programmes the solution? Training is expensive and can be a logistical nightmare. On-line training and work aids, which assist users at the point of need when they are in the midst of accomplishing critical tasks, have a definite advantage over place-based training. However, without human assistance, impatient users (which is everybody using an unfamiliar IT-based tool to accomplish familiar work routines) will often log off and check out.

The real challenge of deploying an intranet or a knowledge base across an organization is getting people to understand how the new system can help them do their work. If it can help them, people will bend over backwards to teach themselves how the system works. For this reason, rather than bring groups of people to a training centre, it makes sense to send trainers out to educate natural work groups in their work environments. Deployment teams can then focus on helping the work group customize the system to their requirements. A side benefit to developers of observing people using the system in the context of real work situations is the opportunity to gather feedback that can be used to make improvements. This was the rationale behind the knowledge management system deployment efforts of ICL, the UK-based technology consulting firm (see Profile).

In large organizations it is impossible to send teams of trainers out to get every individual up to speed on a new system. A 'train the trainer' approach is more realistic. Volunteers throughout the organization receive training on how to use the system and these individuals are then sent out to train their co-workers. Using volunteers lets deployment begin with enthusiasts. When launching its intranet, Global Village, telecommunications giant US West took this 'champion' approach, using what Director Sherman Woo terms a 'pyramid scheme'. Woo gave anyone access to the system who promised to bring two more people into the fold. Thus Global Village began its life with a membership of individuals who believed passionately in the potential of networked communications – people who enthusiastically embraced the new system, rather than those who saw it as an additional burden. What began as a covert operation soon came to include some 30,000 people.

◢◤ PROFILE ▶ *PricewaterhouseCoopers' Financial Advisory Services group*

"When one looks at knowledge management systems they generally come in two flavors," *says Charnell Havens, CKO of PricewaterhouseCoopers' Financial Advisory Services (FAS)* *group. "There's the plain vanilla kind which is light on focused collaboration, but heavy on* *infrastructure. A system is build on the expectation that the faithful will flock to it. Then* *there's the strawberry flavor – knowledge systems that are concerned with solving specific*

business issues. These go beyond mere computing to include both content management and community formation. People gather around key issues, and the metrics virtually fall in your lap. You can't get the strawberry without the vanilla base, but if you stop with the vanilla, you rarely get appreciable results."

When Price Waterhouse and Coopers & Lybrand merged to become Pricewater-houseCoopers (PwC) in 1998, the new entity was faced with the overwhelming task of combining two partially developed knowledge management systems. PwC's solution was to take the best ideas from each of the legacy firms, organizing its information repositories around the work processes of its members. Each line of service took a slightly different approach, but the overarching theme was the same: use the client engagement and its subprocesses as the core organizing framework of the knowledge system.

PwC's Financial Advisory Services group had to vault over some very high hurdles. As a conglomeration of services that are neither under the aegis of the core assurance and tax business or the management consulting business, FAS provides comprehensive financial, economic, interventions (such as disposition of assets) and strategic advice to companies with complex business problems and disputes. "In some ways FAS is made up of cowboys," notes Havens. "It's good because we have a tremendous amount of innovation going on and a huge number of new products being generated. But getting everyone pointed in the same direction can be a challenge. The questions we needed to ask ourselves were 'Where are the leverage points? What are the kinds of things people could do the same way, and where are completely unique solutions required?'"

To answer these questions, the FAS engagement cycle – the way FAS does business – was divided into six subprocesses: 1) Lead to Proposal; 2) Proposal to Contract; 3) Contract to Service Delivery; 4) Service Delivery to Engagement Close; 5) Engagement Close to Relationship Enhancement; and 6) Relationship Enhancement to Lead. To proceed through the cycle it was determined that people needed four basic things as a start:

◆ A reliable window into legacy information repositories

◆ The ability to track client leads

◆ Access to an inventory of service line-wide skills

◆ Document management capabilities.

As a result, four IT tools were integrated into PwC FAS's knowledge management strategy, dubbed Team Power. A Lotus-Notes-based navigator called FAS Link.Power connects users to critical legacy databases and external information links on the Internet. Lead.Power, a global lead tracking systems allows people to manage sales leads, coordinate marketing efforts, and identify staffing needs. Credential.Power is a global repository of professional profiles, experiences, and CVs. It helps those responsible for engagements locate the appropriate skill sets to staff them. Document.Power is a system for housing and managing engagement documents. It allows for sharing of templates, version control of working documents, and real-time collaboration on document development.

This suite of applications, though powerful, is considered only a beginning. The bigger issue, according to Havens, is being responsive to people's wish lists and unique knowledge needs. To address this, the FAS Knowledge Management team conducted a series of workshops over the course of several months, bringing together hundreds of people across professional levels, industries, functions, and geographical regions. The mission: find the answer to the question "If you could wave a magic wand, how would you like to do this work in the future, and what kinds of knowledge would you like to get instantaneously?" The answers gathered from the workshops allowed the team to identify what knowledge needs were global, what were specific to certain countries, industries or services, and what areas required "one-off" solutions.

"Ultimately," says Havens, "it's the ability to customized a knowledge management system to users' business needs that moves you up the food chain from vanilla to strawberry."

> PROFILE *ICL*

Will the training stick? That is the big question when people are trained on new knowledge systems. Will people be using the system three months later or will they revert to their old methods of gathering information? One way to ensure on-going system use is to show people how it relates to their work.

ICL, the global IT systems supplier which is now part of Fujitsu, employs 19,000 people in over 50 countries. Once primarily a computer designer and manufacturer, the company has been transitioning to a service-based organization since the mid-1990s. This transition raised the bar on the need to leverage knowledge across the organization. An analysis of information management initiatives showed that many were already in place, but they were disparate and uncoordinated. In 1996 the CEO approved a plan to create a more formal and intentional approach to knowledge management at ICL. The initiative was dubbed 'Project VIK' (Valuing ICL Knowledge).

The Project VIK team determined that a global information service available to all employees would earn rapid support if it could truly place hard-to-locate information at people's fingertips. The information service was named 'Café VIK' to emphasize the theme of connection. The goal of Café VIK was to reduce the time people had to spend searching for information – estimated at about one day per week. Unlike many of the deployers of most knowledge repository projects, the Café VIK development team spent considerable up-front time interviewing prospective users about *what* information they needed most in order to do their jobs. This 'mission-critical' information formed the framework for Café VIK.

Café VIK was launched at the end of 1996. But the team knew it could not just passively announce the new tool if it wanted it to be adopted. The solution was to create an internal marketing programme that conveyed the critical linkage between knowledge management and the reinvented, service-oriented ICL. These themes were used to introduce the new Café VIK tool.

Taking a unique and whimsical approach, the deployment team set up PCs at small café tables complete with coffee pots and free pastries in conference rooms of various ICL offices. Small groups were brought in first for the knowledge management introduction, and then for the hands-on training. Deployment team staff, who stood out in bright green T-shirts emblazoned with 'Click for VIK', were on hand to coach each individual as needed – but only when asked for help. These sessions were so successful that a year-long roadshow ensued.

Notes Elizabeth Lank, the Programme Director who headed up the VIK initiative, 'Employees felt the tool was something that was being done *for* them rather than *to* them. It was also clear that their feedback was valued and that changes would be made as a result of it.' By November 1998, two years after launch, Café VIK was used regularly by approximately 12,000 of ICL's 19,000 employees, and the number continues to grow.

Think about it!

Conduct a scavenger hunt. Browse though your intranet or one of your organization's databases and identify a list of ten pieces of information. Write them down on a piece of paper, including their specific locations. Then assemble different teams, give them the list without the locations and ask them to find the information. Ask the groups the following questions:

◆ How long did it take to find the information?

◆ Did you use a word search or did you get to the information in some other way?

◆ What path did you take to find this information?

◆ Was the information where you thought it would be? If not, where did you think it would be?

◆ If you had been looking for this information as part of your work, would you have been frustrated, or was this a reasonable process to go through?

Use people's feedback to think about the frameworks your organization is using to house information. Are they logically integrated with the way people think about information?

Quick prioritization of challenge

Based on this section, how much priority should you assign to meeting this challenge?

◆ *Create frameworks that promote knowledge reuse*

Rate your organization on these two factors	Your organization's rating	Rating scale
How much does your organization NEED to respond to this challenge?	*Need*	0 No need 1 Weak need 2 Moderate need 3 Strong need 4 Burning need
What is your organization's ABILITY to respond to this challenge?	*Ability*	0 Unable 1 Slightly able 2 Partially able 3 Almost able 4 Completely able

Need × *Ability* =

★ To do
Transfer your prioritization to box K on page 91.

Prioritization of challenge

(multiply the two ratings)

Notes

1 The distinction between information (articulated knowledge) and knowledge (ideas and know-how embedded in the individual) has already been discussed in Chapter 1. Getting hold of the former may only require the interaction of the seeker and a computer, book, manual, etc. Getting hold of the latter always requires the interaction of a seeker and a holder of knowledge. However, the issues (but not always the tactics) involved in the process of acquiring information and knowledge are essentially the same. We therefore often use these terms interchangeably.

2 *On-Line Communities in Business*, Next Generation Research Group, Arthur Andersen, February 1999.

3 Adapted from 'Intelligent filters to the rescue! (sort of...)', by Jesse Berst, ZDNet AnchorDesk, July 7 1997.

Agenda for action: Get

The action steps presented in the Agenda for action come from the ideas suggested in this chapter. If you believe that your organization needs to focus on improving how well people are able to get the knowledge they need, this template and its suggested action steps are one way to get started.

The Agenda for action is organized in the same way as this chapter. Each imperative and its accompanying challenges are clustered together. Action steps are suggested for each challenge based on the text and profiles. You decide which action steps make sense for your organization and use the empty space to scribble in any additional ideas that come to mind.

Before you begin, make sure that you have transferred your prioritization ratings for each challenge. The prioritization ratings will remind you whether you believed that the challenge was worth pursuing. The maximum prioritization rating is 16, the minimum is 0.

How you use the prioritization ratings is up to you. For example, depending on the range of prioritization ratings, you may decide to ignore all challenges below a minimum threshold and focus only on those challenges above it. Or you may decide that everything that is not 0 deserves at least some thought. We invite you to use this Agenda for action as a place to start acting on your knowledge management priorities.

 **Agenda for action**

1 Articulation

People can describe their information needs

A

Understand and communicate intended use of information	

Prioritization rating

Action step	Who should be involved	My first 'to do'
Work with corporate information specialists or other professional searchers to develop brief interviewing guidelines that will help frame information requests to make them more efficient.		
Scan the intranet or groupware systems to identify instances of poorly articulated requests for information and provide requestors with articulation guidelines for future use.		
Survey teams to determine whether poor information-gathering practices have impacted performance; link up 'problem teams' with an information professional who can help them better understand their information needs.		
Other:		

B

Direct information requests appropriately

Prioritization rating

Action step	Who should be involved	My first 'to do'
Develop a set of guidelines with my work team to direct how information requests are made.		
Identify instances of blanket requests and work with requestors to develop more effective information-gathering approaches.		
Other:		

2 Awareness

People know where to find knowledge resources

C

Provide signposts: directories, Yellow Pages and maps

Prioritization rating

Action step	Who should be involved	My first 'to do'
Prioritize a list of communities or groups in our organization that are most in need of creating a directory of knowledge resources.		
Select a small number for a pilot project, and identify a champion to work with each of these groups.		
Help champions develop a template, either paper-based or electronic, which will gather information about people's expertise and competencies.		
Create training sessions for the purpose of gathering information on expertise.		
Validate sources of expertise by polling groups about where they go for specific types of information.		
Other:		

Use communities of practice to cast a spotlight on organizational knowledge

D

Prioritization rating

Action step	Who should be involved	My first 'to do'
Identify key communities that serve as logical collection points for organizational knowledge.		
Talk with community members about setting aside some resources to support gathering and organizing their mission-critical knowledge to make it available across the enterprise.		
Talk with other organizations that support knowledge management initiatives built around professional communities in order to gather ideas about how their approaches can be adapted to our organization.		
Discuss ways to promote the fact that groups are maintaining and disseminating knowledge related to their communities.		
Other:		

3 Access

People have the tools they need to find and capture information

E

Balance push and pull technologies

Prioritization rating

Action step	Who should be involved	My first 'to do'
Create an information management workshop with the assistance of information specialists to help people understand how to decide what information they need to have pushed to them.		
Assemble an information management team to determine what information needs to be pushed and what information can reside on an intranet or in databases for users to pull when needed.		
Create templates that will help other groups in the organization develop a push vs pull strategy.		
Other:		

F

Prioritization rating

Involve the user in tailoring navigation and capture tools

Action step	Who should be involved	My first 'to do'
Survey people with experience using various information retrieval tools. Gather data on which tools they have found most useful.		
Test tools with less experienced people to determine which are the most intuitive.		
Pilot test a knowledge customization team that works with users to tailor both push and pull information retrieval tools.		
Create training guidelines and tip sheets that can be used by people who have worked with knowledge customization teams. These materials can be used by 'graduates' to educate other team members about customizing tools.		
Other:		

4 Guidance

New organizational roles support information seekers

G

Convert librarians into cybrarians

Prioritization rating

Action step	Who should be involved	My first 'to do'
Collect information on current activities of corporate information specialists.		
Convene a team of information specialists to perform a gap analysis: identify areas where these professionals can help members maximize their information environments.		
Create a pilot programme in which information specialists work more closely with a team or community, implementing some of the activities identified in the gap analysis.		
Other:		

H

Create a new role: the knowledge manager

Prioritization rating

Action step	Who should be involved	My first 'to do'
Identify knowledge positions that currently exist in the organization and compare responsibilities. Assess whether these are commensurate with skill levels of people performing them.		
Identify areas where communities within the organization could benefit from the assistance of someone in a knowledge manager role.		
Bring together groups of people in knowledge roles to exchange ideas and best practices.		
Other:		

Use experts as information filters

Prioritization rating

Action step	Who should be involved	My first 'to do'
Ask groups to identify one or two areas where they think it is worthwhile to divert experts from other responsibilities to improve the quality of information that is archived or sent to others in the organization. Determine whether anyone is already responsible for managing information in these areas.		
Identify experts by asking people who they go to for information identified in previous step. Compare responses. Are these people involved in some form of information management?		
Assemble groups of identified experts to discuss how they can play a role in information filtering. Look for ways to minimize administrative responsibilities.		
Other:		

5 Completeness

The knowledge infrastructure is comprehensive and well-organized

J

Provide access to both centrally managed and self-published information	
	Prioritization rating

Action step	Who should be involved	My first 'to do'
Survey groups to determine whether: ◆ they feel the information in knowledge repositories is credible ◆ they have ample opportunity to contribute information.		
Speak with individuals responsible for centralized information management. How are contributions from members fed into the centralized system? Are there links between the centralized system and other systems which accept contributions from anyone in the organization?		
Other:		

K

Prioritization rating

Create frameworks and processes that promote knowledge reuse

Action step	Who should be involved	My first 'to do'
Soil sample the organization's key information repositories, including the intranet, by examining pieces of information that reside in various locations. Check for currency and redundancy.		
Ask people in the organization how often they find what they are looking for on the intranet or in other information repositories. Try to get a sense of whether people find the organizing frameworks intuitive.		
Select several work teams or groups and survey them about how they use available information resources. Are there opportunities to conduct work-centred training sessions that will improve people's ability to use these resources?		
Other:		

4 Use

But in the interim they had tasted that dangerous fruit of the tree of knowledge – innovation, which is well known to open the eyes, often in an uncomfortable manner.

George Eliot, *Scenes of Clerical Life*

When it comes to using information, effectiveness and efficiency are no longer satisfactory. Innovation has become the byword of the day. How can members of the organization combine information in ways that uniquely satisfy the individual customer? Innovation forces people to climb out of their functional, operating and even process silos to look for ideas under rocks and in nooks and crannies they would otherwise not have considered. The organization can provide many tools to enhance out-of-the box thinking, but most important is establishing an environment in which creativity, experimentation and receptivity to new ideas are encouraged

At a glance . . .

What is new?	Focus on non-traditional sources of insight and out-of-the-box thinking.
What is the problem?	Silo mentality can prevent ideas from crossing organizational boundaries.
What is the individual or team objective?	Innovation that uniquely meets customer needs (the best solution).
What is the organization's responsibility?	Establishing an environment that stimulates creative use of information.
	Providing tools that improve the way in which information is used.

Introduction

Once knowledge has been located and obtained, people are faced with the challenge of applying it rapidly to their specific situation. At this stage of the knowledge management process the focus is on the customer – what does the customer want and how can the organization use its knowledge to meet these demands? The more varied the sources of knowledge and the more contact people have had with others whose perspectives and approaches are different from their own, the higher the potential for a creative and innovative application of knowledge. Using knowledge effectively to create customer value depends upon the organization's ability to respond to the following *imperatives* and *challenges.*

Imperatives and challenges

Permeability	Ideas flow both in and out of the organization, exposing people to many different perspectives and possibilities:
	◆ *Morph the organizational structure to improve communications and knowledge flows.*
	◆ *Design the physical environment in ways that cross-fertilize ideas.*
	◆ *Treat information as an open resource that flows freely to all corners of the organization.*
	◆ *Collaborate on a routine basis with all stakeholder communities.*
Freedom	People are generally comfortable and confident about acting on new ideas:
	◆ *Value the contributions of everyone in the organization.*
	◆ *Create time and space for play.*

1 Permeability

Ideas flow both in and out of the organization, exposing people to many different perspectives and possibilities

Crossing traditional organizational boundaries is important not only for obtaining know-how, but also for using it effectively in new situations. Mastering new ways of building solutions is often the result of combining diverse skill sets and perspectives that reside in equally diverse locations. Rigid organizational boundaries impose high barriers that impede the flow of ideas and the possibility for innovation. Whether it is the hierarchies of authority that influence decisions about who gets what information or the physical barriers of closed doors that literally limit access to the people who know, or a myopic view of who is inside and who is outside the organizational tent, impermeable boundaries can choke the spread of ideas in organizations. Boundaries can also keep old ideas around, cluttering up the space needed for new ones and making breakthroughs hard to imagine, let alone achieve. Of course, when ideas do course through the organization, bad ones may slip in while good ones slip out. Ideas, like choices, make life difficult, but they also enrich the sense of possibilities. To promote the flow of ideas, organization must meet these *challenges.*

Challenges

◆ Morph the organizational structure to improve communications and knowledge flows.

◆ Design the physical environment in ways that cross-fertilize ideas.

◆ Treat information as an open resource that flows freely to all corners of the organization.

◆ Collaborate on a routine basis with all stakeholder communities.

Morph the organizational structure to improve communications and knowledge flows

The 'process view' that swept through organizations in the late 1980s was a reaction to the functional silo mentality of traditional vertical hierarchies that were the norm in most large organizations. In the vertical model, information flows were focused on meeting the needs of senior executives, and were directed steadily and ineluctably upwards. At some lofty level of the organizational food chain, a highly digested version of the facts was shared across functions. Decisions were made and actions were taken as the implications flowed back down the chain. Customer needs were always assumed to be the point of the information flow, but this goal was frequently lost in the scurry to meet internal requirements and to look good to senior executives. It was not important that everyone in the organization understood why they were taking action, it only mattered that they acted as directed.

The process view was supposed to change all that. Putting the customer at the apogee of organizational focus made value creation a foregone conclusion. By rerouting organizational roads to make sure they all led to Rome, the assumption of the process view was that information would flow to the right people and they would know what to do with it. The central irony of the rush to adopt a process-based structure is that for many organizations it has simply turned the silos on their sides. Now information flows horizontally, wending its way through process teams. However, many of the newly constituted process teams remain as impervious to outsiders and outside information as the old functional groups. Process-based structures have for the most part had little impact on improving information flows among organizational groups. Swapping one organizational structure for another does not appear to boost fluid movement of information. Organizations need to be able to adopt many different structures simultaneously in order to achieve the kind of creative use of knowledge that is required to serve customers.

The language that is used to describe organizations today expresses the extent to which complexity and change have become the experience of organizational life. Spaghetti, self-organizing, informal, virtual, learning, networked, viral and dis-organized are among the adjectives that are used to explain organizational structures. These new organizational forms reflect the increasing need for rapid and unobstructed knowledge flows in order to meet customer demands for increasingly complex and one-of-a-kind solutions. Organizations such as Oticon (see Profile) that have adopted these new organizational structures are increasingly the focus of intense scrutiny as others try to glean insights from their experimentation.

Organizational designers are looking far outside the world of business to disciplines such as the social, biological and physical sciences for ideas about how these new structures should be built and how they might be expected to operate. Margaret Wheatley's *Leadership and the New Science* popularized and brought an easy-to-consume version of applied chaos theory and self-organizing systems into the mainstream of business discussion. Peter Senge's *The Fifth Discipline* similarly popularized the recondite and academic area of system dynamics, making 'the learning organization' a common way of describing an organization's aspirations for generative, sustainable growth. Perhaps the most significant contribution of these thinkers has been as a human-centred antidote or counterbalance to the ascendance of information technology in organizational systems. Technology can deliver rapid and unobstructed knowledge flows, but it does so in a highly engineered, low-contact setting and is generally restricted to information that is easy to codify and disseminate. Organizational structures based on social, biological and physical sciences propose sloppy, high-contact experiences as a way to exchange deep and difficult-to-express information. The knowledge flows can be equally rapid and unobstructed, but they move in an entirely different way from those that pass through technology-enabled channels. Both ways of connecting people with the knowledge they need are essential for meeting increasingly complex and unique customer demands.

PROFILE ► *Oticon*

On August 8 1991 at 8 pm, Oticon, a 90-year-old Danish hearing-aid manufacturer, 'dis-organized' its traditional, rigid, hierarchical corporation into a flatter, more flexible one. Everyone lost his or her job. No one had a title, an office, a boss or a job description. August 9 clearly dawned as a new day.

Why explode such a bomb? To ensure that Oticon would exist 90 years into the future. Needless to say, not everyone agreed with the new order. The CEO imposed it in a top-down fashion and it wreaked havoc on the organization, throwing everything into a state of chaos. The experiment garnered worldwide attention, with CNN and the BBC sending camera crews and reporters to document the emergence of a new organizational form. However, reaping the benefits of 'dis-organization' took time. After the initial buzz, the sceptics emerged. Strong financial results did not appear until 1993, one year after the introduction of Oticon's Multi-Focus, the first advanced product to be launched by the new organization. In the interim, only the growing conviction of Oticon's employees that their new organizational form was the way of the future kept the sceptics at bay.

Oticon is the largest of four business units in the William Demant Holding Company. It employs about 1,200 people worldwide. About 850 work in Denmark, with 650 employees in production and research facilities and 200 in corporate headquarters in Hellerup just north of Copenhagen. About 150 of the corporate headquarters group are part of what Oticon calls its Development Organization, the rest perform administrative operations for the company. The Development Organization at Oticon is responsible for new product development and it is this part of the organization that has been dis-organized. The average Development Organization employee is an engineer in his or her mid-30s with a technology, business or audiology background.

Input from Oticon's Eriksholm Research Centre – the world's only basic research centre for audiology and psychoacoustics – as well as from academic and industry R&D groups flows into corporate headquarters. First, a high-level team evaluates the information and determines whether it should be released into the Development Organization for product development. Information that flows into the Development Organization finds its way into self-organizing groups that cluster around tasks. The 150 members of the Development Organization tackle about 100 projects at any given time. Some project teams might have 30 members, such as one working on a next-generation product. A single individual might take on other projects, such as a marketing campaign plan. At all times, members of the Development Organization are part of multiple-project teams working on integrated product development programmes. But how do people know which team to join if no one tells them what to do? How do they know what to do and how to coordinate with other teams if no one is orchestrating the process? How do they make dis-organization work?

The successful dismantling of the former structure was achieved by involving employees directly in the transformation once the process was launched. Starting with the assumption that employees are responsible, honest and interested in knowledge, Oticon rewarded them for taking care of their own education, and let them choose projects. Employees were given responsibility for scheduling their own vacation time and identifying the training needed to assume their new roles. Departments and titles disappeared, replaced by informal groups of interested employees. Jobs were reconfigured into fluid combinations of functions.

The office cubicle atmosphere became an open space filled with workstations. Informal dialogue replaced memos as the main means of communication. Oticon management used the image of '1,000 birch trees', placed on wheels, to define how continually changing project groups would look and feel. This concept evolved into 'the spaghetti organization', a chaotic web of relationships and interactions that has paradoxically uncluttered information flows and clarified the process of innovation.

Blowing up the organizational structure and letting the new one emerge on its own enabled Oticon to become profitable again, reduce price per unit by 20% in under two years, and reduce time to market by 50% (in the early 1990s). Within three years, the newly dis-organized Oticon was the third-largest hearing-aid manufacturer in the world. It had grown 23% in a declining global market and increased its gross profit by 25%.

Think about it!

What is your organization's structure? Use the poles and modifiers to create a description of the predominant characteristics of your organization's structural preference.

	✓		✓			Highly	Moderately	In transition
Rigid	☐	or	☐	Flexible		☐	☐	☐
Formal	☐	or	☐	Informal		☐	☐	☐
Place-based	☐	or	☐	Virtual	To	☐	☐	☐
Fragmented	☐	or	☐	Interconnected	what degree?	☐	☐	☐
Organized	☐	or	☐	Disorganized	(check	☐	☐	☐
Hierarchical	☐	or	☐	Flat	column)	☐	☐	☐
Simple	☐	or	☐	Spaghetti		☐	☐	☐
Orchestrated	☐	or	☐	Self-organizing		☐	☐	☐
Technology-focused	☐	or	☐	Human-centred		☐	☐	☐

Other thoughts about our organizational structure and its impact on knowledge flows:

Quick prioritization of challenge

Based on this section, how much priority should you assign to meeting this challenge?

> Morph the organizational structure to improve communications and knowledge flows

Rate your organization on these two factors	Your organization's rating	Rating scale
How much does your organization NEED to respond to this challenge?	**Need**	0 No need 1 Weak need 2 Moderate need 3 Strong need 4 Burning need
What is your organization's ABILITY to respond to this challenge?	**Ability**	0 Unable 1 Slightly able 2 Partially able 3 Almost able 4 Completely able

Need ✕ Ability =

★ To do	**Prioritization of challenge**	(multiply the two ratings)
Transfer your prioritization to box A on page 124.		

Design the physical environment in ways that cross-fertilize ideas

The corner office with the view was once the ultimate perk for those working their way up the corporate ladder. However, most of us can kiss the corner office good-bye because those at the top are increasingly seated in public spaces located at the centre of a hub of activity rather than in remote and subdued corners of the building.

Workspace designers are now looked to as experts on creating high-impact work environments. The psychology of workspace design has emerged as a real variable that executives consider when determining the value-added from their use of physical space. Physical proximity has received recognition as a major factor in an organization's ability to put its knowledge to use.

Multiple forces have driven this radical change:

1   Growing evidence that the power to boost innovation comes from designing the workspace in ways that augment rather than diminish frequency of inter-personal contact. Few organizations have taken this line of reasoning further than Alcoa (see Profile).

2   A move among service organizations either to insist that their employees spend more time at customers' sites in order to better anticipate needs or to actually locate

their employees at customer sites when they provide an 'outsourced' service. A related movement within organizations co-locates functional professionals with the operating units they serve.

3   The fluid and dynamic nature of work teams in which people are members of more than one team at a time. This has increased the need for people to physically bring their work with them when they meet with different teams throughout the day or week.

4   The demand for rapid response to market opportunities which calls on people to create ad hoc teams that can huddle in physical and cyberspace.

From a cost containment perspective, organizations are looking for ways to maximize their use of very expensive physical space by minimizing idle or unused space. For example, Cisco Systems, a networking systems manufacturer with offices around the world, has eliminated fixed seating arrangements for salespeople in favour of 'hot desks' – a first-come, first-seated system.[1]

Two words of caution about focusing on the cost side of workspace design are in order. First, if employees suspect that the driving force behind clustering them in smaller, less private workspaces is cost containment, the hoped-for benefits of collaboration and spontaneous creativity are unlikely to be realized. While no one working today argues with prudent spending, employees are quick to detect insincerity and lack of real commitment. At Cisco Systems, the company was extremely candid about the dual purpose of the hot desks – saving money and promoting collaboration. They worked closely with the salespeople to try to tailor the workspace design changes to local preferences. In some locations, people wanted storage areas that were portable; in others, they preferred a fixed site. While the change took some getting used to, the salespeople were willing to make the transition. However, when an organization switches to 'hotelling', but has permanently reserved suites for senior executives, no one is fooled. The second caution is that the shrinking of physical space has in many instances been accompanied by a rapidly increasing investment in cyberspace technologies that permit people to work anywhere, anytime. Whether costs are truly being contained in the aggregate is open to speculation.

PROFILE ▸ *Alcoa*

'Alcoa Corporate Center was designed to make the organization more effective. It is different from most office buildings in that we started the design with business ideas, not architectural ideas. Our design principles grew out of business and organizational goals' (Paul O'Neill, Chairman, Alcoa).

In the early 1990s Paul O'Neill, the Chairman of Alcoa, the world's largest producer of aluminum and alumina, faced the prospect of launching the company into a future of continuous change in the way it conducted business. The landmark Alcoa Building that had served as the company's headquarters for 45 years was too static, too resistant to change to suit a company that had to conduct business 24 hours a day around the globe, rapidly responding to subtle economic shifts. 'One of the design ideas for the new building was that everything had to be forgiving of change', recalls Marty Powell, Principal of The Design Alliance, lead architects for the new Alcoa Corporate Center. 'You can't take down or put up drywall fast enough to adjust to changes on the order of magnitude that face organizations at the turn of the millennium.'

Spurred by the Chairman's vision of designing an environment that would help the corporate staff better serve an organization that had to mirror the rapid pace of change in the markets it serves, Alcoa used the process of designing the new building to envision the way the corporate centre staff would work in the future. Employees were invited to participate in the process. Some only decided about the particulars of their individual work area. Others contributed much more substantive ideas. 'If we hadn't involved employees, the process of designing the new building and the new business processes would have failed to achieve its goals. Architecture isn't magic. Processes, people and place must mesh into a workplace ecology,' says Paul O'Neill. 'Alcoa convened several cross-functional teams to sort out the new business processes and the workspace requirements. These teams communicated the results of their efforts to the rest of the headquarters staff through newsletters, web sites, mock-ups, exhibits and frequent tours of the construction site.'

Some of the design elements that were adopted to improve business performance were obvious while others were more subtle. All of them supported the flow of information to people who needed it to make decisions. The underlying theory of the design was that allowing people to see more of each other during the business day would positively impact the decision-making process. Placing magazine racks in central areas so that people congregate around them to promote spontaneous contact is on the simple end of the spectrum. So is installing monitors showing videotapes of news about the company in the communal kitchen areas. Using glass to partition meeting spaces lies on the subtle, structural end of the spectrum. 'When in doubt, make it glass' was another design concept advocated by O'Neill. In their glass-enclosed meeting spaces, the work of the organization is visible and people are naturally curious about what they see. Questions about what was discussed at a meeting have frequently altered the mix of expertise at subsequent meetings. An open seating plan and escalators between floors also promote cross-functional collaboration, communication and spontaneous contact. It is easier to pause for a quick chat between floors and get needed information right then and there than it is deliberately to place a phone call, leave a message and wait for the response. 'One of the more interesting developments at the new building is that the size of many team meetings has grown,' O'Neill states. 'More diverse sets of expertise are brought to bear on decisions because people see each other more frequently during the day. This triggers them to tap into the full extent of our knowledge base when important decisions need to be made.'

Think about it!

Consider the extent to which your workspace design promotes or inhibits knowledge flows by placing a checkmark in the appropriate column.

Promotes ✓	Inhibits ✓	
		Different ways of picturing and solving problems
		Frequent interaction across work teams
		Ability to work with different groups throughout the day and have access to all necessary work tools and information
		Access to customers
		Access to suppliers
		Access to senior management
		Access to middle management
		Access to the front line
		Rapid response to customer needs
		More effective and efficient solutions to problems
		Better relationships with suppliers
		Better relationships with work team members
		Better relationships in general across the organization

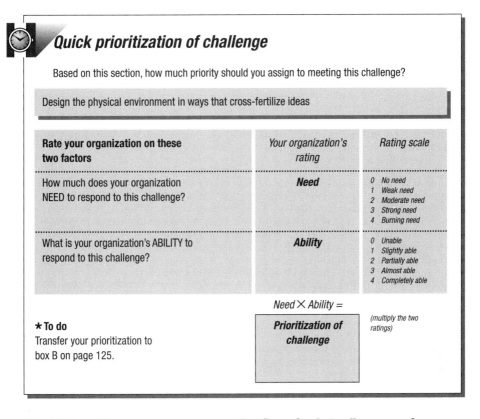

🕐 Quick prioritization of challenge

Based on this section, how much priority should you assign to meeting this challenge?

Design the physical environment in ways that cross-fertilize ideas

Rate your organization on these two factors	Your organization's rating	Rating scale
How much does your organization NEED to respond to this challenge?	**Need**	0 No need 1 Weak need 2 Moderate need 3 Strong need 4 Burning need
What is your organization's ABILITY to respond to this challenge?	**Ability**	0 Unable 1 Slightly able 2 Partially able 3 Almost able 4 Completely able

Need × Ability =

★ To do
Transfer your prioritization to box B on page 125.

Prioritization of challenge

(multiply the two ratings)

Treat information as an open resource that flows freely to all corners of the organization

The tight grip on information that most organizations maintain is another factor that blocks insight into how best to take advantage of opportunities or resolve dilemmas. If employees do not have access to the information they need to make decisions, they lack the tools to create a picture of what is possible. If they do create pictures of possibilities without adequate information, these pictures are often far off the mark. As a result, management tends to disregard employee efforts and a perception builds that the average employee is not capable of contributing to the resolution of these challenges. Ultimately, a self-perpetuating cycle is established in which the more employee efforts to create pictures of possibilities are skewed, the less their efforts are valued, and the less inclined leadership is to share strategic information with them, resulting in even less valuable contributions to the organization.

In many instances the locus of decision making has shifted from the exclusive domain of senior executives to a distributed domain of line managers, but the flow of information has not been equally distributed. In other situations, the inertia that must be overcome to dismantle Byzantine security protocols that guide information flows seems insurmountable. To free information to flow to all corners of the organization, very little of it can be protected. Most information has to be treated as an open resource that only has value if the people who need it have access to it. In addition, senior management must believe that no one in the organization is capable of the omniscience required to know who needs what information and when. None of this means that management will be spared the dilemma of figuring out what information to send through the system in the first place as the executives at Fairchild Semiconductor learned (see Profile).

How many times has a case arisen in which members of an organization know perfectly well where the information they need resides, but it does them no good because they cannot get to it? There are three general categories of 'accessibility dysfunction' that can occur in organizations:

1 **Top down**: Some information, particularly financial, may be considered 'proprietary' and not fit for the eyes of the ordinary worker. While it is often precisely such information that enables good decision making, management does not feel comfortable providing it to everyone in the organization. Top-down accessibility dysfunction generally arises out of security issues or other concerns about misuse.

2 **Cross-organizational**: When people talk about organizational 'silos' they are referring to various functional groups, departments, business units or process teams that refuse to share information. Silos can prevent access not only to information, but also to important resources. Consider the following example: The corporate Yellow Pages of a large financial consulting firm indicate that a prominent expert in foreign exchange is located in the company's New York office. An opportunity arises to set up a financial exchange network for a Milwaukee-based client. But the firm tracks its billings (and ensuing 'rewards') by local offices. The foreign exchange expert is discouraged from working on the project even if her time is covered, because 'credit' will not accrue to her local office. As a result, the firm loses the client to a competitor. Cross-organizational accessibility dysfunction results when holders of information are forced to compete for credit or resources. In these situations, while the organizational benefits of sharing information are clear, there is no personal gain in doing so. The net result is that the organization loses out.

3 **Bottom up**: The lower echelons are not the only groups in organizations that can be hampered by accessibility dysfunction. In some organizations, senior executives are routinely denied access to complete decision-making information. When individuals are rewarded only for communicating the good news (and punished for delivering the bad) they quickly learn what information to pass on to executives and what needs to be buried or 'repositioned'.

Combating accessibility dysfunction requires faith that employees can recognize the value of information and trust that they will use it to benefit the organization. Ironically, organizations that have taken the lead in freeing up the flow of information tend to be relatively small, privately held and tightly controlled. As they struggle to grow, these enterprises have reached the dramatic conclusion that the only way to do it is by abandoning the notion that one person can run the show.

These owner–operators have not only opened their books to everyone in the company but also educated everyone so that they understand what the financial statements mean. In many cases, they have also extended ownership in the operation to employees as a way of underscoring the significance of employee actions.

With financial information in hand, employees can understand the implications of how they plan to use knowledge to meet customer needs. They are in a position to determine if the usage truly results in value creation. However, financial information is not the only kind of information that must flow freely throughout the organization. The process that executives use to reach decisions must also be shared, as well as the 'soft' information that influences their thinking. As organizations ponder how to develop the next generation of leaders, many are arriving at the conclusion that they must make the process of running the organization more transparent. The premise behind transparency is that only when people know what is expected of them and how they are evaluated can they make good decisions for themselves and the organization. For this reason, organizations like SmithKline Beecham have made some of the information about the company's talent pool available on a company-wide basis. The result has been an increase in the number of cross-functional development moves, and an inflow of the best and the brightest into general management positions. The more that this type of information flows through the organization, the more strategically aligned everyone's actions become and the more frequently applications of knowledge yield profitable results.

PROFILE *Fairchild Semiconductor*

As decision making has been pushed down to more people within companies, the need to share knowledge more broadly has increased. However, while information must be an open resource, it does not mean simply opening the floodgates. Employees will not be able to sort it out at the back end if it is not sorted out at the front end.

Fairchild Semiconductor Corporation is a leading supplier of high-performance, multi-market semiconductors. The company's products are used in a wide variety of microelectronics applications, including automotive, telecommunication, computer, peripheral, industrial and consumer products. Fairchild Semiconductor is a reincarnation of its former self. Founded in 1959, the company was purchased by Schlumberger in 1979, then by National Semiconductor in 1987. Fairchild Semiconductor reappeared on the industry scene in 1997 when the combined logic, non-volatile memory and discrete power and signal technologies businesses of National Semiconductor were purchased by private investors and launched as a new company.

Jerry Baker, Executive Vice President and General Manager, has had a long history with Fairchild, extending back through its days as National Semiconductor. When National Semiconductor moved to a more team-oriented work environment, the executive team was forced to think about how information flowed through the organization. They were dismayed to realize that the company's information flows were still directed at them, even though they were no longer responsible for day-to-day decision making. Until the company started to redirect its knowledge flows to reach the teams, it had not truly empowered them to do the work for which they had become responsible. Now that Baker is part of the executive team reinventing the newly spun-off Fairchild, he is once again thinking about what it means to treat information as an open resource that is accessible to those who need it.

'At Fairchild we continued the practices we had established at National Semiconductor. We carefully constructed an environment in which our employees could step up to empowerment. But then, several business crises forced us to switch to a command and control leadership style for a period of time. That style completely contradicts the tenets of empowerment,' recalls Baker. 'There we were, shooting information to the guy at the top who shouted out orders that everyone followed. But eventually we were forced to take another look at what it means to share information that people can act on.'

For Baker, the experience reinforced his belief in information empowerment. Information empowerment is a full equation for information sharing. One half of the equation is getting the right information to the right people at the right time. That half involves making sure that information is a free-flowing, open resource. The other half of the equation is making sure that people can do something with the information when they get it. 'Getting at the data turns out to be such a small part of the problem. Today, few problems go unsolved for lack of data,' cautions Baker. 'Putting information in perspective is the real challenge.' To put information in perspective companies must:

◆ create a common language and platform for information so that people can relate their actions to the results of the overall business;

◆ take the time to discuss not only results, but how specific actions led to them.

'We are not talking about withholding information. We are talking about not overloading people with information. We are constantly working to make sure that the information that gets out is executable.'

Think about it!

Think about your organization's position with respect to treating information as an open resource that flows freely. Put a checkmark in the box that represents how many people in your organization would generally agree with each statement.

	Nearly everyone	Majority	50 – 50 split	Minority	Hardly anyone
People can easily get hold of the financial and operating information they need to make decisions.	☐	☐	☐	☐	☐
Senior management rarely imposes limits on the information to which people have access.	☐	☐	☐	☐	☐
People have the authority to make decisions about all aspects of the work for which they are responsible.	☐	☐	☐	☐	☐
Front-line workers routinely share information with others in the organization.	☐	☐	☐	☐	☐
People can read and interpret our financial statements.	☐	☐	☐	☐	☐
Information is freely shared across the operating units and functional groups of our organization.	☐	☐	☐	☐	☐
Most people treat financial, operating and strategic information as highly valuable.	☐	☐	☐	☐	☐
Strategic decisions are not a surprise to most people because senior management routinely shares this type of information with everyone in the organization.	☐	☐	☐	☐	☐

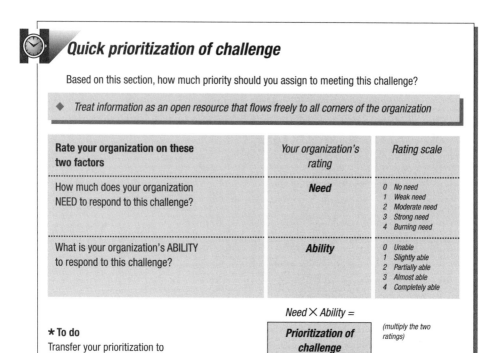

Quick prioritization of challenge

Based on this section, how much priority should you assign to meeting this challenge?

◆ *Treat information as an open resource that flows freely to all corners of the organization*

Rate your organization on these two factors	Your organization's rating	Rating scale
How much does your organization NEED to respond to this challenge?	*Need*	0 No need 1 Weak need 2 Moderate need 3 Strong need 4 Burning need
What is your organization's ABILITY to respond to this challenge?	*Ability*	0 Unable 1 Slightly able 2 Partially able 3 Almost able 4 Completely able

Need × *Ability* =

★ To do
Transfer your prioritization to box C on page 126.

Prioritization of challenge

(multiply the two ratings)

Collaborate on a routine basis with all stakeholder communities

Perhaps the ultimate in crossing organizational boundaries is evidenced by the growth of collaborative activities with customers, suppliers and competitors. The prefix co- has become ubiquitous, paired with strange suffixes to devise terms such as co-opetition and co-innovation that attempt to describe the new ways in which organizations are combining know-how to create value.

The blurring of organizational boundaries has some of its genesis in the cost-cutting measures that became a hallmark of suppliers relations in the late 1980s and early 1990s. Companies were aghast to find that their supplier lists had mushroomed out of control and they were paying a stiff price to administer financial and logistical transactions and manage the effects of uneven quality. Trimming supplier ranks and establishing a handful of preferred suppliers with whom companies negotiated mutually favourable long-term contracts slowly began to affect the nature of supplier relations. It was no longer beneficial to shift problems up- or downstream because both the company and its suppliers were committed to a long-term contract in which neither would benefit by simply off-loading problems to the other. Mutuality of interest replaced zero-sum tactics with win–win solutions. Sharing information and ideas was a necessary precondition to producing mutual wins, and it is increasingly expected that organizations and their suppliers will have this type of relationship.

The growing emphasis on customer intimacy provides a view from the opposite direction. Rather than second-guess customer needs and wants, organizations have begun literally to 'live' with their customers in attempts to involve them in design of new products or services. While this adds more cost to the upfront stages of new product development, it more than offsets the risks of expensive downstream failures, and often produces radically different and much better solutions. In addition to more formal efforts, organizations are also embracing more frequent and casual contact with customers. Employees are encouraged to visit customer sites and customers are invited to drop in on the company when they are in town.

As markets spring into being and just as rapidly flame out of existence, more and more companies are venturing into collaboration with their competitors. Consortia that conduct research in pre-competitive areas such as human safety in the automobile industry, protocol standards in the high-technology industries or environmental practices in the chemical industry have become quite common. Competitors may also cooperate in order to rapidly accelerate the development of a market or transform the nature of an industry's services, product offerings or cost structure. EBS, a manufacturing and engineering business, has been a pioneer of competitor collaboratives among smaller organizations (see Profile). However, collaboration among competitors is not the exclusive domain of the small. For example, in the summer of 1997 British Petroleum PLC and Mobil Corp. kicked off what became an industry trend by merging their European refining and marketing companies – the downstream businesses – which were being pummeled by low profit margins and overcapacity. At the same time, the companies continued to compete in their upstream business lines. In the high-tech arena, American Express and Visa International announced a joint effort to develop a worldwide open standard for 'smart' cards in the summer of 1998. These cards store information on an electronic chip, which has the ability to perform sophisticated functions. The joint venture faces competing technologies, but the race to set the standard will not necessarily be won on technology alone. It will be won by the group that can sustain collaboration over the long haul. Such arrangements are beginning to occur more frequently, and they are changing the very way that companies think about creating value for customers and ensuring their own longevity.

▶ PROFILE ▶ *EBC*

Collaborating with competitors is risky, but not collaborating can be riskier. Without entertaining many diverse perspectives, it is getting harder and harder to imagine the future. However, collaborating with competitors is not for the faint of heart – it requires courage and conviction that there is no other way to succeed.

In 1985 Harry Brown stood at a crossroads. Bethlehem Steel, his employer, had exited yet another in a string of businesses, and Harry had left along with it. Erie Bolt Company (EBC), a manufacturing and engineering business in Erie, Pennsylvania, was for sale. Its owners, like those of Bethlehem Steel, had no further interest in the company's mature and unprofitable products. 'In my opinion, both of these owners had vacated the idea of advancing the entire technology base that underpinned their businesses,' recalls Brown. 'Erie Bolt presented me with a microcosm of the problems plaguing American manufacturing. The great thing about its small size was that I could see the whole system, not just within the company, but within the industry as well. As its owner, I could also experiment in ways that made sense without having to worry about being second-guessed.'

EBC was strapped for capital and striving to regain profitability in a wickedly competitive, global market populated by extremely demanding customers. Cautious, incremental changes were not going to provide the needed boost to lift EBC out of its downward spiral. Instead, Brown initiated a series of sweeping structural changes in the organization, the most dramatic of which was partnering with direct competitors. 'I looked for companies that had complementary weaknesses,' remembers Brown. 'We had a strong marketing group, so I looked for companies that had the equipment and technical expertise we did not. Together we created a better solution for the customer than any of us was able to create separately.' Brown insists that collaboration with competitors is not just for small companies. For a large organization, the impetus to collaborate could occur during a business down cycle that reduces training investment levels and limits skill development. He believes that any organization facing the constraint of needing to grow beyond available capital will eventually consider collaboration with competitors.

Expertise and information flow across company boundaries when competitors band together to serve customers. EBC maintains a lending library of technical information and testing equipment that is available to its collaborators. It has frequently improved its own technical base from observing competitors' processes. 'Few companies in our industry can develop and support the special skills needed to serve customers, so banding together is our best option,' reflects Brown. 'There is an unwritten code of conduct that everyone is expected to live up to. Violators are ultimately frozen out of future work, so the penalty for not behaving in a trustworthy way is severe.' In the final analysis, the goal is to grow the industry by advancing its core technologies so that everyone has a better chance of succeeding. Even when collaboration is not the solution to a particular customer's problem, and EBC loses a specific job in the near term, it stands to benefit in the future. 'Customers come to me because they know that I will solve their problem in the best way possible, whether EBC gets the work or not. That's how I know that we have succeeded in transforming EBC into a reliable and trusted knowledge base within our industry.'

Think about it!

Evaluate your company's ability to effectively collaborate with three key stakeholder communities.

Thinking about your relationships with **customers**, complete these sentences by circling the response that best fits your organization.

1 We have participated in [*no, some, many*] customer collaborations.

2 We [*never, rarely, occasionally, frequently, always*] engage customers early on in the process of new product development.

3 We have [*no, emerging, established*] guidelines or policies for resolving the ownership issues that result from this collaboration.

4 [*None, A few, About half, Most, All*] of our customers would say that they are involved in our organization's product and process improvement efforts.

5 The general consensus in our organization is that collaboration with customers is [*awful, bad, okay, good, great*].

Thinking about your relationships with **suppliers**, complete these sentences by circling the response that best fits your organization.

1 We have participated in [*no, some, many*] supplier collaborations.

2 We [*never, rarely, occasionally, frequently, always*] engage suppliers early on in the process of new product development.

3 We have [*no, emerging, established*] guidelines or policies for resolving the ownership issues that result from this collaboration.

4 [*None, A few, About half, Most, All*] of our suppliers would say that they are involved in our organization's product and process improvement efforts.

5 The general consensus in our organization is that collaboration with suppliers is [*awful, bad, okay, good, great*].

Thinking about your relationships with **competitors**, complete these sentences by circling the response that best fits your organization.

1 We have participated in [*no, some, many*] competitor collaborations.

2 We [*never, rarely, occasionally, frequently, always*] engage competitors early on in the process of new product development.

3 We have [*no, emerging, established*] guidelines or policies for resolving the ownership issues that result from this collaboration.

4 [*None, A few, About half, Most, All*] of our competitors would say that they are involved in our organization's product and process improvement efforts.

5 The general consensus in our organization is that collaboration with competitors is [*awful, bad, okay, good, great*].

Compile your collaborative position here by filling in the response you circled in each of the sentences			
Collaborative stance	Customers	Suppliers	Competitors
We have participated in ____ collaborations			
We _____ engage customers/suppliers/ competitors early on in the process of new product development			
We have _____ guidelines or policies for resolving the ownership issues that result from this collaboration			
____ of our customers/suppliers/competitors would say that they are involved in our organization's product and process improvement efforts			
The general consensus in our organization is that collaboration with customers/ suppliers/competitors is ____			

Quick prioritization of challenge

Based on this section, how much priority should you assign to meeting this challenge?

Collaborate on a routine basis with all stakeholder communities

Rate your organization on these two factors	Your organization's rating	Rating scale
How much does your organization NEED to respond to this challenge?	**Need**	0 No need 1 Weak need 2 Moderate need 3 Strong need 4 Burning need
What is your organization's ABILITY to respond to this challenge?	**Ability**	0 Unable 1 Slightly able 2 Partially able 3 Almost able 4 Completely able

Need X Ability =

✱ To do
Transfer your prioritization to box D on page 127.

Prioritization of challenge

(multiply the two ratings)

2 Freedom

People are generally comfortable and confident about acting on new ideas

We have shied away from calling this imperative creativity because many people are reluctant to call themselves 'creative'. Yet, although people may or may not want to think of themselves as creative, most want to think of themselves as free to act on the best thinking that they or their group has to offer. Freedom to act opens up the creative possibility for new and better outcomes. Whether or not they think of themselves as creative, people have an instinctive sense of what it means to be free to act on their ideas, and they know whether or not their organization encourages or discourages this kind of freedom.

To achieve this imperative, everyone in an organization must not only *feel* free, but also, *be* free to break the rules and wander outside the normal set of everyday activities to 'play with' new and different people and ideas. When this is the case, organizational life can be confusing. With more voices chiming in, it is harder to hear the good ideas over the din of the mediocre and out and out bad. At the same time it is more likely that more good ideas will surface. When serious play becomes the norm, there are dramatically more zany ideas to weed through, but the potential for breakthrough solutions rises dramatically as well. When people are able to 'think different', their understanding of how the organization creates value becomes kaleidoscopic rather than myopic. The world just does not look the same anymore. To open up this worldview and expose its manifold possibilities, these *challenges* must be met.

Challenges

◆ *Value the contributions of everyone in the organization.*
◆ *Create time and space for play.*

Value the contributions of everyone in the organization

It is not easy to value the contributions of every employee and to encourage their active participation in creating value. How does the mailroom contribute to customer value creation? Is that as valuable as the contribution of the CEO? Based on what we pay people in these different positions, the answer is no. But based the possibility of improving the overall system's value-creating potential, the mailroom clerk's motivation to speed the delivery of information within the organization might be underestimated.

Typically, we tend not to think about mailroom clerks and their contribution to value creation. But organizations such as 3M, Motorola and CNN do. At these organizations, everyone is expected to participate in some way in thinking about creating value for customers. At CNN, which has been described as a culture of 'collegiality and … almost compulsive egalitarianism', the behaviour of Tom Johnson, the top executive, models an openness to hearing views from all employees regardless of their pay level.[2] Even more important, though, Johnson's behaviour ensures that everyone at CNN follows suit. CNN is a place where 'a sound technician can openly question the cost of an anchor's hotel expenses and still have a job the next day'. While this type of questioning may be seen as grousing about the pecking order and perks by some, it can also be read as concern about the organization's bottom line. At Motorola, the annual Total Customer Satisfaction competition invites teams from all over the world to enter a contest to select the best team achievement in the organization.[3] A large part of the rationale for conducting the competition is to recognize and honour the great ideas and achievements of outstanding employees – whether they work on the factory floor or in the management suite. The overriding reason for involving everyone in the value-creation process is that organizational systems have become so complex and touch customers in so many different ways, it is virtually impossible to know where the next great idea for adding value will come from.

An ability to absorb new ideas, no matter what their source, and an environment that legitimates all attempts to apply these ideas on behalf of the customer, no matter by whom, are two of the major factors in successful use of knowledge to create customer value. Organizations in which new ideas frequently bubble up from operations are often said to have 'entrepreneurial cultures'. In the mid-1980s large corporations were captivated by the concept of 'intrapreneurship' which promised to unleash the energetic and freewheeling enthusiasm of the small, entrepreneurial organization within the large, well-established corporation. However, the way to entrepreneurial behaviour in large corporations does not seem to be through imitation of small companies. Instead, large organizations that successfully foster entrepreneurialism leverage their large-company strengths by creating structures to provide time, resources and permission for pursuit of new ideas that fit the organization's strategic objectives as epitomized by 3M (see Profile).

> PROFILE *3M*

At 3M the first principle of management is the freedom to pursue creative ideas. Most of what has been written about transforming this principle into work processes focuses on the technical side of how this wildly innovative organization supports a continuous stream of successful new products. However, one of the most intriguing facets of how 3M puts this principle into action is an insistence that everyone in the organization involve themselves in the process.

3M is a $15 billion diversified manufacturing company headquartered in St Paul, Minnesota, with operations in more than 60 countries. Creativity and innovation are distinct territories at 3M. Creativity is an individual act of thinking up ideas. Innovation is seen as a group activity that develops a process for taking good ideas, regardless of the source, and turning them into something of commercial value.

'The reason that we have to involve everyone in the process,' says Dr Geoffrey Nicholson, Vice President, Corporate Technical Planning and International Technology Operations, 'is because we can't schedule creativity. We don't know who is going to have a good idea. But we do know that to have good ideas, we have to have ideas – the good, bad and the ugly. We must empower the individual to pursue his or her dream to help the good ideas survive.'

Lewis Lehr, CEO of the company from 1979 to 1986 was a notable champion of full involvement. Lehr commissioned an in-house study to determine the true state of innovation and enterpreneurialism at 3M. The research uncovered a general consensus among employees that 3M was indeed an entrepreneurial company, but a large segment of the employee population left themselves out of the equation when it came to thinking that their work had anything to do with innovation – finance, sales and marketing, warehouse personnel. For Lehr, exempting anyone in the organization from the struggle to innovate was unacceptable. He insisted that everyone in the organization participate in continuous improvement, not only in the labs but also in the factories and the secretarial pools. 'The result was that people became very conscious of trying to do things differently,' Lehr reported in a regional business journal.[4] 'The key thing is that when you tell people you want them to be entrepreneurs, you have to mean it. You have to give them the resources – it usually doesn't take much – and then a method of recognizing their successes and absolutely no penalty if they fail. In fact, encourage them to try again. If you don't do those things, it is a false message and nobody believes it.'

One powerful way that 3M recognizes success is by enshrining it in a 3M story. 3M is notable for the stories it tells not only about its executives, but also about ordinary folks who have achieved extraordinary things. The discovery of Scotchgard™ brand protectors, used to enhance the stain resistance of fabrics, is one of those stories. 3M had been experimenting with fluorochemicals for a number of years, but a commercial use had not come to light. One day, a lab assistant accidentally spilled some of the fluorochemical solution on her tennis shoes. She became annoyed by her inability to clean off the drops. Patsy Sherman, a researcher in the group was intrigued by the resilience of the compound. With a fellow chemist, Sam Smith, she began to explore a radical new concept – to develop a fluorochemical polymer that could repel oil and water from fabrics. 'In one mistake, Patsy Sherman intuited the possibility for an entire industry where nothing had existed,' says Geoff Nicholson. 'Inspiration can happen at anytime to anyone. We don't want to tell anyone that it's not your job to be creative.'

The stories at 3M sound several themes that describe what empowerment means at the company. They convey a healthy scepticism about management. In many of these stories, senior management is told to 'mind your own business', or 'I'll tell you when I'm ready', when they ask for information about a nascent idea. The stories put individual curiosity and conviction on a pedestal by detailing how people work around obstacles and shrewdly play the culture's hard spots to their advantage as they pursue their dreams. The stories tell of leaders who talk honestly and openly about mistakes and what they learned from them as a way of normalizing the harshness of failure – which is what happens to most ideas. The stories communicate that 3M not only demands but also supports, embraces and remembers each individual's contribution to the organization's success.

Think about it!

Use the following grid to evaluate how widely and deeply your organization values contributions from everyone. Start with the first column and ask yourself to what extent senior executives value input from the group listed in the first row, which is other senior executives. Place a checkmark in the box if they value that input. Move to the next row, which is mid-level executives and ask yourself the same question. When you get to the part of the table in which you are asking about lower level people valuing information from senior level people, consider this: While base-level operating personnel may get input from senior executives and follow it, ask yourself if they really value it. Your organization's hierarchy may require that some people follow orders, but do not let that fact influence your assessment in this case. When you are finished, see how many holes there are in the fabric of your organization's ability to value contributions from everyone.

Value input from:	Senior executives	Mid-level executives	Senior managers	Mid-level managers	Senior operating personnel	Mid-level operating personnel	Base-level operating personnel
Senior executives							
Mid-level executives							
Senior managers							
Mid-level managers							
Senior operating personnel							
Mid-level operating personnel							
Base-level operating personnel							

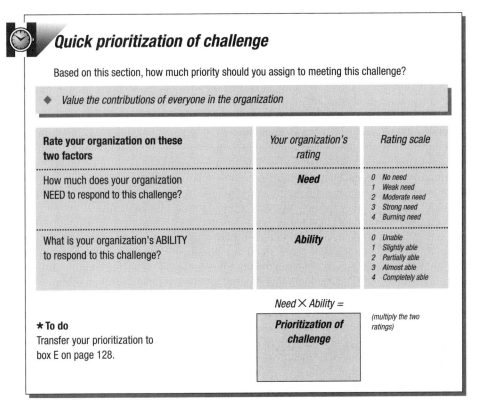

Quick prioritization of challenge

Based on this section, how much priority should you assign to meeting this challenge?

◆ *Value the contributions of everyone in the organization*

Rate your organization on these two factors	Your organization's rating	Rating scale
How much does your organization NEED to respond to this challenge?	**Need**	0 No need 1 Weak need 2 Moderate need 3 Strong need 4 Burning need
What is your organization's ABILITY to respond to this challenge?	**Ability**	0 Unable 1 Slightly able 2 Partially able 3 Almost able 4 Completely able

Need X Ability =

★ To do
Transfer your prioritization to box E on page 128.

Prioritization of challenge

(multiply the two ratings)

Create time and space for play

The buzzword in organizations today is thinking 'out of the box' as if all one had to do to achieve this state was utter the phrase. The reason thinking out of the box is so difficult is because we rely on our boxes for efficiency and effectiveness. If everyone is always operating out of the box, few organizations could get much done in a profitable way. The key is to create space and time for experimentation that permits creative and even wacky ideas to flourish without disrupting the operations of the organization until disruption is desired.

While we are slowly coming to acknowledge that our best ideas may not be generated by going at them head-first, indirect approaches inspire a high degree of discomfort that is difficult to countenance in our hard-charging corporate environments. Even the very word 'play' stands in contrast to the idea of 'work.' Yet an organization's acceptance and promotion of play with its concomitant experimentation and failure are important precursors to successful innovations. David Miller, a professor at Syracuse University who has thought seriously about play, uses an engineering metaphor to argue for its importance. He invokes the image of a bicycle wheel that is either too tightly or too loosely screwed to its frame. A tight fit does not permit the wheel to turn. A loose fit makes it wobble. In either case, the bicycle does not do what it should. But when the screw is fitted correctly, there is sufficient *play* between the wheel and the frame to permit the whole to work. The metaphor extends nicely to organizational systems. Without play, or flexibility, organizations either get stuck in old routines or haphazardly drift from one new fad to the next.

A handful of stories about playful approaches that led to powerhouse innovations are fast acquiring the status of myth among the knowledge management cognoscenti. Nonaka and Takeuchi's[5] story of Canon's invention of the disposable copier drum illustrates many points, one of which is that the purposeful introduction of playfulness can break creative logjams. When the engineers at Canon were grappling with the challenge of developing a disposable copier drum – a totally new technology – the leader of the task force responsible for the design sent out for beer. Mulling over the problem, the task force leader held up a beer can and asked the design team to ponder the similarities between an inexpensive beer can and an inexpensive copier drum. The light-hearted element of this exercise in thinking analogously was carefully orchestrated to help participants climb out of their boxes and view the problem from a different perspective. The Canon story highlights the central significance of sanctioning activity that, despite its ultimate aim of solving a critical business challenge, can often feel like a meandering, irrelevant exercise.

More modest, but no less effective, are techniques such as agendaless or unstructured meetings, which are used to discuss pressing issues but also to surface those niggling doubts and shadowy thoughts which rarely make it into traditional corporate meetings. Facilitation skills that support new ways of examining situations are also making their way more frequently into standard meetings. Mindscaping or mindmapping uses graphical or illustrative representations of the meeting's topics to stimulate new ways of associating ideas that potentially lead to a flash of insight that is unlikely to occur when using traditional recording techniques (see Point of view). Casual dress and informal settings are increasingly used to break down barriers and level the playing field among participants who might operate in different hierarchical positions outside of the meeting. Toys, theatre games, story telling and simulations are slowly being adopted as tools for helping people connect with all of the skills that they possess for problem solving, not just those most commonly used in day-to-day business settings. To raise the bar above effectiveness and efficiency to innovation, organizations are stretching as never before to become comfortable with ways of seeing and being in the world that are more often associated with children at play than adults at work.

> POINT OF VIEW *Mindscaping*

Organizations are looking for ways to boost creativity and innovation. The ability to tap into the rich core of knowledge that lies below the level of consciousness is one reason that they are finding value in disciplines more typically associated with the arts.

Mindscaping is a system that uses pictures, visual metaphors, symbols, colour and the space on a page to create a graphic representation of ideas. Nancy Margulies, the creator of mindscaping, believes that organizations are seeking different approaches to problem solving in part because we now have a more sophisticated understanding of how the brain works. 'The process of non-linear note taking itself reflects the way the entire brain works. It engages both the logical, sequential processing style and the creative, holistic style of the brain,' Margulies explains. 'But the strange thing is that the mindscapes themselves end up looking like a network of neurons. They are visual representations of the way we think.'

When problems are confronted using most standard analytical techniques, people must first identify what they believe the key variables are and then work in a sequential fashion to achieve outcomes. They may or may not identify the correct variables and interrelationships on the first pass. However, by the time most people have wandered through a lengthy analysis, they have become highly invested in this particular way of thinking about the problem. Mindscaping, in contrast, supports a much more free-flowing and random generation of ideas. It permits people to delay pattern making until relationships among variables emerge. By the time this occurs, many different relationships suggest themselves, as do many possible solutions.

'Mindscaping's main strengths are that it: 1) reflects a whole system, 2) uncovers patterns and connections and 3) generates many options,' says Margulies. 'Seeing the widest universe of possibilities is a much more solid base from which to make decisions if you operate in a volatile marketplace where you might have to make a different choice tomorrow.'

Mindscaping has been used in many organizational settings. One of the most interesting for Margulies is her work with several Maori tribes in New Zealand who are petitioning the government to reclaim tribal lands. To be successful in their claims, the tribes need to present a complex system of land rights and history that clearly proves their case. Mindscaping was used to record ideas and then organize them for presentation to the government's tribunals. The tribes also used mindscaping to create a shared vision of how they wanted the reclaimed land and new resources to be used for the betterment of all. A page-sized version of this mindscape will be included with the tribe's other documents when they are submitted to the government. 'There is no better way for someone to immediately grasp the Maori tribes' vision than looking at this visual depiction,' says Margulies.

Mindscaping taps into the intelligence that operates below the level of consciousness. Margulies believes that this non-linguistic intelligence is deeper and richer than the limited aspect of our intelligence we bring to bear on most problem solving. 'Mindscaping asks people to approach their problem from an odd angle. Many don't believe that it will get them from point A to point B. But after putting themselves in an initially uncomfortable situation, almost everyone ends up at point D, farther than they thought they could go toward reaching innovative solutions' (see Figure 4.1).

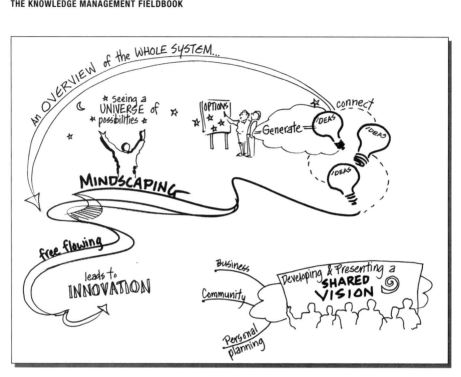

Fig 4.1 ◆ Mindscaping

Think about it!

Think about your organization's position with respect to creating time and space to play. Put a checkmark in the box that represents how many people in your organization would generally agree with each statement.

	Nearly everyone	Majority	50–50 split	Minority	Hardly anyone
We often talk about how we come up with new ideas as playing around.	☐	☐	☐	☐	☐
We no longer believe that an exclusively analytical approach is the best way to solve problems.	☐	☐	☐	☐	☐
We often meet off-site in relaxed settings to discuss work-related issues.	☐	☐	☐	☐	☐
We are genuinely creative and original thinkers when it comes to exploring new ideas.	☐	☐	☐	☐	☐
We believe that work and play are mutually reinforcing activities.	☐	☐	☐	☐	☐
More and more of us have training and experience as meeting facilitators.	☐	☐	☐	☐	☐
We have a flexible approach to developing new products or services from which we feel free to deviate.	☐	☐	☐	☐	☐

Quick prioritization of challenge

Based on this section, how much priority should you assign to meeting this challenge?

◆ *Create time and space to play*

Rate your organization on these two factors	Your organization's rating	Rating scale
How much does your organization NEED to respond to this challenge?	*Need*	0 No need 1 Weak need 2 Moderate need 3 Strong need 4 Burning need
What is your organization's ABILITY to respond to this challenge?	*Ability*	0 Unable 1 Slightly able 2 Partially able 3 Almost able 4 Completely able

Need × Ability =

★ **To do**

Transfer your prioritization to box F on page 129.

Prioritization of challenge	(multiply the two ratings)

Notes

1 'Cisco's staff conquers separation anxieties after losing desks', Thomas Petzinger, Jr., *The Wall Street Journal*, February 21, 1997, page B1.

2 'The people's network', Peter J. Boyer, *The New Yorker*, August 3, 1998.

3 'Motorola brings fairy tales to life', Leigh Ann Klaus, *Quality Progress*, June 1997, pp. 25–28.

4 'Captains of industry: four of the state's most powerful business leaders reflect on their careers and give their prognoses for the coming decade', Britt Robson, *Minneapolis–St. Paul Magazine*, 20 (7), s.1, p.44.

5 Ikujiro Nonaka and Hirotaka Takeuchi. *The Knowledge-Creating Company*. Oxford: Oxford University Press, 1995.

Agenda for action: Use

The action steps presented in the Agenda for action come from the ideas suggested in this chapter. If you believe that your organization needs to focus on improving how well people use knowledge to create innovative solutions for customers, this template and its suggested action steps are one way to get started.

The Agenda for action is organized in the same way as this chapter. Each imperative and its accompanying challenges are clustered together. Action steps are suggested for each challenge based on the text and case studies. You decide which action steps make sense for your organization and use the empty space to scribble in any additional ideas that come to mind.

Before you begin, make sure that you have transferred your prioritization ratings for each challenge. The prioritization ratings will remind you whether you believed that the challenge was worth pursuing. The maximum prioritization rating is 16, the minimum is 0.

How you use the prioritization ratings is up to you. For example, depending on the range of prioritization ratings, you may decide to ignore all challenges below a minimum threshold and focus only on those challenges above it. Or you may decide that everything that is not 0 deserves at least some thought. We invite you to use this Agenda for action as a place to start acting on your knowledge management priorities.

Agenda for action

1 Permeability

Ideas flow both in and out of the organization, exposing people to many different perspectives and possibilities

A

Morph the organizational structure to improve communications and knowledge flows

Prioritization rating

Action step	Who should be involved	My first 'to do'
Find out whether any groups within our organization use 'emerging forms' such as spaghetti, self-organizing, informal, virtual, learning, networked, viral and disorganized. If they are used, find out how these managers believe the structures impact performance.		
Ask a cross-section of managers from our major organizational units to complete the Think about it! exercise to determine the range of opinion about our organizational structure and its impact on knowledge flows within and across the organization.		
Determine if and how we might productively experiment with some new organizational forms to support our strategic objectives.		
Other:		

B

Design the physical environment in ways that cross-fertilize ideas

Prioritization rating

Action step	Who should be involved	My first 'to do'
Examine our current workplace design to determine both how well it promotes the flow of ideas and how well it utilizes 'idle space'. Include our information technology and communications infrastructure in this review.		
Evaluate the interest in and potential impact of locating work teams on-site with their customers and with our suppliers.		
Experiment with flexible workspaces that permit co-location of work teams for variable lengths of time.		
Other:		

C

Treat information as an open resource that flows freely to all corners of the organization

Prioritization rating

Action step	Who should be involved	My first 'to do'
Evaluate the mechanisms we use to share financial and strategic information with employees. Determine the extent to which employees believe that they have the information they need to make decisions.		
Determine what actual policies and procedures prevent and support our sharing this type of information.		
Begin discussions with key operating, functional and process managers to explore the current validity of these policies and procedures in light of our strategic challenges.		
Determine if programmes exist within the organization to educate employees about the meaning and use of financial and strategic information. If there are none, find out if trade or industry groups provide such training.		
Design experiments to share more information with groups engaged in strategically critical activities and monitor the results.		
Other:		

D

Prioritization rating

Collaborate on a routine basis with all stakeholder communities

Action step	Who should be involved	My first 'to do'
Review our current plans for process and product/service improvements to determine how much impact and involvement our customers and suppliers have had on them and whether more or less might be desirable.		
Evaluate the type and extent of contact we have with our customers, suppliers and competitors – mostly formal or casual, one-way information sharing or dialogue, proactive or reactive, etc.		
Discuss the feasibility and desirability of collaborating with competitors to grow our industry – what are the pros and cons, how have past experiences coloured our opinions?		
Assess the state of the industry with respect to these practices. Are we leading, lagging or tagging along with others? Are there areas in which we should be setting the standard? Identify the groups within our organization whose business would be most positively impacted by changing the current level of collaboration with stakeholders. Approach those managers to discuss the possibility of conducting a focused pilot project.		
Other:		

2 Freedom

People are generally comfortable and confident about acting on ideas

E

Value the contributions of everyone in the organization

Prioritization rating

Action step	Who should be involved	My first 'to do'
Evaluate current programmes that provide support (resources, time) for moving from idea stage to experimentation. How widespread are these programmes? Can anyone apply to use them or is access limited?		
Examine the ways in which we support and undermine contributions that come from unlikely sources. Do we tell stories of innovations that single out not only our leaders but also the rank and file?		
Circulate the table from the Think about it! exercise in this challenge to create a 'snapshot' of our organization today in terms of who listens seriously to whom. Compile the results and circulate them electronically or on paper to solicit feedback about how our current state helps and hinders innovation.		
Other:		

F

Prioritization rating

Create time and space for play

Action step	Who should be involved	My first 'to do'
Interview several key managers and ask them to describe their typical process for generating and developing new ideas. Identify similarities and differences across our organization.		
Determine how frequently we use 'playful' and 'informal' techniques to generate and develop new ideas. Find out how comfortable people are with the concept of 'playing'.		
Discuss how we might experiment with these new techniques and find a group or sponsor who would be interested in launching a pilot.		
Other:		

5 Learn

> The rate at which individuals and organizations learn may become the only sustainable competitive advantage.
>
> **Ray Stata**[1]

The processes 'learn' and 'contribute' are relatively new to organizations. This is not to suggest that in the past no one learned from their experiences or contributed to the organizational knowledge base. However, the formal recognition of these processes as a means of creating competitive advantage *is* new. The challenge for organizations is to find ways to embed learning into the way people work. This means resisting the crisis mentality that places short-term needs ahead of engaging in structured reflection that has the potential to pay off in the longer term. In this chapter we have limited our discussion of learning to those elements that affect the flow of knowledge as an organization meets the tactical demands of responding to the marketplace. Human resource development issues such as leadership development and training which are mostly strategic in nature are discussed in Chapter 8 of the *Fieldbook*.

At a glance . . .

What is new?	Creating an 'organizational memory' and an ability to acknowledge and learn from failure as well as success.
What is the problem?	Short-term pressure to move on to the next task makes it difficult to embed learning that has value to the organization into the way people work.
What is the individual or team objective?	Improving the outcomes of future projects by investing more heavily in understanding how actions affect outcomes in current projects.
What is the organization's responsibility?	Fashioning an environment that embraces the full range of learning styles. Facilitating the learning experience.

Introduction

Getting and using information occurs in some fashion and to some degree in all organizations. However, despite the hype about learning organizations that has dominated the business media during the past ten years, learning in organizations is rarely intentional or leveraged. This may be because the links between learning and creating value are harder to establish than those of getting and using information. External triggers such as customer demands activate the process steps of getting and using information, and the output from these process steps can be traced back to a marketplace transaction. The pressure to respond to these external triggers is relentless. One set of needs follows the other without interruption. Completing the knowledge management process by following through with learning and contribution often feels nice but not necessary. Even when these process steps are completed, the links to a particular outcome are tenuous at best.

Learning is important to organizations because, along with contribution, it is the transition step between the application of ideas and the generation of new ones. It is a lever that can boost the potential value of a local successful solution or a local abject failure into an insight with global implications. Learning is the mysterious activity that many organizations believe will fuel growth in a future where emerging market opportunities must be imagined and intuited into being. However, for most organizations, the knowledge management process ends when people use the knowledge that they have acquired to meet their immediate needs. Having solved the pressing problem, people move on to face the next challenge. The drive toward action, understood as doing something visible, so dominates business culture that the act of learning, which is fundamentally invisible, is seen as doing nothing. Yet, in organizations where leadership has embraced learning as critical to achieving competitive advantage, there is an emphasis on making the invisible visible. In these organizations, taking time to reflect on experience and consider its possible value elsewhere is sanctioned, and people do not consider a fire to be out until they have thought about why it happened in the first place.

Organizations in which individual learning benefits the entire enterprise engage in a multitude of activities that can be clustered around the following *imperatives* and *challenges*.

Imperatives and challenges

Visibility	The link between strategy and the learning derived from everyday actions is obvious:
	◆ *Picture the complexity of human systems.*
	◆ *Engage the mind and the body to connect 'soft' issues to strategy.*
Habituation	The practice of learning is commonplace:
	◆ *Promote the pleasure principle at work.*
	◆ *Embed reflection mechanisms into the habit of work.*
	◆ *Capture the benefits of mistakes, failures and disagreement.*
	◆ *Nurture the art of learning by doing.*

1 Visibility

The link between strategy and the learning derived from everyday actions is obvious

Visibility functions on an organizational and on an individual level. At the organizational level, learning has been identified as a means of achieving strategic objectives. Organizations that make learning visible have not abandoned the more familiar means of reaching goals – productivity, process efficiency and customer focus. Rather they use learning to add question marks to these approaches. Productivity, how? Why, exactly? Where does it start, proceed and finish? Learning at the organizational level asks individuals to go beyond just accomplishing a task to asking questions about it.

Some organizations have come to the conclusion that having the capacity for learning is, in the end, the only way to grow and renew themselves. The good news is that people's capacity for learning is an infinitely abundant resource. It does not deplete itself through use, but paradoxically replenishes itself. However, like underused muscles, if people are not asked to use their capacity for learning, when they need to use it, they experience discomfort and are unable to sustain the activity for long. In addition to being an abundant resource, people's capacity for learning ranges across an infinite field of interests. People learn all the time, but what they learn may or may not be important to the organization.

Learning and contributing are increasingly critical if organizations are to achieve the desired outcomes of the knowledge management process. Getting and using without learning and contributing creates a vast repository of byproducts that end up as waste. Know-how goes nowhere as people discard what they obtained and used to solve one set of issues and move on to the next. The organization's leadership must doggedly communicate how the strategy of the organization is achieved through the learning that derives from everyday decisions and actions. Connecting the dots between strategy and everyday actions is a state of strategic nirvana called 'alignment'. When the connections are visible, they become the 'rules' for how to practice learning in a way that benefits the organization.

To secure a bias toward learning and to focus it in ways that benefit the entire enterprise, organizations face these *challenges*.

Challenges

◆ *Picture the complexity of human systems.*
◆ *Engage the mind and the body to connect 'soft' issues to strategy.*

Picture the complexity of human systems

Simulations have emerged in the past ten years as an increasingly popular technique for instilling 'in the bones' understanding of organizational strategy. Simulations run the gamut from those closely mapped to the business experience to those that range far afield in an attempt to create an observable 'feeling' among people.

System dynamics is a field of study that helps people picture complexity in simple ways. System dynamics falls on the clinical or scientific end of the 'in the bones' understanding of strategy. It hails from a discipline that was brought to the attention of business enterprises through the work of Peter Senge and others at the Massachusetts Institute of Technology, but has been known to social scientists since Jay Forrester established the field of study in the 1940s. In a nutshell, system dynamics suggests that what people view as isolated actions are always part of interconnected systems. For example, when people try to fix problems, they frequently find that the fix only works for a limited period of time. Inevitably, the problem reappears, often in a more aggravated form. The 'fix that fails' is a common system dynamic. The fix works at first because most systems have delays built into them; in the long run it fails because eventually it triggers other elements of the system which amplify the problem state. Not all fixes fail; some stabilize or minimize the problem state. The dilemma is that people cannot tell what impact their actions will ultimately have because they cannot visualize the system in which those actions are taken.

To develop an awareness of the systems in which we make decisions and take action, system dynamics practitioners bring groups of people within organizations together to construct models of the way their system works. The system is described as a set of interrelationships among various levers which when pushed up or down cause reactions that lead to growth, decline or stasis. These systems are pictured visually as causal loop diagrams. Some system dynamics practitioners translate the causal loop diagrams into software applications which simulate the way in which members of an organization believe their system behaves when decisions are made. By 'playing' with these simulators, people can begin to see how discrete decisions affect the whole and understand how strategic objectives are achieved or missed.

At Ford, simulations have been used for more than a decade by engineers wishing to test such questions as whether a particular automobile design might survive a crash test. Now the company's product development group is experimenting with how simulation concepts can be adapted to management decision making or project management. A typical management simulation might ask such questions as: 'What would happen if the team suddenly had six weeks lopped off its deadline to deliver a new model?' or 'What might be the effect of failing to recruit a particular kind of full-time expert for this project?' or 'What would be the impact of a last-minute change to the design specs for a new headlight?'

'In today's world where people don't stay at the same company forever, simulations are an excellent way to capture organizational learnings and pass them on to people who may be new to the organization or less experienced', says Bob Matulka, Director of Product Development Process Leadership at Ford. Ford tries to mine the knowledge of its experts and feed this knowledge into its simulation models. It also uses historical data to test how well the model predicts outcomes. Simulations are considered works in progress: the more they are used, the more feedback you can gather, and the more this feedback can be incorporated into the model to improve its predictive ability.

Simulations have a range of potential uses at Ford. They can test alternative scenarios which combine both external factors and inputs that can be controlled by the organization. They can also be used to objectively demonstrate to stakeholders the potential impact of their decisions – for example, what the impact on revenues might be if the engineering department gets its way and makes that final tweak to a door handle. But Matulka thinks one of the most exciting uses is to help train new project managers to run good projects. 'You'd be hard pressed to find a NASA shuttle pilot launching into orbit without having gone through rigorous simulation training. Yet companies put people in charge of running projects who have little or no experience in the process itself. We think simulations can really help those folks up the learning curve.'

Engage the mind and the body to connect 'soft' issues to strategy

We have grouped a set of simulations that fall on the other end of the 'in the bones' understanding of strategy under the rubric of kinetic experiences. Kinetic experiences range from the physically aggressive Outward Bound-type courses to the less athletic off-site retreat to the board-based activity of a Celemi simulation (see Profile). All are designed to help people become more aware of group process and how it affects decision making and outcomes by removing them from familiar settings and asking them to engage themselves fully – both their minds and their bodies – in a simulated experience.

Outward Bound pits teams against nature in the pursuit of an outcome – completing a whitewater rafting trip or surviving several days in the wilderness with just the basics or rappelling down a cliff-face. The experience is physically challenging and the only way to succeed is by working effectively as a team. Throughout the experience, participants are encouraged to observe the way in which group process affects performance and results. A company founded by two US Army Rangers called Leading Concepts received considerable press coverage in the spring of 1998.[2] Leading Concepts offers a variation on the Outward Bound theme, bringing military combat concepts to bear on understanding decision making and teamwork. Companies send groups composed of members from different functions and from different levels of the organization to a one-week simulated combat experience. Each day the group completes a series of missions under the leadership of a different team member. Each day they debrief their experience, seeking to understand how decisions and actions undermined or supported their ability to achieve the mission.

Some branches of the military turn the process upside down and send their members into the realm of the business world to learn about decision making in high-stress situations. For example, groups of US marines have spent a day as traders on the US mercantile markets in New York and Chicago to experience making split-second decisions with imperfect information. These scenarios turn out to be remarkably similar to those in which contemporary warfare takes place. 'Just as savvy traders size up the market, commanders need to decide which messages demand immediate responses. Just as traders deploy their capital judiciously, commanders must husband their munitions. And just as traders cut their losses, commanders have to decide when to back off and evacuate casualties.'[3] Experiencing life in the trading pits helps future commanders learn about the challenge of communicating effectively under severe pressure.

Taking a more playful and light-hearted approach to simulating experience, Xerox Business Services (XBS), a 15,000 person, billion dollar (US) document-management unit of Xerox, created Camp Lur'ning.[4] A week-long learning experience, Camp Lur'ning was conducted on at least two occasions for several hundred XBS employees. Designed to mimic the summer camp experiences of American youths, Camp Lur'ning eschewed formal classroom training for hands-on activities. Each group faced the task of creating a plan for getting close to a specific XBS customer. They were given carte blanche to gather information and formulate their plan, but were strongly encouraged to have fun and let their creative juices flow. Workshop experiences exposed the campers to new ways of thinking about their tasks, and each night the groups met to reflect on their experiences. Like the more aggressive military or athletic simulations, the less physically strenuous XBC camp simulation invited people to engage their minds in a relaxing off-site environment in pursuit of insights about how everyday actions and decisions lead to the achievement of strategic objectives.

> **PROFILE** ▶ *Celemi*

During a Celemi learning process, participants have the opportunity to share their own experience and learn from those of others in a highly realistic and competitive situation. When learning like this takes place, people are extremely receptive to new information and want to work with it to discover its implications for their own assignments. The enthusiasm and interest generated in this way is also a valuable source of inspiration and creates a positive flow of knowledge.

Celemi creates learning processes based on the philosophy that commitment to company goals is generated when people are allowed to take responsibility for their own learning and its application in the workplace. These processes are non-computerized to ensure a gut-feel understanding of strategies and systems, as well as to promote person-to-person interaction which enhances the learning process.

Celemi's methodology addresses the natural requests we all have when trying to acquire new knowledge:

1   Awaken my curiosity! Let me see for myself what is so interesting.

2   Give me only as much information as is necessary, no more, no less.

3   Let me think about the information, discuss it, work with it, so I can come to my own conclusions.

4   Help me see the whole context so I have a complete understanding.

5   Help me be able to apply what I've learned so that I build on it and don't forget it!

Taking these requests seriously has enabled Celemi to create effective learning experiences which target specific business goals – implementation of a strategy, the launch of a new product, the enhancement of a branding campaign. Participants spend anywhere from a few hours to a few days, depending on the depth of the seminar, actively gaining new knowledge, both on the theoretical level as well as the practical level. A very positive side-effect of the way these learning processes are designed is the generation of spontaneous and freely flowing information between colleagues who, in other situations, do not communicate well. In this way, the Celemi experience can be used to open new channels of communication based on a better understanding of the big picture and the situation one's colleagues face in their day-to-day work. The improved communication that results from this learning process is especially critical to successful knowledge management, where clear and effective communication must be part of the company culture.

One large professional services company uses one of Celemi's learning processes, Tango™, to introduce new consultants to project management. Several teams of four consultants each convene for a two-day session to participate in a simulation of running a company based not only on hard assets, but also intangibles. The teams set a strategy and compete for employees and customers in the session, just as they would in the real world. Using a game board, cards and other playing pieces, they simulate several business years, managing an abridged income statement, balance sheet and intangible assets monitor. During the session, some companies merge, others go bankrupt, some forge strategic partnerships. At various points throughout these 'years', discussions are held related to the real company's specific issues. In this way, Tango provides the consultancy's new hires with an enriching, almost first-hand experience of running a company.

Think about it!

With your work group in mind, consider the following ways in which participating in simulations helps people make the link between everyday actions and strategy. Place a checkmark in the box that describes how important achieving each type of insight might be for your group as a whole.

	Very important	Important	Somewhat important	Not important
Understand group dynamics	☐	☐	☐	☐
Understand the work process	☐	☐	☐	☐
See how group dynamics affect the work process	☐	☐	☐	☐
See how group dynamics affect outcomes	☐	☐	☐	☐
See how the work process leads to outcomes	☐	☐	☐	☐
Link our group's work to the strategic objectives of the organization	☐	☐	☐	☐
Experiment with different scenarios to see what outcomes they achieve	☐	☐	☐	☐
Practice new approaches to develop confidence about applying them	☐	☐	☐	☐
Develop deeper relationships among group members	☐	☐	☐	☐
Develop a wider network across the organization	☐	☐	☐	☐

Quick prioritization of challenge

Based on this section, how much priority should you assign to meeting these challenges?

- ◆ *Picture the complexity of human systems*
- ◆ *Engage both mind and the body to connect 'soft' issues to strategy*

Rate your organization on these two factors	Your organization's rating	Rating scale
How much does your organization NEED to respond to this challenge?	**Need**	0 No need 1 Weak need 2 Moderate need 3 Strong need 4 Burning need
What is your organization's ABILITY to respond to this challenge?	**Ability**	0 Unable 1 Slightly able 2 Partially able 3 Almost able 4 Completely able

Need ✕ *Ability* =

★ **To do**

Transfer your prioritization to box A on page 160.

Prioritization of challenge

(multiply the two ratings)

2 Habituation

The practice of learning is commonplace

Individuals reflect on experience all the time and this is the essence of learning. What distinguishes the learning people are hard-wired to do from the kind of learning that organizations desire is that it occurs naturally and is undirected. The proverbial water cooler or coffee break experience in which gossip serves as the conduit for a flow of information and a platform for making meaning out of organizational events is the typical unstructured, invisible learning experience. All too often, the insights that emerge from these experiences are based on incomplete and incorrect information. The decisions and actions that flow from these insights can be deeply flawed, sometimes leading to missteps that could be avoided by engaging in a more intentional learning process.

The conundrum that bedevils all organizations is how to motivate individuals sufficiently to find and invest the time that allows them to make more of their everyday work than completing the task at hand. As we just discussed, one piece of the puzzle is providing people with a clear grasp of how fulfilling organizational goals is connected to their own everyday actions and decisions. If people cannot literally see how the kind of learning in which the organization wants them to engage improves the way in which they get their everyday work done and at the same time nudges them one step closer to the next level of personal accomplishment, learning will languish. It will never become part of the routines that help beat back the constant commotion of meeting today's demands. Learning must become a habit, not a one-time event.

To develop the habit of learning in ways that benefit the enterprise as well as the individual, organizations must find ways to face these *challenges* head on.

Challenges

♦ Promote the pleasure principle at work.
♦ Embed reflection mechanisms into the habit of work.
♦ Capture the benefits of mistakes, failures and disagreement.
♦ Nurture the art of learning by doing.

Promote the pleasure principle at work

Linking everyday actions and decisions to strategic objectives helps people see how the tasks that they perform within the narrowly construed 'work hours' impact the larger organizational system. But what happens during non-work hours, in the unstructured moments when learning also occurs? With the advent of information and communications technologies, worklife and homelife increasingly bleed into each other, making the distinction between them a moot point. People carrying beepers or paging devices who are not engaged in life-saving work has reached epidemic proportions such that *The Wall Street Journal* carried an etiquette editorial on the correct use of these devices during live theatrical, dance and music performances. (FYI: The correct use is to leave them at home.) Work is always with us these days and we are always at work.

Unisys, a $7 billion US-based computer company, released a new ad campaign in late 1998 that showed its employees as committed workaholics, always thinking about the customer. Their bodies may be at home or on the golf course, but their minds are at work which the ads depicted by giving them computers for heads. People rail against this as the final insult of the 21st century – that we are once again organization men (and women), owned by the organizations for which we work.

However, it is true that at some companies and for some people, being involved in work is not a chore, it is a pleasure. People in these organizations tell a palpably different story about worklife than others. For them, mulling over a work-related problem during off-hours and picking up the phone or getting on-line to engage a colleague in the process just makes sense because learning happens whenever and wherever. They do not tell stories of being browbeaten into becoming workaholics by unrelenting corporations fixated on squeezing productivity from their every waking hour. They talk about curiosity and collegiality and express the enjoyment that they derive from their work. The organizations that inspire this 'continuous learning' have transformed the burden of work into the pleasure of work and in so doing, they have pushed the temporal boundaries of work beyond eight or ten or twelve hours to let learning happen any time and any place.

For example, Melissie Rumizen, the Assistant to the Chairman for Knowledge Sharing at Buckman Laboratories International, describes the excitement that most people at the highly profiled specialty chemicals company feel about being connected to the company and each other all the time. Everyone has a laptop that is almost a third appendage. This is especially important given the geographic dispersion of most of the company's 1,200 associates who are spread across 90 countries around the globe. But more than that, everyone is encouraged to let their families play with their laptops and use the Internet connection provided by the company for personal use as well as for business. This means that whenever Melissie has a good idea, even if it comes to her on Sunday afternoon while lazing around the house, all she has to do is boot up her laptop and use the modem to share her thinking with others in the company. People might say that the scenario could also be looked at another way: Buckman Laboratories gets much more than it pays for by creating a cultural norm that promotes work at any time and at any place. But Rumizen would demur. For Buckman Labs associates there is great pleasure in working at a place where the majority of your colleagues share your enthusiasm and curiosity about work. What the company gets from the associates is more than fair given what they get in return.

Think about it!

Use the following matrix to think about your group's work style and the extent of the pleasure they derive from the work. Position your group where they fit best on the matrix and consider the questions beside it.

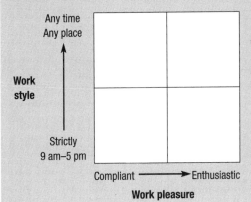

◆ Are work style and work pleasure correlated for your group?

◆ Which seems to have more impact on work product? Is the impact positive or negative?

◆ What impact do you believe that a change in either of these variables might have on work product?

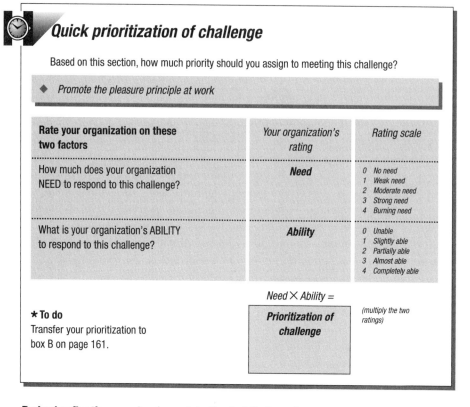

Quick prioritization of challenge

Based on this section, how much priority should you assign to meeting this challenge?

◆ *Promote the pleasure principle at work*

Rate your organization on these two factors	Your organization's rating	Rating scale
How much does your organization NEED to respond to this challenge?	**Need**	0 No need 1 Weak need 2 Moderate need 3 Strong need 4 Burning need
What is your organization's ABILITY to respond to this challenge?	**Ability**	0 Unable 1 Slightly able 2 Partially able 3 Almost able 4 Completely able

Need ✕ Ability =

★ To do
Transfer your prioritization to box B on page 161.

Prioritization of challenge

(multiply the two ratings)

Embed reflection mechanisms into the habit of work

When confronted with the challenge of reflecting on an experience, most people complain that their organizations make no time for this to happen. Although organizations pay lip service to learning by requesting that people 'make time' for reflection, for those who must wring another hour out of an already crammed 10-hour day and set it aside for 'learning', the idea seems ludicrous. Anything that is 'set aside' is a luxury, a nice but not necessary part of the day that one never gets to because necessary always trumps nice. Furthermore, if the organization asks people to set aside their personal time for learning, unless work is a pleasure rather than a chore, the odds are that it will not happen.

Organizations that use learning as a means of leveraging individual experience on behalf of the enterprise do not ask individuals to set aside time for learning. In these organizations, learning is tightly integrated into the habits and routines of work and is indistinguishable and inseparable from the work process itself. Learning is not fitted into the real work of the organization – it *is* the real work of the organization. The US Army's after-action review is frequently cited as an example of embedding reflection mechanisms into the habit of work. When the US Army conducts training exercises at Fort Leavenworth, Kansas, the lessons learned are gleaned by stepping back from the simulated experience of the training exercise and reflecting on it. A probing, sometimes combative analysis of what decisions were made and how they affected outcomes yields insights which are then codified, collected, stored and ultimately disseminated. The Center for Army Lessons Learned, also at Fort Leavenworth, maintains a knowledge base which houses not only information at the 'news flash' level but also training scenarios which are used to get military units rotating through tours of duty quickly up to speed. The US Army considers the training exercise and the military operation incomplete until lessons have been learned and documented.[6]

Perhaps of even greater significance, however, is the role of Fort Leavenworth itself as a centre for learning, pondering the future and imagining how the US Army will continue to fulfill its mission. Officers on the rise, the majority of whom spend at least several months on the base, assiduously study military history, on the look out for patterns that repeat themselves. These patterns harbour lessons to be learned about the future because they reveal how competing interests have come to terms with one another. Reflecting on experience – one's own and that of the organization in the past and in the present – is deeply embedded in the habit of daily work and the cumulative habits that constitute a career in the Army.[7]

The US Army is not the only organization that embeds reflection mechanisms into its work process. At Steelcase, a manufacturer and designer of office furnishings, the entire sales and service process for key customers receives extensive analysis on an ongoing basis specifically to derive learnings and diffuse them throughout the organization (see Profile). Examples from the oil industry cover both a back-end mechanism similar to the US Army, and a front-end one. At Chevron, exploration teams conduct post-drilling assessments that review the entire process of searching for new petroleum sources. They examine the sources of information that were used to select drilling sites and the interpretations that the teams made of the geographic data to see whether there may be new ways of interpreting the data in the future. At Shell Oil, scenario planning is used to envision the future by drawing on collective insight from past experience. Shell's use of scenario planning to anticipate how the company could respond to extreme volatility in crude oil prices, when no one had any inkling that this scenario would ever come to pass, has entered the realm of corporate myth, and justly so. It remains one of the best examples of the value of collective learning that comes from embedding reflection mechanisms into the habit of work.

PROFILE ▶ *Steelcase*

Many people in companies try to figure out why things work the way they do, but the learning rarely transcends the level of the individual. Steelcase has transformed the traditional sales review of wins and losses into a powerful learning mechanism that is part of the way individuals collectively achieve the company's strategic objectives.

Steelcase Inc. is the world's leading designer and manufacturer of office furnishings. Its mission is to create high-performance work environments designed to help people work more effectively.

Steelcase not only advocates a focus on learning and knowledge flows when it creates innovative work environments for its clients, it also practices what it preaches. Like most companies, Steelcase tracked client wins and losses by sales region, circulating aggregated numbers among members of the company's management team. 'To be honest, the numbers were sterile,' reflects Dave Lathrop, Manager of Knowledge Initiatives. 'The rich learnings took place at the ground level in the local sales office in St Louis or Philadelphia. While the numbers from St Louis made it to Philadelphia, the insights about what worked and what didn't were not transferred. There was no way to leverage those insights to another local sales office, let alone the entire company.'

The Win Room is Steelcase's answer to leveraging insights. In the spring of 1998 Steelcase created the Win Room, a physical and virtual location in which employees huddle on a weekly basis to get beneath the numbers to understand what causes them. Every Monday morning one of four regional sales vice presidents and his or her area sales directors preside over a discussion of successes and problems they are facing in their efforts to secure mission-critical clients. They present their status, sharing what has worked and soliciting input from other participants about how to handle difficulties. Win Room participants range from senior executives to functional experts. But anyone at Steelcase who is interested can participate in the Win Room sessions. Agendas for each session are posted about a week or more in advance on the Win Room server. The strategy and tactics for winning clients are also stored on the server to give participants time to brief themselves *before* the debrief.

'Win Room sessions can be intense,' warns Mike Palmer, Director, Southern Region Sales Resource Team. 'All of the sales executives are there, and sometimes, if we are talking about a huge global customer, all of the company's executives are there. It is not the time to be unprepared.' While the pressure is high at these sessions, the company's emphasis on collective action and problem solving helps to keep the focus on what counts – moving the company toward its strategic objectives by learning faster and better than the competition. To ensure that the insights from the Win Room sessions are acted on and reapplied, Steelcase has established a Sales Resource Team composed of members representing the many disciplines that are needed to win and maintain clients – yield management, product presentation, proposal response, design and application, utilities specialists, contracts/agreements, etc. After the Win Room sessions, the Sales Resource Team codifies insights and posts them in the Win Room files. The Team also monitors resources to make sure that they get to the local sales offices. Palmer concludes, 'Capturing what we've learned, leveraging it to the global level and reapplying it are what Win Room sessions are all about.'

Think about it!

Most organizations engage in some practices that permit them to reflect on their work process, but they are frequently informal, exclusive and erratic. Nonetheless, these practices are a good place to start when building a formal, inclusive and reliable reflection mechanism into the work process.

Use the following table to think about existing practices in your part of the organization that could be converted or expanded to become formal reflection mechanisms as well as practices from elsewhere in the organization that could be transferred in and adapted.

We have filled in some generic practices that most companies use in some way to get you started. If your group uses them and does a fairly good job, fill in the 'Adapt' column, describing how you can expand and enhance these practices to become reflection mechanisms. If another group (from your organization or a supplier, customer or competitor) uses them, fill in the 'Adopt' column, noting a first step or two that you should take. Note from which group you plan to steal shamelessly. In some cases, you will use both columns, electing to adapt your practice and adopt some elements from elsewhere.

Existing practices from which to build reflection mechanisms	Adapt our practice	Adopt practices from another group
Sales or prospecting meetings		
Current customer status meetings		
Marketing focus groups		
Employee evaluations		
Budgeting		
Business performance reviews		
New product development meetings		
Customer service reviews		

Quick prioritization of challenge

Based on this section, how much priority should you assign to meeting this challenge?

◆ *Embed reflection mechanisms into the habit of work*

Rate your organization on these two factors	Your organization's rating	Rating scale
How much does your organization NEED to respond to this challenge?	*Need*	0 No need 1 Weak need 2 Moderate need 3 Strong need 4 Burning need
What is your organization's ABILITY to respond to this challenge?	*Ability*	0 Unable 1 Slightly able 2 Partially able 3 Almost able 4 Completely able

Need × *Ability* =

✶ To do
Transfer your prioritization to box C on page 162.

Prioritization of challenge

(multiply the two ratings).

Capture the benefits of mistakes, failures and disagreement

When was the last time you read a quotation from a chief executive of a major organization that contained the word 'mistake' placed near the word 'failure?' If you have not yet, we predict that you will see more and more quotes like this one from Jack Greenberg, CEO of McDonald's Corp.: 'In his zeal to attract health-conscious diners, he isn't at all discouraged by the 1996 *failure* of the low-fat McLean Deluxe burger. "That's the kind of *mistake* I want to make more of," he says.'[8] You know that something different is going on when a chief executive is willing to go on record as looking forward to making more mistakes. The usual drill is to word-smith mistakes or failures into a new kind of success. Distinguishing between failures that lead to learning and failures that lead to system collapse is one way to avoid papering over the problem of failure altogether. This is the approach taken by US West's Global Village Labs (see Profile).

A relentless emphasis on 'best practices' has dominated the corporate world for the past decade and has even exerted its influence on not-for-profit and other institutions. 'Best practices' are seen as an antidote to mistakes and failures. The result of scouring the organization for successful process performance, best practices offer a way to tighten up the organizational system by making it more effective and efficient. 'Best practices' imply that success is the best teacher. However, implementing 'best practices' may not be the best way to learn because we tend to move rapidly from success to success. 'If it ain't broke, don't fix it' carries the message, 'No use thinking about something that works so well – Move on!' Failures, on the other hand, stun us into learning, while mistakes help us stumble into it. The full stop of failure or the hiccups of mistakes give people time to adjust their mental models – their accepted way of thinking about their world. Small adjustments that allow new information to flow in and reframe a situation have been proven to make the difference between catastrophe and containment in nuclear power plants and life and death in the military. Ironically, failures and mistakes teach us how to make better use of best practices, by suggesting that especially when success is assured, time should be taken to ask critical questions.

Part of the reluctance to label failures as such is tied to an inability to tolerate disagreement. Disagreement is often confused with disintegration, when in reality it is the most potent tool for achieving high-functioning systems. A research team at the University of California, Berkeley, has been studying 'high reliability organizations', those that operate with zero-failure tolerance.[9] US Navy nuclear aircraft carriers, the US air traffic control system and nuclear power plants must conduct operations without a hitch because hitches can be lethal. Things do go wrong in all of these systems, but they rarely result in lethal failure. One important contributing factor to the 'rightness' of these systems is that they are designed to encourage constructive disagreement. For example, the researchers have concluded that on nuclear aircraft carriers, 'The collision of fresh, sometimes naïve approaches with a conservative institutional memory produces a creative tension that keeps safety and reliability from degenerating into a mechanical following of the rules.'[10] In these organizations, institutional memory captured in policies and procedures (the forerunners of 'best practices') are not a template cast in stone. People are asked to bring their judgment and opinions to the workplace on a daily basis and to exercise them. Small things that go wrong are dragged into the open and examined. Disagreement is expected and used as a tool to create a new, shared understanding of group experience.

While this way of approaching learning is new to most business organizations, the roots of thinking about the imperfection of human systems go back at least to the 1940s. With a wave of new workers (mostly women) taking over assembly lines at factories supporting the war effort in the US, the imperative to reduce errors birthed a new field of study called human factors analysis. The fundamental principle of human factors analysis is that perfect human performance cannot be achieved.[11] Human systems should be designed with fallibility in mind. Blame-free environments in which honest reporting of errors and mistakes can occur are the best way to rout out the possibility of total system failure in the future. Systems designed for perfection squeeze out learning. Perfection also excludes the possibility of creative tension and disagreement – two powerful ingredients for learning. Hospitals, where failure can mean life or death, are tough environments in which to sustain mistakes, failures and disagreement, but at Hermann Hospital in Houston, Texas, deliberate approaches are being taken to build a capacity for doing just that (see Profile).

Admitting that things go wrong when people are involved and that efforts to perfect systems are no talisman against mistakes is hard to do. However, when organizations view mistakes, failures and disagreement as the cradle of innovation and insight, they are able to find ways to incorporate them into the model of how work gets done.

PROFILE   *US West Global Village Labs*

'At Global Village Labs we either succeed or we obtain new knowledge. But we seldom experience "true" failure, which is continuing to spend money without knowing why you are doing it. Throwing good money after bad rarely results in new knowledge,' says Sherman Woo, Director of Global Village Labs.

US West is a telecommunications company based in Denver, Colorado. Its 47,000 employees serve 25 million customers in fourteen states. As in many other nations, the telecommunications industry in the United States is experiencing the effects of deregulation. The shift from compliance to customer focus has been difficult for all players in the US market, and the roaring tide of technology innovations has further agitated an already turbulent environment. One way that US West meets the challenge of change is through the work of its Global Village Labs (GVL).

GVL is a research and applications group with a broad mandate to improve US West by applying information technology solutions to business problems. All projects are funded by US West business units which are not required to use GVL. This arrangement makes GVL the partner of choice rather than the partner of record. GVL operates according to a radically different set of rules than the rest of the organization, the most important of which is that GVL seeks solutions that are best for the entire US West enterprise, not just its business unit customers.

In this environment, success is not a foregone conclusion. In fact, failure is the more likely result. At GVL, failure that leads to new knowledge must be embraced. To help the group learn from failure, one of GVL's bedrock principles is 'fail fast'. To fail fast, GVL team members are encouraged to rapidly iterate through different approaches to problem solving. Approaches that do not work are quickly discarded, unencumbered by the fear of failure that makes people reluctant to abandon an obviously unpromising approach because failure is unacceptable. Working harder is eschewed in favour of working easier. The hallmarks of success are ease and obviousness. When confusion and increasing difficulty reign, GVL team members know that it is time to pull the plug.

Not only do GVL project teams pull the plug, sometimes they reject projects altogether. When business units approach them to develop a software application, GVL steps back from the IT solution to examine the business problem. It is an article of faith at GVL that most business problems do not get solved by writing code. If the business unit is not willing to scratch beneath the surface to examine the real problem, the GVL team will not waste its time or the business unit's money applying an IT band-aid. GVL team members feel a sense of ownership about US West. They keep their eye on the big picture and constantly seek major breakthroughs that can be leveraged across the organization, not incremental improvements limited to a specific business unit.

Rapid iteration and careful project selection are supported by a constraint that all projects have a specified time frame for completion – a 'time box' – that is as short as possible. The typical time box at GVL is ten weeks which is further spliced into shorter project phases. Measurable objectives must be achieved for each phase of the project. When objectives are not met, tough questions get asked about the approach and the project. Should the approach be changed? Should it be abandoned in favour of a different approach? Should the project be scrapped? Asking these questions is part of the habit of work at GVL. 'Social wisdom dictates that public failures are the smart way to learn,' says Woo. 'When bridges were state-of-the-art engineering, if structural collapse was imminent engineers would gather to observe it. Observing failure was accepted as an opportunity to learn. Of course, there isn't anywhere to hide when a bridge collapses, while many business mistakes can be swept under the carpet. But this is a distinct disadvantage. We strive to make our failures public so we can do a better job learning from them.'

PROFILE ▶ *Hermann Hospital*

When organizational performance literally results in life or death, failure tends to result in blame seeking. It is a tremendous challenge to stay focused on learning and improving overall organizational performance.

Hermann Hospital, located in Houston, Texas, is one of a group of healthcare institutions in the United States that has chosen to rethink the meaning and purpose of mistakes and failures in the context of improving organizational performance. The hospital suffered through the agony of inadvertently causing the death of an otherwise treatable 2-month-old infant. A series of doctors and nurses failed to notice that the dosage of a potent heart medication was overprescribed by a factor of ten. By the time the infant reacted to the overdose, it was too late to save his life. In researching the events that led to the infant's death, the hospital's Chief Quality and Utilization Officer, Dr Joanne Turnbull, focused not on where to lay blame, but on the way in which the hospital system failed to detect and prevent the error before it resulted in tragic consequences.

Many cultural elements of the healthcare system work against a learning and improvement culture. The most pernicious is a belief in the perfection of the system. However, to become a high-reliability organization, one that performs high-risk activities without engendering catastrophic failures, capturing information about adverse events and near misses is imperative. 'The tricky part is that in a hospital setting, sometimes bad outcomes have nothing to do with errors,' remarks Dr Turnbull. 'For example, a neurosurgeon might perform a flawless procedure, but the patient may die. On the other hand, surgical mistakes might occur and the patient recovers from his ailment. For this reason, we need to divorce outcomes from actions to truly improve our system's performance. This is not easily done in a culture in which people are trained to understand performance based on cause and effect patterns.'

The other difficulty for many institutions, not just hospitals, is that maintaining a database of mistakes exposes the organization to the risk that the information can be used against it as part of a lawsuit. To reduce those risks, Hermann Hospital looks to approaches used by other disciplines and industries. For example, it borrows the market research practice of 'blinding' data so that no piece of information can be directly linked to a specific person or group. On the national level there is discussion about contracting with a third party to maintain a database that follows the model of the US airline industry which has hired the National Aeronautics and Space Administration (NASA) to maintain a database of near misses. Another approach might be to conduct this type of reporting on a state-wide level. For example, in the case of hospitals that voluntarily report all failures and near misses, penalties might be much less stringent than those of hospitals that do not contribute their data on a routine basis.

How the information is gathered for the database is equally important to the hospital. 'Much to their surprise, physicians liked the programme. It was a relief to finally have a sanctioned process for discussing mistakes without blame. The process also gave many of our professionals and physicians their first experience of working together as a multi-disciplinary team with a trained facilitator,' recalls Dr Turnbull. As the information gathered from the process made its way into the database and then through monthly reports to the hospital's Performance Review Council, substantive corrective actions were made to its operating processes. The results have been impressive. Adverse events have been reduced by 50% in the two years since the root cause analysis process and database were established. Greater improvement is expected as equally blame-free initiatives are launched that focus on areas such as routine care provided by the nursing staff. Concludes Dr Turnbull, 'Establishing a climate in which true learning takes place is possible when blame is removed from the picture and outcomes are divorced from actions while still maintaining accountability.'

Think about it!

Think of a disagreement, mistake and failure that have become well-known in your organization. Use the following table to reflect on how well your organization captured the benefits that could have come from learning more fully about these incidents. We have listed a series of responses that organizations have to these events and left a few blank slots for you to write in your own. Place a checkmark in the boxes for the responses that apply for each of the three incidents.

To take your organization's pulse in this area, copy this table and circulate it with a cover sheet that describes the disagreement, the mistake and the failure you want others to evaluate. Tally the responses and calculate the percentage that report in each category.

Organizational responses	Disagreement	Mistake	Failure
Covered it up	☐	☐	☐
Did not talk about it	☐	☐	☐
Changed the story	☐	☐	☐
Assigned blame	☐	☐	☐
Accessed a database of incidents for insight about how to deal with it	☐	☐	☐
Someone tried to figure out what happened	☐	☐	☐
A few people tried to figure out what happened	☐	☐	☐
Talked about it within the group	☐	☐	☐
Talked about it outside the group	☐	☐	☐
Documented it for use within the group	☐	☐	☐
Documented it for use by others outside the group	☐	☐	☐
Reported formally on it	☐	☐	☐

Quick prioritization of challenge

Based on this section, how much priority should you assign to meeting this challenge?

◆ *Capture the benefits of mistakes, failures and disagreement*

Rate your organization on these two factors	Your organization's rating	Rating scale
How much does your organization NEED to respond to this challenge?	**Need**	0 No need 1 Weak need 2 Moderate need 3 Strong need 4 Burning need
What is your organization's ABILITY to respond to this challenge?	**Ability**	0 Unable 1 Slightly able 2 Partially able 3 Almost able 4 Completely able

$Need \times Ability =$

★ To do
Transfer your prioritization to box D on page 163.

Prioritization of challenge

(multiply the two ratings)

Nurture the art of learning by doing

'Experience is a great teacher'. Daily experience is the crucible in which individuals learn and formulate what they know. People intuitively understand that experiential knowledge is valuable to organizations. On-the-job training (aka learning by doing) carries more weight than simulations because real risk commands more attention than pretend risk (which is why in some instances learning by doing should be avoided). Simulations are an experience, but they are one step removed from the real thing. Experiential knowledge comes into play when the stakes are high and decisions must be made quickly. For this reason, experiential knowledge may be the most critical type of knowledge for members of the organization to possess. At Gillette, experiential knowledge has been the foundation for the company's leading-edge innovations for almost 100 years (see Profile).

What exactly is experiential knowledge, and how do people acquire it? Some have argued that the best way to develop deep understanding is to strip away all mundane tasks, allowing people to focus on the more profound aspects of the work process. Automating away drudgery was supposed not only to drive down cost and inefficiency, but also to free up the time and energy that could be devoted to the truly important work of the organization best handled by a human brain. Ironically, in an age that seeks to computerize all routine functions, experiential knowledge may be best acquired by engaging in a combination of mundane as well as challenging tasks. Investigation into the automation of decision making and plant processes has shown that the more the operator and the system are removed from one another, the more the operator's judgment is impaired and expertise is stunted. The more closely connected human beings are to the work they perform, the more they are allowed to make mistakes and correct them, the more accountable they are for their work, the less likely the system is to collapse and the more likely it is that the individual will learn.[12]

This is not just a theoretical nicety. When executives as high profile as Herb Kelleher, the CEO of Southwest Airlines, make a point of doing the work of their business that connects with the customer on a routine basis – in his case handling baggage and serving snacks on board the airplane – the rationale goes beyond public relations. When Triarc Co., a New York City-based consumer food and beverage company, tried to revive the once-trendy Snapple fruit drink line, its head of sales devoted himself to spending half of his week in the field at retail and distribution locations because 'the proof is to be found in the marketplace'. Staying connected to the mundane and repetitive tasks that deliver value to the customer is as important for the CEO as it is for everyone else in an organization. First-hand knowledge is the most solid foundation for understanding how to respond rapidly and appropriately in a crisis when there just may not be time to think.[13]

Another problem is that the experiential knowledge base needs to be widespread and dense enough in an organization for it to deliver results. If only a handful of people possess enough knowledge to see patterns and act on them rapidly, and they are all collected in one unit or scattered individually across the organization, there will not be enough momentum to make their decisions matter. Solving this problem calls for redundancy. However, redundancy has become a 'no-no' for the contemporary organization. Organizations that understand how to develop an experiential knowledge base by nurturing individuals are learning to say 'yes' to it.

For the US Marine Corps redundancy gets translated into an emphasis on developing 'generic' leaders rather than specialists and experts. Marines are routinely transferred to positions that range far outside their base of expertise so that in times of crisis, the base of experiential knowledge is wide enough and deep enough to respond effectively. Rather than seeing this as a pendulum swing back toward 'everyone a cog in the machine' from 'everyone a unique individual', it can be seen as the more flexible middle ground that is capable of embracing a paradox that everyone is both at the same time. During day-to-day operations, redundancy drives down efficiency, but it raises efficiency dramatically during crunches. For the US Marines, these are the times that count most.[14] In an entirely different industry, the Danish professional cleaning company ISS also overstaffs its jobs relative to the competition. Sending two or three people to a job site that could be handled by one person reduces the cost competitiveness of its contracts. However, the redundancy pays off in terms of overall corporate flexibility. When opportunities arise that require redeployment of a team member to another job site, all of the expertise that is required to achieve superior performance does not leave with that person. The ability to consistently deliver superior performance allows ISS to command a premium in the marketplace and appear on the short lists for contract bids.[15] Both ISS and the US Marines nurture the individual's capacity to learn as a way of keeping their experiential knowledge bases vital. To do so, they manage the discomfort of holding a paradoxical view of people as unique and interchangeable and cleave to their strategic priorities which tell them what matters most and how to keep it alive in their organizations.

PROFILE ▶ *Gillette*

At Gillette, the product is the hero, not any particular person. The company's stories are about breakthrough improvements in business processes and the resulting product innovations, not about an individual inventing something. The paradox is that at Gillette a focus on the collective frees the individual to participate more fully in the learning process. When the product succeeds, everyone at Gillette succeeds. However, the product can only succeed if everyone at Gillette bests their best, and that happens by learning faster and better than they did the last time.

The Gillette Company is a worldwide leader in shaving technology, renowned for breakthrough products that transform the industry. In 1998 the company rolled out its newest razor – the Mach 3 – that boasts entirely new engineering design and materials. The story of how this razor was invented and brought to market touches on every important aspect of learning that we have highlighted in this chapter so it is a natural way to bring our discussion of this step of the knowledge management process to a close.

Gillette commands a unique position within its industry. It has been the industry leader since 1903. Every major shaving advance since that time has come from Gillette. Few organizations in any industry can rival this legacy. When Gillette innovates, it does so by besting its best. Everything that it knows must be improved upon, dramatically, to move the organization forward. Al Zeien, its CEO, mandates that every new razor must achieve superior performance over the existing best shave in order to become the next generation Gillette razor. This relentless push to set new standards fuels Gillette's learning process.

The spark that ignited the Mach 3 razor innovation did not come from the most obvious source or from the most obvious person. Instead, the creative flame burns steadily at Gillette because the company has been able to hew close to the concept that led to its founding – the razor as a highly engineered instrument. Gillette's holy grail is the perfect shave. If there is a better way to shave, Gillette will find it. Using this concept as a divining rod, Gillette scientists are able to stay focused on developing product innovations that lead the market. In the words of its CEO, the markets in which Gillette sells its delivers 'yield to technology' – the market belongs to the company that delivers a highly engineered product. This clear and compelling strategic message guides the way in which Gillette scientists design and conduct their experiments, providing a tight link between strategy and the learning derived from everyday actions and events.

Gillette's R&D groups are populated by many long-timers – 20 to 30 years' tenure with the company is not unusual. In part, people stick around because they delight in applying advanced metallurgy and physics to the very real-world problem that billions of men around the world (not to mention billions of depilating women) face everyday – removing facial hair. These people get a charge out of their work and it imbues the atmosphere in which product development takes place. They work for an organization that reveres technology and manufacturing even as it wields such marketing clout that it is the sixth best-known brand name in beauty and toiletry products. 'The technology that is delivered in a $7 razor would surprise the average person. It is every bit as leading edge as the technology in a $3,000 computer system,' says Eric Krause, Director of Communications, North Atlantic Group. 'For example, the coating that we applied to the Mach 3 blades uses ion deposition technology borrowed from the semiconductor industry. It represents the first time that this technology was successfully used on a non-flat surface.'

What is remarkable at Gillette is that the experience of these R&D veterans does not create blinders, but seems to enhance their ability to peer into the future and leverage the core strengths of the organization to maintain its relevance. The long-standing relationships among these researchers, built up from many years of successful and failed experiments, have fashioned a web of knowledge that holds their collective tacit experiences. Mulling experiences over together through the years, reflecting on outcomes not just once, but continuously, has embedded a learning orientation in the process of how work gets done. Operating in this environment not only stimulates the obvious 'stars', but also the less obvious contributors to unselfconsciously share their ideas. As a result, a quite competent, but otherwise quite regular, scientist felt free to ask the question that contained the germ of the Mach 3's breakthrough concept. When strategically directed learning becomes as pleasurably integrated into the fabric of daily worklife as it is at Gillette, breakthrough ideas not only surface, but also stand a good chance of being recognized for what they are and acted on.

Think about it!

Nurturing the art of learning by doing is a companion to ensuring that everyone in the organization understands how their work links to strategic objectives. The former emphasizes the routine aspects of work and the latter, the more abstract ones. Both are important components of learning which matter to the organization. Rate each group listed below that applies to your organization on the basis of how well it understands strategy, the day-to-day operations of the organization and the linkage between the two. Use the scoring guidelines at the bottom of the chart to get a rough measure of your organization's learning position.

To take your organization's pulse in this area, copy this exercise and circulate it. Tally the responses and calculate the percentage that report in each category.

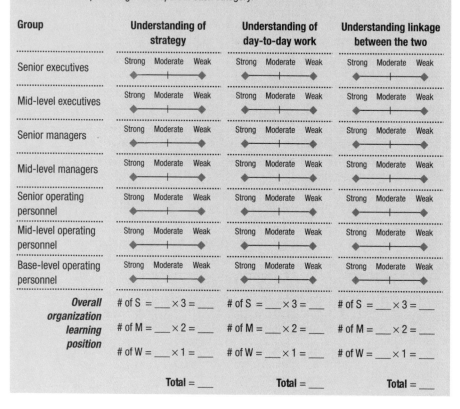

Group	Understanding of strategy	Understanding of day-to-day work	Understanding linkage between the two
Senior executives	Strong Moderate Weak	Strong Moderate Weak	Strong Moderate Weak
Mid-level executives	Strong Moderate Weak	Strong Moderate Weak	Strong Moderate Weak
Senior managers	Strong Moderate Weak	Strong Moderate Weak	Strong Moderate Weak
Mid-level managers	Strong Moderate Weak	Strong Moderate Weak	Strong Moderate Weak
Senior operating personnel	Strong Moderate Weak	Strong Moderate Weak	Strong Moderate Weak
Mid-level operating personnel	Strong Moderate Weak	Strong Moderate Weak	Strong Moderate Weak
Base-level operating personnel	Strong Moderate Weak	Strong Moderate Weak	Strong Moderate Weak
Overall organization learning position	# of S = ___ × 3 = ___ # of M = ___ × 2 = ___ # of W = ___ × 1 = ___ **Total = ___**	# of S = ___ × 3 = ___ # of M = ___ × 2 = ___ # of W = ___ × 1 = ___ **Total = ___**	# of S = ___ × 3 = ___ # of M = ___ × 2 = ___ # of W = ___ × 1 = ___ **Total = ___**

Quick prioritization of challenge

Based on this section, how much priority should you assign to meeting this challenge?

◆ *Nurture the art of learning by doing*

Rate your organization on these two factors	Your organization's rating	Rating scale
How much does your organization NEED to respond to this challenge?	**Need**	0 No need 1 Weak need 2 Moderate need 3 Strong need 4 Burning need
What is your organization's ABILITY to respond to this challenge?	**Ability**	0 Unable 1 Slightly able 2 Partially able 3 Almost able 4 Completely able

Need ✕ *Ability* =

★ To do

Transfer your prioritization to box E on page 164.

Prioritization of challenge

(multiply the two ratings)

Notes

1 'Organizational learning: the key to management innovation', Ray Stata, *Sloan Management Review,* Spring 1989, pp. 63–74.

2 'I want to be a Chairborne Ranger: boot camp for the office', Abby Ellin, *The New York Times,* Sunday May 24 1998, p. BU 9.

3 'Halls of Montezuma … to the pits of Chicago', Greg Burns, *The Chicago Tribune,* Business Section C1, January 17 1999.

4 'XBS learns to grow', Alan M. Webber, *Fast Company,* October:November 1996, p. 113–124.

5 Klas Mellander, *The Power of Learning: Fostering Employee Growth.* Business One Irwin, 1993, pp. 76.

6 'Lessons learned: Army devises system to decide what does, and does not, work', Thomas E. Ricks, *The Wall Street Journal,* Friday May 23 1997, p. A1.

7 'Fort Leavenworth and the eclipse of nationhood', Robert D. Kaplan, *The Atlantic Monthly,* September 1996.

8 'The new chief is ordering up changes at McDonald's', Kevin Helliker and Richard Gibson, *The Wall Street Journal,* August 24 1998, p. B1.

9   'When failure is not an option', Robert Pool, *Technology Review*, July 1997, p. 40–45.

10   'When failure is not an option', Robert Pool, *Technology Review*, July 1997, ibid.

11   'How can we save the next victim?', Lisa Belkin, *The New York Times Magazine*, June 15 1997.

12   'Programmed for disaster', Lawrence Hunter, *The New York Times Book Review*, September 7 1997 (review of *Trapped in the Net: The Unanticipated Consequences of Computerization* by Gene I. Rochlin).

13   'Snapping back: soft-drink marketers at Triarc deftly give Snapple back its "buzz"', Nikhil Deogun, *The Wall Street Journal*, December 14 1998, p. A1.

14   'Corps values', David H. Freeman, *Inc.*, April 1998, pp. 58–64.

15   'Service with a smile', *The Economist*, April 25 1998, pp. 63–64.

Agenda for action: Learn

The action steps presented in the Agenda for action come from the ideas suggested in this chapter. If you believe that your organization needs to focus on improving how well individual learning leads to developing intellectual capital, this template and its suggested action steps are one way to get started.

The Agenda for action is organized in the same way as this chapter. Each imperative and its accompanying challenges are clustered together. Action steps are suggested for each challenge based on the text and case studies. You decide which action steps make sense for your organization and use the empty space to scribble in any additional ideas that come to mind.

Before you begin, make sure that you have transferred your prioritization ratings for each challenge. The prioritization ratings will remind you whether you believed that the challenge was worth pursuing. The maximum prioritization rating is 16, the minimum is 0.

How you use the prioritization ratings is up to you. For example, depending on the range of prioritization ratings, you may decide to ignore all challenges below a minimum threshold and focus only on those challenges above it. Or you may decide that everything that is not 0 deserves at least some thought. We invite you to use this Agenda for action as a place to start acting on your knowledge management priorities.

Agenda for action

1 Visibility

The link between strategy and the learning derived from everyday actions is obvious

A

Picture the complexity of human systems
Engage the mind and the body to connect 'soft' issues
to strategy

Prioritization rating

Action step	Who should be involved	My first 'to do'
Canvass our major operating and functional or process managers to find out the extent to which they believe it is important for everyone in their area to understand the link between strategy and their individual or team tasks.		
Determine if we have used any type of simulation as a skill-building experience to make the strategy–everyday task link. If we have, find out if we still do it and how people evaluate its effectiveness and rationalize the cost. Also find out how the simulations are structured and their exact purpose.		
Structure an experiment or pilot with an interested manager who uses simulations to compare the performance of his or her group with other groups in our organization that do not use any type of simulation. Discuss the ways in which performance ought to be improved and the lag time until such improvement will be visible. If no one uses simulations, find a manager willing to experiment on a small scale and create a simple simulation experience that we can use to get started.		
Other:		

2 Habituation

The practice of learning is commonplace

B

Promote the pleasure principle at work		

Prioritization rating

Action step	Who should be involved	My first 'to do'
Canvass the major operating and functional groups to identify one or two in which there is a high percentage of people who 'really like their work' and 'are willing to do whatever it takes to get the work done'.		
Obtain permission from the groups' management to convene a few roundtable discussions with a cross-section of members. Probe what factors they believe create an atmosphere in which they enjoy their work more than other groups in the organization.		
Circulate the findings from the roundtables to other groups (post on intranet bulletin boards, if we have them) and invite comment from other groups.		
Share the findings and comments with our operating management to open up a discussion about the issue of 'pleasure at work' for the entire organization.		
Other:		

C

Embed reflection mechanisms into the habit of work

Prioritization rating

Action step	Who should be involved	My first 'to do'
Use the Think about it! exercise from this challenge as a starting point for thinking about practices in which we already engage that could serve as springboards for creating reflection mechanisms.		
Canvass major operating and functional or process groups to surface any stories with specific information about outcomes that were improved as a result of groups taking the time to reflect on their activities. Document these stories and circulate them either electronically or on paper.		
Solicit one or two interested managers to create a formal reflection mechanism that will become part of their standard work process. Adapt or adopt existing practices from our organization if possible. Identify a small set of metrics that will be tracked over a period of time to monitor the impact of making this change.		
Obtain senior management support for this initiative, even if it is only to review the results of the experiment. Find out what metrics senior management would find compelling as evidence that reflection mechanisms benefit the organization.		
Other:		

D

Capture the benefits of mistakes, failures and disagreements

Action step	Who should be involved	My first 'to do'
Use the Think about it! exercise for this challenge as a starting point for using mistakes, failures and disagreement as an opportunity for improving performance.		
Canvass major operating and functional or process managers to find out if any group(s) within our organization are considered good at dealing with adversity in constructive, positive ways.		
Interview people in these groups to identify the factors that encourage them to publicly and honestly acknowledge mistakes, failures and disagreement and to discuss the impact on their work.		
Circulate the findings from these interviews electronically or on paper and capture reactions.		
Identify an interested manager and work with him or her to make minor changes in the work process so that mistakes are more visible and discussions about them are integrated into status meetings. Monitor performance over time to determine if, when and how it changes.		
Other:		

E

Nuture the art of learning by doing

Prioritization rating

Action step	Who should be involved	My first 'to do'
Review our organizational practices for ensuring that executives and managers stay connected with the realities of operating work.		
Consider how our development practices ensure that we have a solid base of know-how across our organization and within major operating, functional or process groups that will withstand the loss of specific individuals.		
Take information from the first two steps and cluster these practices into major categories. Interview several managers to find out how they believe these practices contribute to organizational performance.		
Use the Think about it! exercise from this challenge as a starting point for obtaining organization-wide input about how well we are positioned to benefit from learning. Change the row headers to fit the way our organization identifies its groups.		
Other:		

6 Contribute

> Diffused knowledge immortalizes itself.
>
> **Sir James Makintosh**

The need to inspire contribution – to make individual knowledge available across the entire organization – is the bellwether of the knowledge management movement because it gets to the heart of the matter: how people feel about being part of organizations. As with learning, contribution is a process step that most organizations find difficult to implement. While the existence of powerful networking technologies makes it theoretically possible for everyone to contribute their knowledge to the communal pool, in practice, sharing individual know-how is beset by complications and hurdles.

At a glance . . .

What is new?	Technology has enabled far greater exchange of information, permitting organizations to focus on concepts such as knowledge leveraging and knowledge re-use.
What is the problem?	Contribution is time consuming and value to the individual and teams is unclear, making contribution a low priority for them.
What is the individual or team objective?	Increasing efficiency and innovativeness of future projects based on willingness to collaborate and share ideas.
What is the organizational objective?	Creating a culture of contribution and supporting the contribution process through roles and structures.

Introduction

'How can we get people to share?' It is the perennial lament of the knowledge practitioner, and thousands flood knowledge management conferences every year looking for an answer. It is hard to argue with the benefits of contribution. But facilitating the contribution process does have its drawbacks – namely time and money. Giving people time away from 'real work' to contribute know-how ends up costing the organization, since those same individuals do not spend time creating new knowledge. Likewise, building up a large infrastructure of people to assist with contribution costs money that could be spent on other resources. The organization must monitor whether contribution achieves one of the following two goals:

1 People spend their time generating more innovative and more valuable ideas instead of recreating basic knowledge blocks.

2 People are able to combine contributed knowledge to create something new and valuable.

When managers approach the knowledge-sharing question, they invariably begin with a number of assumptions. The granddaddy of all assumptions is that people are not sharing. They point to the multitude of empty databases that litter the information technology landscape as evidence. The only thing this proves, however, is that people are not sharing their knowledge in databases. Sharing goes on in many other ways, much as it always has in organizations. Knowledge exchange may also occur electronically on a one-to-one basis with E-mail, or in smaller groups with distribution or mailing lists. Empty databases are frequently symptomatic of an underlying condition other than the unwillingness to share – for example, systems that are poorly integrated with work processes.

Adding contribution into the knowledge management process depends on the following *imperatives* and *challenges*.

Imperatives and challenges

Motivation	Members want to contribute their knowledge:
	◆ *Remove barriers to sharing.*
	◆ *Link contribution to opportunity and advancement.*
	◆ *Withhold benefits from non-contributors.*
	◆ *Find points of mutual benefit.*
Facilitation	Systems and structures support the contribution process:
	◆ *Allow employees the time and space to contribute their best work.*
	◆ *Create dedicated roles that support the contribution process.*
	◆ *Support transfer of tacit knowledge.*
	◆ *Weave an organizational web.*
Trust	The organization promotes understanding of and respect for the value of contributed knowledge:
	◆ *Support a contract of reciprocity.*
	◆ *Create explicit policies on the use of intellectual assets.*
	◆ *Use self-publishing to promote ownership.*
	◆ *Overlap spans of trust.*

1 Motivation

Members want to contribute their knowledge

In general, people will only share their knowledge if they feel sharing has some benefit to them, although how people define 'benefit' varies widely. Thus, motivation is the crux of the sharing issue, and it engenders considerable debate. When organizational and individual benefits are not linked – or as may sometimes be the case, are at odds – motivation becomes a serious problem.

While much of this chapter seems like basic common sense, it is surprising how many organizations espouse such values as collaboration, teamwork and community while providing incentives that compel precisely the opposite behaviours. An organization that has set up barriers to contribution needs to take a close look at what it values most highly from its members. This is not an easy exercise; it requires senior management commitment. If the contribution problem stems less from barriers than from a dearth of ways and means, solutions tend to be simpler and more tactical in nature. The Think about it! exercise on page 181 provides a Contribution Assessment Guide which can help you undertand why contribution may not be occurring in your organization.

Motivating employees to share involves the following *challenges*.

Challenges

◆ *Remove barriers to sharing.*
◆ *Link contribution to opportunity and advancement.*
◆ *Withhold benefits from non-contributors.*
◆ *Find points of mutual benefit.*

Remove barriers to sharing

Every organization that bewails the lack of sharing among its members must grapple with the question of whether to reward sharing as a means of inspiring the behaviour. There are two schools of thought. One is that sharing is hard to do and at odds with human nature, especially in western cultures that celebrate the Lone Ranger as a hero. The other is that people in knowledge organizations share easily and willingly. The first school of thought proposes rewards – sometimes money – when people share their ideas, work or personal resources. The second school rejects rewards, arguing that they set up a dysfunctional precedent, motivating people for the wrong reason – personal gain rather than collective good. Others, such as Tom Davenport, Professor at Boston University's Graduate School of Management, fall somewhere in between. During presentations, Davenport frequently quips, 'Sharing is an unnatural act, but people commit unnatural acts all the time.'

Setting up reward systems to get people to participate in a particular type of sharing activity can be a good way to get people involved. The key is to ensure that rewards do not become a short-term fix that cannot be sustained. Another pitfall is a reward structure that results in elaborate ways for members to 'game the system'. The result of these 'dollars per share' programmes is often quantity over quality.

Hewlett-Packard has come up with an elegant way of rewarding employees for knowledge sharing. It has established a 'microeconomy' in which members who contribute information can have actual monetary payments funnelled to their departments when anyone views or downloads the material. The HP solution, because it is buyer driven, ensures that only quality information is rewarded (see Profile).

No enterprise believes that it consciously sets out to discourage sharing and contribution, yet many organizational systems, structures and environments do just that. Barriers to contribution generally arise when individuals, groups or units compete for resources that may be withdrawn or redirected if they share ideas or information with one another. Organizations walk a fine line between encouraging aggressive entrepreneurialism – which may call for internal competition and small decentralized groups of employees – and supporting collective knowledge building – meaning people must share ideas and information even when they do not benefit directly from doing so.

Many organizations find that 'knowledge economies of scale' cannot be achieved when individual groups are pitted against one another for resources. Decentralized and autonomous groups raise even more challenges when they compete for the same customer. These groups rarely share customer information across boundaries and often offer customers competing solutions that undermine the credibility of the company as a whole.

One highly publicized example of how erecting barriers to sharing can cause serious damage comes from electronics giant Motorola. What former CEO Bob Galvin referred to as Motorola's autonomous 'warring tribes' were once its key strength – lean and mean from competing internally for resources and fanatically focused on developing outstandingly engineered products. In 1998, however, Motorola was castigated for turning a deaf ear to customers and for its inability to offer them integrated solutions that depended on sharing information across business division boundaries. For example, while one division moved swiftly to install digital cellular infrastructure equipment, Motorola's cellular handset division failed to respond to the demand for digital technology and developed yet another analogue product. Had the two divisions shared their plans, Motorola's subsequent loss of share in the cellular handset market might have been averted. Motorola's lack of internal cooperation led CEO Chris Galvin to restructure the organization and consolidate divisions around major businesses. By reducing the control of all-powerful division heads and adjusting executive compensation to reflect company-wide performance, Galvin is trying to jump-start a more collaborative culture.

PROFILE ▶ *Hewlett-Packard*

It is one thing to share knowledge with others on your team, department or business unit. But these days organizations are saying economies and innovations can be achieved by sharing information across the entire enterprise. The problem is, it takes time to help out and it is hard to justify when you're managing to a tight departmental budget. At Hewlett-Packard a newly instituted micropayment system has firmly established the benefits of knowledge sharing.

How can organizations make it worthwhile for people to share information? Pay them for it. 'On the Internet, everyone is trying to figure out how they can get people to pay small amounts to view chunks of content, but the privacy and security issues are huge,' says Chuck Sieloff, an internal knowledge management consultant. 'So a couple of years ago we asked ourselves, "why not do something like this internally at HP?" Without those bigger issues it was mostly just a technology challenge.'

The idea was to develop an electronic payment system in which individuals wishing to view or download information would be charged a small fee. The payment would flow to the department of the individual or team that had supplied the information. The solution was an elegant one for a variety of reasons. First, one of the trade-offs of Hewlett-Packard's decentralized structure is a reliance on internal fund transfers to pay for services, from training to travel. However, from an accounting perspective, billing for small services rendered is very costly. Many shared services are rolled into overhead, and business units are charged a set amount regardless of how often the services are used. The microeconomy concept eliminates the trade-off for information products that can be accessed electronically. It creates a 'pay per view' situation in which consumers of information are charged for precisely what they use.

The microeconomy addressed another problem at HP: getting people to share information outside their local environment. Sieloff points out that deliberate knowledge hoarding is not an issue at HP. What blocks sharing is the extra effort it takes to share knowledge with people in a different part of the organization. It often means finding the time to provide additional documentation, context setting or personal support. Furthermore, the payback is not always easy to trace. 'The microeconomy helps offset the expense of providing knowledge. What's more, the fact that people are willing to pay for the information demonstrates that it has value, and we can see exactly *how much* value,' says Sieloff.

Development efforts, which began in 1997, were funded out of the corporate IT department. Within a year the programme had been piloted, and it was launched in November 1998. More than 90,000 employees have been issued an electronic credit card called NetCard. At the end of each month, individual charges are consolidated. Each participant receives a single electronic credit reflecting all the usage charges from around the company. At the same time, each department receives a single bill, reflecting the charges incurred by all of its NetCard users. While usage detail is preserved in a web-accessible database, none of the detail flows through the accounting system. According to Sieloff, the system creates an infrastructure that supports payments of as little as a few cents.[1] Charges can either be transaction based, in which each instance of access results in a charge, or subscription based, whereby subscribers have unlimited access to material for a specified period of time.

The system is a real benefit for contributors because it makes the impact of their contribution visible. In addition, while in the past there was no way to demonstrate that certain knowledge resources benefitted the organization – other than collecting testimonials – the microeconomy offers both the proof and the funding to continue supporting them. Sieloff points to a community of practice that had been struggling for some years to achieve organization-wide knowledge sharing for corporate training professionals. The community provided trainers with a range of web-based information, including evaluations of new training technologies. The individual who managed the community and its web pages was somewhat reluctantly funded by his home department. Now his time spent on community activities is paid for by the revenues collected from individuals who access its web pages. 'The community wouldn't have survived without the microeconomy', acknowledges Sieloff. 'Finally we have a way to demonstrate and support efforts that lie outside traditional organizational budgets. It really opens up the pipeline for knowledge sharing.'

Think about it!

Consider how barriers to sharing could be lowered in the following two scenarios. Read the scenario and questions. Jot down your thoughts in the space provided.

Scenario 1   Think of a group within your organization from which your work team could benefit if they shared information with you.

    1   What could you do to encourage them   1
        to share with you?
    2   What explicit rewards could you   2
        provide?

Scenario 2   Flip this exercise around and think of a group within your organization that would benefit if your work team shared information with them.

    1   What could you do to encourage your   1
        team to share with them?
    2   What explicit rewards could they   2
        provide?

Quick prioritization of challenge

Based on this section, how much priority should you assign to meeting this challenge?

◆ *Remove barriers to sharing*

Rate your organization on these two factors	Your organization's rating	Rating scale
How much does your organization NEED to respond to this challenge?	**Need**	0 No need 1 Weak need 2 Moderate need 3 Strong need 4 Burning need
What is your organization's ABILITY to respond to this challenge?	**Ability**	0 Unable 1 Slightly able 2 Partially able 3 Almost able 4 Completely able

Need ✕ *Ability* =

✳ To do

Transfer your prioritization to box A on page 210.

Prioritization of challenge

(multiply the two ratings)

Link contribution to opportunity and advancement

When an organization has built a culture that truly encourages individuals to share knowledge, contribution occurs naturally. The bad news (or the good news, depending on your organization) is that this kind of culture comes about through leadership. If leaders have achieved their positions of authority through individual heroics and knowledge hoarding, then the contribution step of the knowledge management process will be considerably weakened in their organizations. This does not mean knowledge management is a lost cause. But it will be harder to do well, and the approach will probably be more mechanistic. There is also a tendency in contribution-poor organizations to substitute technology for the failings of environment or culture.

In organizations that foster contribution, there are clear incentives to knowledge sharing that go beyond mere rewards. Rewards tend to be short term and matched to a specific result, while incentives are longer term and focused on achieving a more comprehensive set of outcomes. Incentives for contribution can range from promotions to professional growth opportunities to heightened visibility within the organization. Organizations in which contribution occurs naturally evaluate members based on this criterion. People who fail to contribute – either by working well in teams or by sharing their individual knowledge with others in the enterprise – do not thrive or even survive. While individual performance may be excellent, the organization considers such results to be short term, narrow gains taken at the expense of achieving sustainable, more sweeping objectives.

At General Electric, CEO Jack Welch has coined the term 'boundarylessness' to convey the organizational need to cross departmental and business borders in both getting and giving ideas. Boundarylessness is more than a buzzword. Employees are evaluated on how well their behaviours model this value. When someone has a new idea, the first thing they are expected to do is share it. Likewise, those who borrow best practices from other business units and apply them are singled out for recognition. Much of GE's sharing initiative focuses on its highly visible Six Sigma quality programme. Every January the organization's most successful executives are invited to present the results of their Six Sigma projects to one another and to Welch. This is a prime opportunity to exchange ideas for cost cutting and increased productivity. An invitation to the annual meeting is an important feather in any executive's cap. The lessons learned there also cascade down to the rest of the organization where ideas continue to be transferred via presentations and on-site visits among the company's highly diverse business units.

Even more significant, in a culture of contribution, sharing knowledge is the accepted and preferred way of doing business. At specialty chemicals manufacturer Buckman Laboratories International, the salesforce, which spends most of its time at customer sites around the world, relies on the participation of Buckman associates in the company-wide virtual discussion forum called K'netix. Anyone can post a question on this network and receive a response within 48 hours. Bob Buckman, Chairman of Bulab Holdings which contains Buckman Laboratories, spent a good part of the system's inaugural year as an active contributor. Several years into K'netix's life, he was still showing up in lists of the top 50 knowledge sharers. Given Buckman's relentless focus on getting information into the hands of those directly engaged on the front lines with customers, most people do not think about *not* participating. But there is nothing like the participation of the person at the top of the organization to convince people that contribution will get noticed.

Think about it!

Think about how your organization links contribution to opportunity and advancement. Put a checkmark in the box that most closely matches your assessment of the proportion of people who would agree with the statements that are listed.

	Nearly everyone	Majority	50–50 split	Minority	Hardly anyone
Senior managers and executives actively participate in knowledge sharing.	☐	☐	☐	☐	☐
Borrowing ideas and practices innovated elsewhere in the organization is viewed positively.	☐	☐	☐	☐	☐
Our promotion policies take knowledge sharing into account.	☐	☐	☐	☐	☐
Some of our senior managers or executives have achieved their current positions based not only on how well they managed their part of the organization, but also on how much they contributed to overall organizational success.	☐	☐	☐	☐	☐
Failure to share knowledge is ultimately penalized through limited opportunities for advancement.	☐	☐	☐	☐	☐

Quick prioritization of challenge

Based on this section, how much priority should you assign to meeting this challenge?

◆ *Link contribution to opportunity and advancement*

Rate your organization on these two factors	Your organization's rating	Rating scale
How much does your organization NEED to respond to these challenges?	**Need**	0 No need 1 Weak need 2 Moderate need 3 Strong need 4 Burning need
What is your organization's ABILITY to respond to these challenges?	**Ability**	0 Unable 1 Slightly able 2 Partially able 3 Almost able 4 Completely able

Need × Ability =

★ To do
Transfer your prioritization to box B on page 211.

Prioritization of challenge

(multiply the two ratings)

Withhold benefits from non-contributors

Encouraging contribution becomes easier if it can be used as a point of leverage. Consider a discussion forum that participants view as a valuable information source. It is relatively simple to require participation as a condition of membership. Long before there was any hint of today's ubiquitous computer databases, professional services firm Arthur Andersen required individuals who were being considered for partnership to prepare a detailed paper for the company's 'Subject Files'. These documents, which explored some aspect of the tax or audit practice, were then cross-referenced and indexed for the benefit of others who frequently consulted them in the course of client work. No paper, no partnership.

Clearly there are many ways to 'force' participation, but denying non-contributors access to the organization's intellectual capital sends an unmistakable message. In the case of on-line systems, it is both relatively easy and devoid of confrontation, since the technology does the dirty work of keeping tabs on who contributes and denying access to those who do not.

In a fascinating experiment in cross-organizational on-line community building called the Community of Inquiry and Practice, Peter and Trudy Johnson-Lenz, founders of Awakening Technology, built a system in which various software agents played a role sometimes reserved for human beings. If members failed to provide basic registration information such as filling out a personal profile, the agent would gently return them to the orientation procedure if they attempted to enter the discussion space. The profiling information was considered a critical way of linking the community together (for example, it helped identify areas of mutual interest within the group). This minimum level of contribution was required before participants were granted access to the communal thinking of the group (see Point of view).

The Community of Inquiry and Practice consisted of a relatively small group of people who had explicitly agreed to be active participants, but the concept of reciprocity – which is central to knowledge management – can be supported on a larger scale. Several years ago, the finance organization at Shell Malaysia began a Lotus Notes-based discussion forum, called the Leadership Development Network, for employees to share ideas about leadership. While the network was open to all employees regardless of rank, participants were required to contribute one 'leadership learning' every month in order to continue as members. Because senior leadership participated enthusiastically in the forum, it was considered a place to 'see and be seen'. As a result, contribution was consistent and ongoing.

Denying access to non-contributors can be a useful 'stick', but organizations should use it sparingly. Keep in mind that databases also exist for knowledge seekers who may not be able to contribute much to the organization at a particular point in time – for example junior members who are conducting research. Knowledge recipients are as important a part of the knowledge landscape as knowledge givers. Rules about contribution must take into account the time lag that exists between the need to take and the ability to give back.

▶ POINT OF VIEW ▶ *Motivating participation in an on-line community*

Motivating people to share knowledge can be especially challenging in a groupware environment, where individuals are required to take the extra time and effort to write up new ideas or contextualize old ones. Peter and Trudy Johnson-Lenz of Awakening Technology have had more than two decades of experience using groupware in business settings. They believe that no external motivation is effective without the motivation that comes from within.

Asking how to motivate participation and knowledge sharing in on-line communities is a trick question. It assumes people need to be motivated from the outside. Harvard's organizational behaviour elder, Chris Argyris, says that internal commitment is far more effective than external commitment to empower and engage people's best thinking and action.

If we are the ones being motivated, that is good news. As managers, however, we read the bad news. We are not in control! So, even though we know better, we motivate from the outside, the classic carrot/stick way:

◆ **Carrot**: Change the compensation and promotion structures and reward contributions in whatever ways you can. Select expert knowledge practitioners and give them perks such as bonuses, peer recognition, micropayments for each contribution, positive evaluations and promotion paths. Tie participation and contribution to performance reviews.

◆ **Stick**: Penalize people for not contributing by withholding the same kinds of things.

You get the idea. It feels a lot like school – gold stars and demerits. Maybe even detention if you really drag your mouse. All of this may be necessary sometimes with some people. But it is not the answer in all cases. It does not achieve the breakthrough results we are all hungry for. As Argyris notes, offering the 'right' rewards creates dependency, and their potency diminishes with use.

Robert Gilman, a leading thinker in the area of sustainable development, has put forward an 'equation of change and innovation' which provides some insight into a different approach:

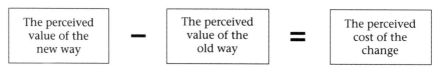

We change when the value-added of the new is greater than the cost of change. Using the assumption in our trick question, we might:

◆ Use the carrot by building up the perceived value of the new.

◆ Use the stick by increasing the pain of the old.

◆ Make the change as easy and effortless as possible.

But these still work from the outside. If people fail to participate or share knowledge, it is our fault as managers for not motivating them properly. What else can we do? We can build from the inside out, by appreciating the internal motivations, knowledge and experience that everyone has. Find out what is already working and increase (appreciate) its value. Instead of trying to motivate others, our job is to help develop their natural motivations and commitment. We might apply our leverage to:

◆ Encourage others openly to evaluate the old way: what is working? What is not?

◆ Engage them in creating the new way: what is really needed? What will work best?

◆ Compare the costs of changing the old ways and adopting the new ones.

We all know that learning how to work together effectively in cyberspace is expensive. It is easy to throw money and technology at people, but that does not work very well. The short-term added cost of involving knowledge workers in designing their virtual workspaces and processes is a bargain compared with the higher price of excluding them and being forced to make changes or risk user rejection. Given the opportunity to influence their future, some of those who do the work will prove they know best what is needed, what is not and what is actually going to work. Priceless knowledge.

In practice, a mixed strategy of internal and external motivations may lead to the best organizational performance, as long as these are not contradictory. Be clear about what is possible and appropriate in your organizational culture, what is working and what is not, and where the greatest leverage points are for all concerned. Then, appreciate it!

Peter and Trudy Johnson-Lenz of
Awakening Technology contributed this section.

 Think about it!

Think of ways in which you could stimulate knowledge sharing in the organization using penalties and rewards. Use your work team as a frame of reference and think about getting members to share with each other. Most organizations are adept at the 'stick' approach to encouraging people to behave in specific ways, but less inventive when it comes to using 'carrots'. If you are like most people, you will find it easier to fill out the left-hand column than the right-hand column, but try to complete both.

Ways to stimulate knowledge sharing within our work team

Sticks	Carrots
1	1
2	2
3	3

Quick prioritization of challenge

Based on this section, how much priority should you assign to meeting this challenge?

◆ *Withhold benefits from non-contributors*

Rate your organization on these two factors	Your organization's rating	Rating scale
How much does your organization NEED to respond to these challenges?	**Need**	0 No need 1 Weak need 2 Moderate need 3 Strong need 4 Burning need
What is your organization's ABILITY to respond to these challenges?	**Ability**	0 Unable 1 Slightly able 2 Partially able 3 Almost able 4 Completely able

Need $\times$ Ability =

★ To do
Transfer your prioritization to box C on page 211.

Prioritization of challenge

(multiply the two ratings)

Find points of mutual benefit

A culture of contribution does not blossom overnight. If reducing internal competition seems impossible, organizations can learn from some of the new forms of collaboration that have evolved in the business world – particularly from what has been dubbed 'co-opetition'. Co-opetition is cooperation among competitors. It flourishes in 'pre-competitive spaces'. These are areas of research and exploration that have the potential to grow the industry as a whole but are not well-enough established to compete in. Progress in the pre-competitive space generally benefits all parties, making it logical for rivals to collaborate, since not doing so forces all players to slice up a static or shrinking market pie instead. The best place to start collaborating across groups within a single enterprise is in an area where rapidly shared knowledge will benefit the entire organization without dampening the competitive spirit that drives it.

In large organizations, however, it may be difficult for individual employees to see how their knowledge sharing benefits either the company overall or themselves personally. Alignment of individual and organizational interests, while a worthy goal, is often elusive. Rather than insisting on 'universal sharing', a better approach is to identify smaller groups within the organization where knowledge sharing is likely to yield more visible results. Such groups need not be the same departments or sub-units that already fit neatly into the organizational chart. In fact, groups of knowledge sharers that cut across an enterprise may actually be a more efficient way to achieve universal sharing than trying to force an 'everything into one pot' approach to contribution.

In organizations such as Sun Microsystems (see Profile), groups often organize informally for the purpose of sharing knowledge and information in particular areas. One reason such groups, sometimes referred to as communities of practice, work so well as knowledge-sharing entities is that individuals can clearly see the benefits of mutual knowledge exchange.

PROFILE ▶ *Sun Microsystems*

Knowledge sharing within communities of practice generally takes place without any organizationally imposed rewards and incentives. Where professionalism serves as its own incentive, as in Sun Microsystems' Java Center Organization, points of mutual benefit are easily identified.

Sun Microsystems' Java^2 Center Organization is a virtually linked group of about 150 Java specialists operating out of more than a dozen geographically dispersed Java Centers. The Java Center Organization is part of the Sun Professional Services Organization, which consults with customers who either sell Java solutions to their own clients or who are Java end-users themselves. The Center is made up of the leading Java developers who exchange solutions and serve as an expert resource for the rest of the Professional Services Organization and its customers.

A range of sophisticated technology tools allows members of the community to operate from any location. Nevertheless, the group's mode of knowledge sharing is surprisingly low-tech, with an emphasis on efficiency. They use a form of E-mail distribution list, called an E-mail alias, to disseminate information and personal web sites to house information. E-mail alias discussions are archived on the Java Center Organization's web site where they are available to the larger organization. A powerful search engine allows people to locate information quickly.

Java is a relatively new language which is used extensively for Internet applications. Its continued acceptance and development by programmers both inside and outside the organization is critical to Sun. For this reason it is imperative that the company disseminate as much information and support for Java as possible. The community of Java experts is pivotal to this initiative, and knowledge sharing is the fuel that fires the engine. Each day some two dozen questions will go out via the E-mail alias from all corners of the globe. It is a rare for there to be fewer than three or four responses.

'The way we add value is through our ability to quickly diffuse expertise and the latest developments across the organization. Expertise is a currency that everyone around here understands and respects,' says Mark Bauhaus, Director of Worldwide Java and Internet Consulting. 'For most people in the Java Center Organization, it is their own pride in being on the cutting edge that drives them to share. Sharing information with others, or responding to questions is what makes their expertise visible and gives them credibility.' As people develop reputations for certain types of expertise, the community begins to know itself. Even when an expert does not respond to a query personally, it is likely to land on his or her doorstep through the recommendation of other members.

There is another reason that knowledge hoarding simply makes no sense within the Java Center Organization, notes Bauhaus. Much of the information that is shared is in the form of lines of code, and in the fast-paced world of Java programming, code becomes obsolete with alarming rapidity. It is therefore in everyone's best interest that it be disseminated as quickly as possible.

Java developers within Sun face a unique challenge. Development efforts for the Java language are going on in many other leading organizations, such as Hewlett-Packard and Microsoft. The language has evolved as quickly as it has through a willing exchange of expertise and knowledge. As a result, Sun has to run fast, just to keep up with its own customers and other developers. 'No one has a corner on knowledge in this market,' says Bauhaus. 'Only by combining what everyone in the community knows can we continue to stay several steps ahead.'

Think about it!

Consider the group or organizational unit in which you work. List the practices or situations that motivate or de-motivate people from sharing knowledge and ideas *within* the group.

Sharing knowledge within the group

Motivators

De-motivators

Consider your organization as a whole. List the practices or situations that motivate or de-motivate people from sharing knowledge and ideas *across the entire organization*.

Sharing knowledge across the organization

Motivators

De-motivators

Quick prioritization of challenge

Based on this section, how much priority should you assign to meeting this challenge?

◆ *Find points of mutual benefit*

Rate your organization on these two factors	Your organization's rating	Rating scale
How much does your organization NEED to respond to these challenges?	**Need**	0 No need 1 Weak need 2 Moderate need 3 Strong need 4 Burning need
What is your organization's ABILITY to respond to these challenges?	**Ability**	0 Unable 1 Slightly able 2 Partially able 3 Almost able 4 Completely able

Need × *Ability* =

★ To do

Transfer your prioritization to box D on page 212.

Prioritization of challenge

(multiply the two ratings)

Think about it!

Getting at the root causes of non-contribution is the first step in maximizing this step of the knowledge management process. A good way to begin is by asking people in the organization whether they do share; if so, how and with whom, and if not, why not.

Use the following assessment guide with members of your organization to help you pinpoint contribution roadblocks.

Contribution Assessment Guide

1   What percentage of your time do you spend working on projects, answering questions or putting together materials that will not benefit you or your group directly?

2   What form does this 'helping' activity take? How many people does it ultimately reach?

3   With whom are you most likely to share information? What factors influence your decision to share information?

4   How often do you contribute material to an organization-wide database?

5   Complete the following sentence by checking the three phrases that hold most true for you.
    'I would share more of my work, ideas, expertise, etc. with other members of the organization if':

    ☐ I had more time.

    ☐ my boss explicitly told me to contribute.

    ☐ I knew what other people were interested in.

    ☐ someone could help me get everything organized.

    ☐ I knew where to put or send my contribution.

    ☐ someone else took care of the details of submitting it.

    ☐ the process of contributing was more integrated with work I already do (I didn't have to go to another 'place' to contribute it).

    ☐ I knew what people did with it once they had it.

    ☐ I got some tangible reward for contributing it.

    ☐ I got more credit for contributing it.

    ☐ more people thanked me for contributing.

    ☐ I got feedback on what I contributed.

    ☐ the amount of contributing I did was reflected in my performance review.

    ☐ I didn't think someone else was going to take credit for my work.

    ☐ I felt like my contribution made a difference.

    ☐ other people contributed things too.

    ☐ Other: ....

2 Facilitation

Systems and structures support the contribution process

Lack of time is almost as important a reason as lack of motivation for failure to contribute. The fast-forward pace at which most organizations operate leaves individual employees with little leisure to consider such big picture questions as 'what have I done lately that others can benefit from?' or the time to put these accomplishments into a universally accessible, explicit and contextualized format. Slapping an electronic presentation, devoid of explanatory notes, on the corporate intranet rarely benefits anyone.

Since 'there aren't enough hours in the day', organizations that value contribution find ways to facilitate the process by meeting these *challenges*.

> **Challenges**
>
> ◆ Allow employees the time and space to contribute their best work.
> ◆ Create dedicated roles that support the contribution process.
> ◆ Support transfer of tacit knowledge.
> ◆ Weave an organizational web.

Allow employees the time and space to contribute their best work

We have already discussed the concept of allowing people the time to reflect on what they have learned from their work experience. Contribution, like learning, also takes time. The valuable knowledge that could benefit others in the organization may not be written down. Or, it may need to be re-contextualized – set in a more universal frame that will be relevant for the organization at large rather than for a specific group. Re-contextualizing involves everything from providing background information, to changing language and terminology, to adding commentary and recommendations – all time-consuming tasks. Some organizations penalize employees for taking time away from their own work to assist others whose work is not directly related. At best, organizations treat contribution as an afterthought – something employees ought to be doing on their own time as a mark of corporate citizenship. Yet the unwillingness of organizations to 'pay' for contribution time stamps it as low value. The result is that people turn their attention to matters that do pay off.

One of the central premises of knowledge management is that the give and take of sharing do not necessarily coexist. Giving may precede taking or vice versa. People give with the tacit understanding that someday they will be able to take; they take with an implicit acknowledgement that at a later date they will be obliged to give back. In their book *Working Knowledge*,[3] Davenport and Prusak refer to knowledge markets as those based on 'credit' rather than cash, precisely because of the delayed gratification of contributors. Managers must accept this reality before censuring employees who spend time on work not directly related to their official jobs. Allowing employees to assist other individuals, groups or the organization as a whole is a way to build up equity for future assistance. Establishing some simple practices can help deliver the message that contribution is a legitimate activity:

✓ Ask individuals or teams to spend an hour each week writing down and disseminating (or posting) information that might benefit others in the organization. Consider establishing a time period – a day or a week – during which the entire group, division or organization focuses on contributing reusable material.

✓ Encourage employees to make a habit of perusing areas of the intranet or corporate bulletin boards where others have posted questions, and providing answers wherever possible. Once again, this needs to be an understood and accepted allocation of employee time.

✓ Set up a system of 'contribution credits' which individuals can earn by spending time helping out or contributing specific expertise to groups other than their own. Like continuing education credits, employees might be asked to accumulate a certain number each year (see the Profile of Hewlett-Packard on page 166 which describes how an actual monetary compensation system works).

Another frequent complaint about the contribution process is that it is too much make-work – an additional step for people who are already overburdened with the daily details of getting their job done. If people are forced to launch a new application in order to contribute information electronically, or if they have to learn a new technology in order to do so, contribution invariably slows down. Even well-established efforts can be affected by changes in technology. After Buckman Laboratories switched to new technology following years of using the simple Compuserve system, there was a drop in contributions to the knowledge-sharing forums. The company formed a problem-solving team to address the issues. One immediate action was to develop a 'cookbook' to give people a quick start guide for the new system. The team also collected data from a small sample of users about the difficulties they had encountered with the new system. Lastly, the team was chartered to look for ways to increase the perceived value of the system within Buckman.

Buckman is not alone in looking for ways in which contribution can be seamlessly integrated into the process of work itself. In many organizations, a lot of knowledge is exchanged on a one-to-one, or a one-to-few basis via E-mail. To boost contribution, some companies have added features so that when employees push 'Send' on their E-mail tool bar, a button pops up asking whether the sender would like to submit the message to the corporate intranet for archiving. All they need to do is click 'yes'. Someone else worries about how to categorize and clean up the information. The next time the person gets asked the same question by others, he can refer them to the intranet for an already codified answer. At Sun Microsystems, lead developers at the Sun Java Center Organization – a globally dispersed group of Java programmers – communicate largely through 'E-mail aliases', a customized mailing list application. All such communications are archived by the system administrator on the Center's web site. In this way, contribution becomes automatic, and no additional steps are required of the sender.

Teltech, a research and consulting firm which develops expert directories and other knowledge tools for clients, looks for ways to integrate updating into existing work processes. For example, it works with human resource departments to tweak performance review forms so that information from them can be fed directly into databases containing experts' biographies. It is relatively simple to build contribution capabilities directly into on-line systems that workers use on a daily basis. Electronic feedback and contribution forms allow users to comment and offer suggestions for improving specific content immediately after reading it, rather than at some later point in time. Providing feedback to facilitators is also a good way to encourage future contribution.

Think about it!

Imagine you've been given an additional hour a week to work on something that you can make available to everyone else in your organization. Consider these questions:

What would you contribute?

Why do you think this is what you
need to work on?

How will the organization benefit?

How would others use this
information?

Who might you ask to work with you?

How could you integrate contributing this
information into your work process?

What support could the information
technology system provide?

What support could other people in the
organization provide?

Quick prioritization of challenge

Based on this section, how much priority should you assign to meeting this challenge?

◆ *Allow employees the time and space to contribute their best work*

Rate your organization on these two factors	Your organization's rating	Rating scale
How much does your organization NEED to respond to these challenges?	*Need*	0 No need 1 Weak need 2 Moderate need 3 Strong need 4 Burning need
What is your organization's ABILITY to respond to these challenges?	*Ability*	0 Unable 1 Slightly able 2 Partially able 3 Almost able 4 Completely able

Need × Ability =

★ To do
Transfer your prioritization to box E on page 213.

Prioritization of challenge	(multiply the two ratings)

Create dedicated roles that support the contribution process

Everyone in the organization has something valuable to contribute, but it is often those who are busiest – people who must constantly spend time with customers, the top salesperson, the lead research scientist – whose contributions are most in demand. There are ways the organization can make it easier for such people to contribute. One is to ensure that they do not have to worry about tasks that are extraneous to the knowledge transfer process, such as deciding where text-based information should be housed or how it should be formatted. Organizations like Booz Allen & Hamilton have built a knowledge management infrastructure which includes specialized positions for people who organize and summarize the knowledge contributions of others (see Profile). Many of these information professionals have dedicated their careers to information management and are far more qualified for the task than the contributors themselves.

Some organizations have formalized the role of specialists or experts in the knowledge management process, using the title of knowledge 'steward', 'gatekeeper' or 'gardener'. One of the keys to making this role work is minimizing the administrative component of the position. In Chapter 3 we discussed the role of the knowledge manager as consisting of two levels, the knowledge coordinator and the true knowledge manager who has fewer administrative responsibilities and more content knowledge. If we add the knowledge steward, or expert, to this mix, it is easy to visualize a position that calls for almost no administration, only in-depth content knowledge. In other words, the more the organization values an individual's content knowledge, the less difficult it should be for the individual to contribute that knowledge. The trade-off is depicted in Figure 6.1.

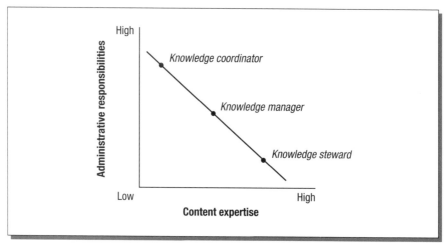

Fig 6.1 ◆ **Aligning knowledge management roles to maximize expert contribution**

▶ PROFILE ▶ *Booz Allen & Hamilton*

Contributing individual knowledge to the organization can be greatly enhanced if specific jobs support the process. At consulting firm Booz Allen & Hamilton, information profession-als – people with degrees in library science – serve as knowledge managers, helping teams think about what and how they should contribute learning from client projects.

In 1994 Booz Allen brought its traditional library and research functions under the auspices of the Chief Knowledge Officer, creating an Information Professional Community with an expanded mandate. Not only would the group be responsible for conducting research to support client-service teams, but also – through the new position of knowledge manager – for gathering, synthesizing and organizing the knowledge generated in the process of serving clients. Intellectual capital in the form of text-based documents is housed on Booz Allen's intranet, called 'Knowl-edge On-Line' (KOL).

Information professionals have a dotted-line reporting relationship to a practice area or industry in which they have expertise. They work closely with client-service teams, ideally from the outset of an engagement. One group of Booz Allen informa-tion professionals, researchers, is responsible for locating specific information both externally and within the firm. Knowledge managers, in contrast, must have a slightly different set of skills: they must be top-notch facilitators and communicators.

'The knowledge managers are not the ones who write the content that goes onto KOL,' explains Lois Remeikis, Director of Knowledge and Information Management. 'Nevertheless, their intimate understanding of the firm, the consulting business and their particular industry helps them guide the consulting teams who do develop the content.' Together with the client-service teams, knowledge managers determine what critical knowledge should be contributed to KOL. According to Remeikis, a rigorous review process ensures that only the highest quality contributions make it onto the intranet.

Selecting the best information requires a group that can look across the entire organization and identify who knows what. As a tightly knit global community, Booz Allen's information professionals are able to do just that. When the Information Professional Community was first formed, the far-flung members had frequent face-to-face meetings. Now the group communicates more often via frequent conference calls and electronic bulletin boards. 'We make aggressive use of our community network to track down information,' says Remeikis. 'Networking is critical to our role as knowledge managers.'

Think about it!

If your organization moved ahead to create dedicated roles for supporting the contribution process, which members of your work team or group would be best suited to filling the three main roles that were identified in the previous section? What qualifications make them best suited to these tasks? Use the following space to list a few candidates and their qualifications.

Roles	Candidates from our work team	Qualifications/skills for role
Knowledge coordinator	A	A
	B	B
Knowledge manager	A	A
	B	B
Knowledge expert or steward	A	A
	B	B

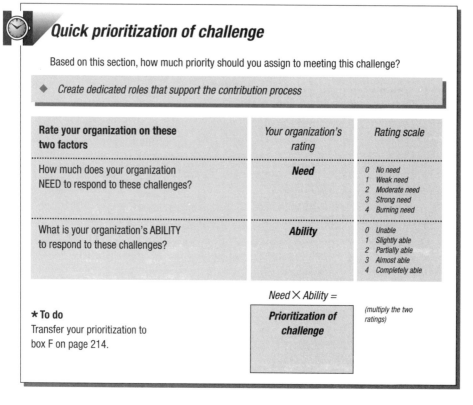

Quick prioritization of challenge

Based on this section, how much priority should you assign to meeting this challenge?

◆ *Create dedicated roles that support the contribution process*

Rate your organization on these two factors	Your organization's rating	Rating scale
How much does your organization NEED to respond to these challenges?	**Need**	0 No need 1 Weak need 2 Moderate need 3 Strong need 4 Burning need
What is your organization's ABILITY to respond to these challenges?	**Ability**	0 Unable 1 Slightly able 2 Partially able 3 Almost able 4 Completely able

Need × *Ability* =

★ To do	**Prioritization of**	(multiply the two ratings)
Transfer your prioritization to box F on page 214.	**challenge**	

Support transfer of tacit knowledge

Organizations generate vastly different forms of knowledge that can be segmented into two major types – *explicit*, which can be articulated using written words and graphics, and *tacit*, which generally cannot be articulated because it is embedded in the mind of a particular individual. Explicit knowledge is often described as 'know what' or knowledge *about* something, while *tacit* knowledge can be described as '*know how*', or an understanding of *how* to do something. An example of explicit knowledge is the set of directions for creating a particular chemical compound. Tacit knowledge, by way of contrast, resides in the mind of the technician who is able to adjust the necessary equipment to precisely the right calibration and can tell by the smell of the solution when there is a problem. Another example of explicit knowledge is a consulting firm's activity-based costing methodology. For this organization, tacit knowledge is possessed by the consultant who almost never has a 'bad' client because she instinctively detects early on when things are beginning to go sour and intuitively knows what steps to take.

It is relatively easy to support contribution of explicit knowledge, so it is hardly surprising that most knowledge management efforts in today's organizations focus on its storage and transfer. But a great deal of organizational knowledge – and many argue, the more valuable or mission-critical knowledge – is tacit in nature. The best way to move tacit knowledge from one individual or group to another is not through a database, but rather through human interaction. 'Mushy' knowledge calls for mushy methods to move it around the organization.

Realistically, knowledge exists on a continuum, with most of it lying somewhere inbetween tacit and explicit. Much of what is referred to as "tacit" is simply knowledge that has not been articulated. Contributing unarticulated (but articula*table*) knowledge calls for one approach, while contributing tacit knowledge calls for another. For example, experts often possess deep knowledge of a subject area, which can be made explicit, but rarely is. The knowledge may be too hard to contextualize, or the expert may have trouble combining all the pieces to create a useful picture. In this case, successful contribution depends on the use of professional facilitators and interviewers who are adept at eliciting expertise – asking the kinds of questions that will enable the expert to begin the process of articulation. The ability to elicit expertise – ask the right questions, dig below the surface, interpret the answers and identify common themes and patterns – is a valuable skill, and one which organizations need to nurture. However, these skill sets are not always resident in the organization.

For instance, when Arthur Andersen, the professional services firm, launched its Global Best Practices knowledge base in the early 1990s, it made the decision to hire teams of editors and journalists on a project basis rather than rely on auditors and consultants to create content. Not only were these individuals better suited to conducting secondary research and writing, they also had strong interviewing skills which they used with firm experts to translate their know-how into a cogent set of best practice information.

When eliciting true tacit knowledge is the objective, the organization will need to adopt some unconventional approaches. 'Storytelling', an informal accounting of events that embraces the personal or experiental as critical to transferring knowledge, has become increasingly popular. For example, IBM brings together teams that have succeeded in securing new large global accounts. The teams are asked to relive the experience by recounting it verbally, complete with interruptions, corrections and dialogue among team members. The recounting is videotaped. The tapes have become a rich source of learning as well as a way to pass on tacit knowledge to others. Another storytelling example comes from the Marine Corps. At the Basic School, a six-month experience for new Marine lieutenants, almost 300 hours are devoted to storytelling by instructors. Telling stories and talking about them is a form of scenario planning that helps less experienced members understand the complex set of facts and feelings from which life and death decisions are made.

Ultimately, transfer of tacit knowledge requires significant face time between individuals or small groups. We address some of the ways to achieve this type of connection in the next challenge.

Think about it!

Consider how you might support the transfer of tacit knowledge in the two scenarios that follow. Read each scenario and list three responses to the question that is posed.

Scenarios	Three responses
Consider your team's most recent significant achievement. Imagine that you have been asked to tell a story about it, rather than write a report. What three pieces of information might you express verbally in a story that you would never write in a formal report?	1 2 3
Consider the last really boring meeting that you organized at which you were hoping that people would share what they had been working on and then talk about how to work together to solve a particular problem. If you could do it all over again, what three aspects of how the meeting was conducted would you change to inspire the exchange of more tacit knowledge?	1 2 3

Weave an organizational web

Today's organizations are like vast neural networks in which any individual cell is connected to other cells through a variety of pathways. If a cell sends a message along a pathway that is no longer functional, it quickly looks for another. The more connecting pathways there are, the faster the message travels. This analogy reflects a very simple tenet of knowledge management – it is not just about connecting people to information, it is also about connecting people with other people. The more linkages that can be created among individuals in the organization, the greater likelihood that knowledge will flow.

Technology has an especially firm grip on the organizational imagination when it comes to knowledge management because of its powerful ability to connect people. But non-technological approaches to connecting people have always been around. Organizations that are serious about knowledge management need to use them as well. Creating links among members of the organization has another benefit in terms of increasing contribution: people tend to share more freely and deeply with people they trust, and they tend to trust people with whom they have connected personally (usually face to face). Increasing organizational linkages increases the 'span of trust' for individuals and groups, resulting in greater contribution and sharing.

The best approaches to weaving an organizational web are those which create connections that might not otherwise have occurred without some form of intervention:

✓ **Mentorship programmes**: Many organizations pay lip service to mentorship, although an increasing number have instituted formal programmes. However, most think of it as a way to get young people 'up to speed' or to teach them leadership behaviours. If viewed as a form of knowledge transfer, the concept of mentorship becomes more fluid. Experts swap perspectives with younger workers, each providing the other with a window into a different world. When mentors are matched to mentees with very different backgrounds and experiences, unexpected organizational networks begin to take shape, stimulating new knowledge flows.

Mentors are not necessarily senior executives. In fact, when it comes to technology, a number of organizations have instituted 'reverse mentorship' programmes, in which young, computer-savvy employees provide assistance to organizational elders who want to get beyond the paperweight stage with their computers. Mentors need not even be employees. One consulting firm instituted an 'Emeritus Program', providing former employees with offices and an invitation to continue to drop in and share knowledge.

✓ **Sabbaticals**: Organizations that have adopted such leave of absence programmes generally do so to re-energize employees by allowing them to work on something that might be unrelated to their jobs. But an additional advantage is forging new ties outside the organization. When the employee returns to work, these new relationships extend the web of relationships beyond traditional organizational boundaries, creating new and valuable linkages. Organizations that are intentional about leveraging these newly established contacts will benefit accordingly.

✓ **Exchange programmes and internships**: It is hardly rocket science that getting people to move around and work with other groups or disciplines helps break down calcified 'us versus them' allegiances. Networks become simultaneously stretched and strengthened, and information flow and transfer is stepped up in the process.

✓ **Temporary project teams**: In the same way that exchange programmes get people and ideas moving around more freely, teaming up people with diverse backgrounds to solve problems or work on short-term projects also helps extend networks across the entire organization.

✓ **Training programmes**: Face-to-face training programmes, seminars and workshops also bring people together. Professional services firm Arthur Andersen considers its state-of-the-art training facility in St Charles, Illinois to be one of the cornerstones of its culture. While the cost of bringing members of a worldwide organization to a single facility has led it to consider an array of distance learning approaches, the firm continues to bring new employees to the St Charles facility for several weeks of orientation and training. The rationale for shouldering this expense is that the experience permits new employees to network with others from around the world. Many of the relationships formed at St Charles become the bedrock of the future partnership.

✓ **Mix 'n' match meetings, sans agenda**: Meetings have become the drudge work of the modern manager. One of the dreams for networking technology is that it can be used to reduce the amount of time everyone needs to spend in such corporate purgatory. However, meetings do have at least one advantage over E-mail distribution lists. People come together face to face, raising the potential for a more complex interchange. By all means, reduce the amount of time people spend in meetings where they swap information with people they already interact with on a daily basis. Instead use the face-to-face format to bring together people who *do not* normally interact. Or get people who *do* work together regularly to connect with one another in different ways. For example, organize meetings with no formal agenda other than stimulating the flow of ideas. At Monster Board, which produces one of the Web's biggest hubs for those seeking and selling talent, every once in a while the weekly morning meeting is replaced with a 'Monday Morning Unplugged' session.[4] The point of the meeting is to get ideas flowing more freely. People tell stories and work together in teams playing games that depend on group communication.

✓ **Open-space environments**: Visual contact nudges people to talk more often to one another – particularly up and down the organizational ladder. Open-door policies are easier to take seriously when the doors disappear altogether. Many organizations have found that establishing lounge areas where people feel comfortable just sitting and talking has increased the level of knowledge sharing. Danish hearing-aid manufacturer Oticon went a step further by closing down its elevators to increase the rate of happenstance – instances of people bumping into one another in the hallway or on the stairs and bouncing around ideas or tidbits of information.

✓ **Vive the knowledge broker**: Some people have a particular talent for hooking other people up – they are organizational matchmakers and network catalysts. They cannot be replaced by databases and knowledge maps. Organizations that fail to recognize the importance of knowledge brokers – or even worse, who downsize them – are overlooking an important benefit.

Think about it!

Depict the trade-off between your organization's *comfort level* with adopting one of the contribution practices described in the section you have just read and the degree to which that practice *supports the transfer of tacit knowledge* in your organization by placing the letters for each practice on the matrix.

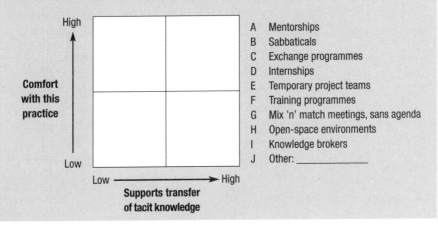

A   Mentorships
B   Sabbaticals
C   Exchange programmes
D   Internships
E   Temporary project teams
F   Training programmes
G   Mix 'n' match meetings, sans agenda
H   Open-space environments
I   Knowledge brokers
J   Other: _____

Quick prioritization of challenge

Based on this section, how much priority should you assign to meeting these challenges?

◆ *Support transfer of tacit knowledge*
◆ *Weave an organizational web*

Rate your organization on these two factors	Your organization's rating	Rating scale
How much does your organization NEED to respond to these challenges?	**Need**	0 No need 1 Weak need 2 Moderate need 3 Strong need 4 Burning need
What is your organization's ABILITY to respond to these challenges?	**Ability**	0 Unable 1 Slightly able 2 Partially able 3 Almost able 4 Completely able

Need × Ability =

★ To do
Transfer your prioritization to box G on page 215.

Prioritization of challenge

(multiply the two ratings)

3 Trust

The organization promotes understanding of and respect for the value of contributed knowledge

Trust is an emotion-laden word to use when talking about business enterprises. But it is the linchpin upon which the entire premise of knowledge sharing hinges. Without it the knowledge-sharing organization is an oxymoron. Trust comes in many forms, all of which grease the wheels of the contribution process:

♦ Trust the organization: It will not take a drain and discard approach.

♦ Trust the system: It will facilitate a return on contribution.

♦ Trust the people: They will make ethical use of contributed knowledge.

Achieving trust within organizations and using it to increase individual contribution depends on the following *challenges*.

Challenges

♦ *Support a contract of reciprocity.*

♦ *Create explicit policies on the use of intellectual assets.*

♦ *Use self-publishing to promote ownership.*

♦ *Overlap spans of trust.*

Support a contract of reciprocity

Few organizations have not responded to competitive pressures by laying off at least some percentage of their employees, and in so doing, increased the need to foster contribution and rapid knowledge transfer to achieve productivity gains. Ironically, employees in today's 'You're on your own' era may feel that the knowledge between their ears is also the only thing between them and the unemployment line. If they believe that their employers want to drain them of their expertise only to discard them, they are unlikely to be cooperative when it comes to sharing what makes them employable. While people no longer expect lifetime employment, they do expect to be treated fairly.

In an insightful article in the *Harvard Business Review*[5] W. Chan Kim and Renee Mauborgne explain how organizations fail to appreciate the importance of fair process in gaining the trust and commitment that leads to knowledge sharing. Most organizations continue to operate under the premise that what people want is 'distributive justice' in which they are paid what they deserve. The problem with distributive justice is that it encourages people to restrict themselves to following directions and meeting expectations. Fair process, or 'procedural justice', in contrast, is very different:

> Fair process builds trust and commitment, trust and commitment produce voluntary cooperation, and voluntary cooperation drives performance, leading people to go beyond the call of duty by sharing their knowledge and applying their creativity.

The concept of fair process is abstract. But it is a constant of change initiatives that many organizations are undertaking to improve performance. Change initiatives and knowledge management initiatives are both predicated on a committed group of employees who are willing to do just about anything to get information and ideas flowing like an elixir through the organization.

Fair process implies that that the 'rules of the game' are understood. People know where they stand and agree to be judged by those rules. To foster contribution there needs to be a pervasive and felt understanding – a set of norms -- that embodies expectations surrounding knowledge sharing. A successful knowledge system is based on a balance of payments: I give, therefore I get back. This contract holds true whether it is between the individual and the organization or between individuals themselves.

Knowledge-based organizations understand that employees are not only valuable for what they know, but for what they continue to learn. If the culture sanctions continuous learning, rather than making it something employees are forced to do in their own time, employees are far more likely to offer up their knowledge for the general good of the organization. The implicit contract between these organizations and their employees reads: 'In exchange for sharing your knowledge, we promise to provide you with learning opportunities. You will get a continuing supply of new knowledge, increasing your value to us or to others should you decide to leave.'

Contribution is a voluntary activity, but it is not endlessly philanthropic. People contribute in the expectation that eventually they will get something in return. Likewise, receiving knowledge from another person implies that at some point you will give them something back. If this contract is broken, contribution will fall by the wayside – one individual at a time.

Think about it!

With your work group in mind, consider the following ways in which participating in simulations

	Nearly everyone	Majority	50–50 split	Minority	Hardly anyone
The organization encourages people to advance their careers by gaining new knowledge					
People are generally willing to pitch in because they know they can rely on others when they need help					
The norms of our organization clearly spell out the rewards for the individual who share knowledge					
Learning new skills on company time is an accepted way to enhance one's value to the organization					
When people go above and beyond the requirments of their jobs, it is recognized and rewarded					
Most people who leave this orgaization go on to a better opportunity elsewhere in part because of the skills and experiences they have obtained here					

Create explicit policies on the use of intellectual assets

One of the revolutionary aspects of the knowledge era is the sheer volume of people who now spend the majority of their time developing knowledge. Yet the difficulty of placing a monetary value on most knowledge causes its value to be underestimated. Few people would consider co-opting a fellow worker's computer or desk chair, but ideas and knowledge are 'up for grabs'.

In many ways, of course, inspiration *should* be up for grabs, because shared ideas frequently turn into better ideas. At the same time, people who contribute their ideas are far more likely to continue the practice if their contributions are acknowledged in some fashion by those who build upon or use them. The research community – which is driven by intellectual assets – has always understood this concept. Violations of the etiquette of acknowledgement are looked upon with consternation. Every paper published in a scholarly journal includes copious bibliographic notes citing previous research that has led to the work at hand. But the business world, in its drive to turn ideas into dollars, has yet to understand the subtleties of intellectual assets as they relate to individuals.

Ultimately, members of the organization must have a healthy respect for intellectual assets and an understanding of what constitutes appropriate use of the ideas of others. One way to develop this attitude is through explicit policies and procedures. Once these are internalized, they become almost second nature, and fewer problems arise.

Paradoxically, the enterprise-wide knowledge base is probably the *last* place the organization should start trying to model contribution behaviours. Groupware removes a sense of personal indebtedness on the part of the user. When people download information, there is a feeling that it is there for the taking – they do not necessarily 'owe' the contributor anything. The conviction that information on the corporate intranet is 'free' and comes without strings stems from the availability of oceans of free information on the Internet. The contract of reciprocity breaks down in groupware systems unless deliberate policies and procedures are in place. Here are some to consider:

✓ **Maintain attribution**: From a technology perspective it is not difficult to ensure that the name of the contributor is always associated with contributed knowledge in a groupware system. This is precisely what happens at IBM Consulting. Any piece of information that is contributed to the organization's intranet remains attached to the name of the contributor. In this way, no matter how many times information is forwarded, it retains the identity of the orginal creator. It also helps the organization monitor the contribution behaviour of each individual.

✓ **Require notification or permission**: It is a simple idea. By making it a requirement that users let contributors know that they wish to use their material, the organization achieves two things in addition to preventing knowledge misappropriation. First, contributors receive the satisfaction of hearing that others value their work. Second, another link is forged in the organizational network – between giver and taker. Making this relationship visible also reinforces the reciprocity contract by establishing a sense of obligation on the part of the taker. In their experimental on-line community, the Community of Inquiry and Practice, Peter and Trudy Johnson-Lenz of Awakening Technology crafted a covenant that read: 'Keep confidential other people's items (unless permission is explicitly given by the author to do otherwise); each person's words are his or her own.' Of course, requiring people to notify contributors that they would like to use their information is not always practical or realistic. However, in the case of particularly important contributions – for example, formal reports or white papers – contributors may want to know when their material is being used. One workaround solution is to have the contributor drive the decision by including a mechanism that allows him or her to specify the conditions under which notification or permission is required.

✓ **Institute feedback mechanisms for contribution**: In some organizations, 'getting credit' for ideas is not considered an issue. Ideas are for sharing and building upon. Nevertheless, for those who do contribute their ideas, knowing how those ideas are used, by whom, and what the users reactions are, is a tremendous incentive. Not only does it generate a communal creative process, it defines what types of knowledge are most valuable to others in the organization, making the overall contribution process ultimately more efficient . For organizations that encourage people to contribute knowledge to an electronic environment, it is relatively straightforward to examine which postings are downloaded most frequently. It is an easy next step to convey this information back to the contributor. Emerging groupware tools now allow people to rate the helpfulness of a particular contribution and to build on it. Some organizations, such as Hewlett-Packard have even devised ways to funnel small payments to contributors when their material is used (see Profile of Hewlett-Packard on page 168).

Think about it!

Evaluate the policies of your organization regarding the use of shared knowledge. Put a checkmark in each box that applies to your organization's current status.

Our organizational status

Policy	Have a policy	Do not have a policy	Policy is explicit	Policy is implicit	Most people practice it	Most people do not practice it
Maintain attribution of contributed knowledge	☐	☐	☐	☐	☐	☐
Require notification or permission for use of contributed knowledge	☐	☐	☐	☐	☐	☐
Establish feedback mechanism to alert contributor	☐	☐	☐	☐	☐	☐

Quick prioritization of challenges

Based on this section, how much priority should you assign to meeting these challenges?

◆ Support a contract of reciprocity
◆ Create explicit policies on the use of intellectual assets

Rate your organization on these two factors	Your organization's rating	Rating scale
How much does your organization NEED to respond to these challenges?	**Need**	0 No need 1 Weak need 2 Moderate need 3 Strong need 4 Burning need
What is your organization's ABILITY to respond to these challenges?	**Ability**	0 Unable 1 Slightly able 2 Partially able 3 Almost able 4 Completely able

Need × Ability =

★ To do
Transfer your prioritization to box H on page 216.

Prioritization of challenge

(multiply the two ratings)

Use self-publishing to promote ownership

People are generally proud of their ideas. Studies repeatedly indicate that what truly motivates knowledge workers is not money, but being recognized and appreciated for their thinking. In the previous challenge we talked about using explicit policies and procedures to ensure that people get credit for their contributions. A self-publishing model of contribution is another way to help people maintain a feeling of ownership over their knowledge.

It is interesting that the concept of self-publishing – often in exchange for nothing more than the gratification of having a stage and a receptive audience – has blossomed on the Internet. About.com, an Internet-based content provider, has assembled some 650 individuals who both mine the Internet for subject-specific information and create their own newsletters, discussion groups and commentaries. These guides set up their sites on About.com's platform for relatively small compensation and a portion of ad revenues. They exemplify the desire to share expertise that is not driven solely by financial incentives.

A web site is not necessary to share ideas in cyberspace. Many people create specialized distribution lists or subscription services, E-mailing their thoughts and expertise in newsletter format either to the select few or anyone who wishes to subscribe. David S. Bennahum, a contributing editor to *Wired* who distributes his newsletter *Meme* via Listserv (a mailing list application), writes:

> What is exchanged on a list, where money rarely is the prime measure of success or failure? Ideas, time, and attention – the sometimes vast numbers of subscribers, or powerful people on a list – are all part of a complex ecology in an environment remarkably separate from traditional markets, where getting something for nothing remains a paradox.[6]

This passion for sharing ideas has been slow to catch on in most organizations. What can businesses learn from the Internet's more successful model? One idea is to give people more control over how their knowledge is packaged or distributed, by providing them with the tools to create home pages or disseminate information to subscribers. This approach has been adopted at such organizations as Sun Microsystems and US West, where individuals and teams are responsible for maintaining their own web sites. When people retain their position as the source of ideas, number of 'hits' to a home page, downloads, people on a distribution list or E-mail responses all become meaningful and rewarding measures.

From the standpoint of the organization, one drawback of self-publishing is that it can be messy and redundant. If individuals and groups all have home pages on the corporate intranet, the system needs a powerful search engine and organizing framework to help people get where they need to go. Organizations have to accept that a certain amount of duplication is bound to occur using a self-publishing model. Obvious redundancy can be dealt with on a case-by-case basis, but it is not worth the time and resources to stamp it out altogether. Furthermore, redundancy is not all bad. It can be a catalyst for forming new networks and highlighting subtle but important differences in approach that lead to breakthrough thinking. As for that organizational bugbear, 'reinventing the wheel' – sometimes it is just what the doctor ordered.

PROFILE ▶ *IBM Global Services*

Communities of practice are 'distributed centres' of expertise that fit nicely into the world of electronic knowledge sharing. At IBM Global Services, these communities are logical gatekeepers for specialized knowledge, and they are responsible for managing and publishing that knowledge. Individuals are encouraged to maintain ownership of contributed information even after it goes through a quality review process. Ownership carries both the benefit of being an acknowledged expert and the responsibility of fielding questions and keeping the information up to date.

IBM Global Services is the division of computer giant IBM that includes a range of service-based businesses, including consulting, systems integration, outsourcing, product support services, e-business and learning services. In the mid-1990s, the consulting business instituted a knowledge management group which was so successful that it has expanded to about 40 people worldwide who are now responsible for increasing the level of knowledge contribution and reuse throughout the entire division.

One element that makes IBM Global Services' approach to the contribution process unique is its focus on reuse. 'Reuse was a central issue from the beginning for us,' explains Barbara Smith, the division's Director of Knowledge Management. 'We wanted people to start thinking about reuse as soon as a new opportunity arose. They need to be asking questions like "Where did we go head-to-head with this competitor before?", "What have we already done that we can leverage?" Once people begin thinking about reuse, their whole mind set changes, and this in turn influences what and how they choose to contribute to the organizational knowledge base.'

IBM's explicit knowledge – from code to proposals to methodologies – resides in a variety of databases and is accessible via a Domino application.[7] A key organizing framework for this knowledge uses the division's communities of practice. Communities of practice may focus on an industry, such as automotive; a technology, such as SAP; a business area, such as e-business; or even a process, such as project management. Each community of practice has a leader and a core team – a group of eight to ten people who spend about 10% of their time managing the community's intellectual capital and knowledge.

When people contribute intellectual capital it goes to the core team, which asks the question 'How can we package this information so that it is most useful to the community?' As a result, they may massage the information to 'genericize' it. Every piece of intellectual capital that is made available electronically to the community has a contact name. This is generally the name of the original contributor. Insisting that each contribution be attached to an owner achieves two goals. First, it gives credit to the originator. Second, it puts interested parties in touch with a more in-depth information source. In order to be the acknowledged owner, the contributor must be willing to take phone calls regarding his or her contribution. If contributors do not want to take on this responsibility, then a member of the core team becomes the owner.

Communities of practice are explicitly acknowledged groups at IBM sponsored by a business unit. Once a group is sponsored, the leader contacts the knowledge management team which assigns a relationship manager to the group. The relationship manager's responsibility is to work with the community's core team to develop a strategy and plan for managing the community's intellectual capital. The first step in this process is to define the community's business priorities and strategic initiatives. Then, the team identifies members of the community. The community needs to be global in scope, attracting the 'best of the best' who can contribute expertise related to the practice area. Next, the team works with the relationship manager, both virtually and face to face, to define the community's domain of knowledge and intellectual capital – specifically what the community requires to operate and what knowledge resources it will need. The group then engages in a hunting and harvesting exercise, determining what intellectual capital already exists and developing an action plan to close knowledge gaps. The relationship manager also takes the core team through a crash course on knowledge management. The objective is to show the group how knowledge management can help it achieve its business goals. Once the core team has set operating guidelines and assigned roles and responsibilities, it is ready to launch to community members.

The role of core team members has gone through several iterations at IBM. Initially, they were paid out of a central budget because the community development process was introduced mid-year, and without the ability to bill for their time, core members would have been penalized professionally. However, in 1997 bonus incentives were put in place worldwide to recognize and reward core team participation. The measures used to evaluate core team members were rejiggered: either utilization targets were adjusted down, or different criteria were used to determine bonuses. In addition, evaluations were changed to reflect the need for all professionals both to contribute and reuse intellectual capital.

Performance criteria were also developed for the communities themselves. A 'health check' process was used by the knowledge management team to assess core team effectiveness and the degree to which the community was active. For example, the team looked at total number of contributions from community members to the core team and the number of core team approvals and rejections. They also looked at how much new material was contributed within the past 30 days. Interviews were conducted with both core team and community members. As the number of communities grew from a handful to more than 40, and relationship managers became responsible for some ten communities each, the health check task was turned over to the communities for self-monitoring.

Looking back on the evolution of the communities approach, Smith reflects on the need to provide these groups with incentives to both share and reuse one another's knowledge. 'It's really a combination of a carrot and a stick approach. The stick approach sometimes works better in the beginning. But once people see the value, the behaviour gets incorporated, and you focus on the carrot. In fact, the process becomes a reward in itself.'

Think about it!

Identify three areas of knowledge that would be beneficial to your work team if they were more frequently and freely discussed and if good information were readily available. Consider which of the mechanisms described in the previous section might stimulate knowledge sharing in these areas and who would be involved.

	Who would be involved with these mechanisms for stimulating knowledge sharing		
Area of knowledge	*Personal web site*	*E-mail distribution lists*	*Community web site*
1			
2			
3			

Quick prioritization of challenge

Based on this section, how much priority should you assign to meeting this challenge?

◆ *Use self-publishing to promote ownership*

Rate your organization on these two factors	*Your organization's rating*	*Rating scale*
How much does your organization NEED to respond to these challenges?	***Need***	0 No need 1 Weak need 2 Moderate need 3 Strong need 4 Burning need
What is your organization's ABILITY to respond to these challenges?	***Ability***	0 Unable 1 Slightly able 2 Partially able 3 Almost able 4 Completely able

Need × Ability =

★ To do
Transfer your prioritization to box I on page 217.

Prioritization of challenge

(multiply the two ratings)

Overlap spans of trust

It is hardly earthshaking to say that people are more likely to share information with those they trust. Social networking specialists have shown that trust has significant impact on how information flows in organizations. If no one trusts the people who are responsible for processing and disseminating information, serious communications breakdowns can occur.

Trust is generally based on personal relationships. Every person has a 'span of trust' – a group of individuals with whom he or she is willing to share deep knowledge. These spans of trust tend to be relatively small. In fact, evidence indicates that 'natural groups' – clusters of individuals who all have some kind of relationship with one another – do not expand beyond about 150 people.[8] This is one rationale behind the policy of some organizations to spin off operations that grow beyond a particular size. Yet companies consistently make the mistake of assuming that the simple fact of membership in the organization is basis enough for trust.

If an individual's span of trust is only a few hundred people, this could be bad news for most organizations which are seeking to launch knowledge-sharing initiatives on a far greater scale. Earlier in this chapter we talked about ways to increase personal connections – effectively enlarging the individual's span of trust. Yet this can only go so far; to leverage critical knowledge across the enterprise, organizations will need to look for ways to ensure that these new connections result in *overlapping* spans of trust.

Many organizations have had dismal experiences with matrix-style management in which dual reporting relationships point people in both a functional and an operational direction. Take away the reporting requirement – which can result in schizophrenic allegiances – and the idea is a sound one. For example, at 3M researchers who serve in the role of technology owners are responsible for finding ways to use a particular technology across the entire organization. As a result, they develop relationships with research scientists in many different divisions, not only increasing their personal spans of trust, but also creating overlaps among many separate communities.

Of course no two people in an organization have identical spans of trust, so there is always some overlap. But when there is talk of 'too many silos' you can be sure that the problem is caused by spans of trust that are far too similar and isolated from one another. The solution is not to throw everyone into one pot – the main drawback of the organizational knowledge repository – but to look for ways to insert key individuals into a range of natural groupings. This can be achieved through special assignments, providing more people with cross-organizational responsibilities or supporting communities that do not conform to the standard organizational chart of departments, functions and processes.

While working to overlap spans of trust will not result in the kind of universal access to knowledge that would occur if everyone dutifully contributed their knowledge to a single knowledge-sharing system, the knowledge transfer that does occur is certain to be deeper and more meaningful in nature.

Think about it!

Consider a few of the communities in your organization that you believe *need* to have a high degree of overlap with other communities. (Try to choose communities of which you are a member. It will make it easier to think of other communities with which they need to overlap.) Using the following boxes, list those communities in the left hand boxes and the communities with which they need to overlap in the right hand boxes. On the scale beside each community set, position a 'C' on the scale to indicate the degree to which overlap currently exists.

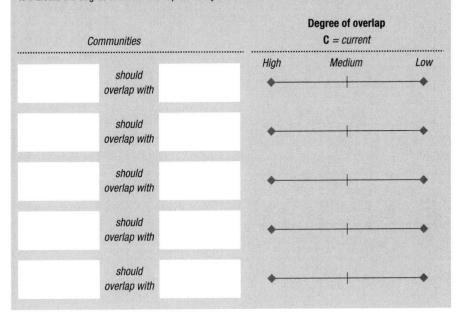

Quick prioritization of challenge

Based on this section, how much priority should you assign to meeting this challenge?

◆ *Overlap spans of trust*

Rate your organization on these two factors	Your organization's rating	Rating scale
How much does your organization NEED to respond to these challenges?	*Need*	0 No need 1 Weak need 2 Moderate need 3 Strong need 4 Burning need
What is your organization's ABILITY to respond to these challenges?	*Ability*	0 Unable 1 Slightly able 2 Partially able 3 Almost able 4 Completely able

Need × *Ability* =

★ **To do**
Transfer your prioritization to box J on page 217.

Prioritization of challenge

(multiply the two ratings)

Notes

1 There are four ways that these electronic payments are collected:
   ◆ a Java applet referenced on the web page triggers a charge
   ◆ developers can build 'calls' into an application – that is, each time an individual uses a particular function in an application they are charged a nominal fee
   ◆ a general 'wrapper program' can be used to launch applications that HP purchases externally. For example, the organization subscribes to the *Official Airline Guide*. Now whenever anyone accesses it they pay 12 cents
   ◆ groups that have already been billing for their services can use the system to simplify their billing procedures. For instance, competitive intelligence report charges can be placed on a department's consolidated NetCard account instead of being invoiced separately.

2 Java is a software language developed by Sun Microsystems.

3 Thomas H. Davenport and Laurence Prusak. *Working Knowledge: How Organizations Manage What They Know*, Boston: Harvard Business School Press, 1998.

4 'It's story time at Monster Board', Cathy Olofson, *Fast Company*, August 1998, p. 50.

5 'Fair process: managing in the knowledge economy', W. Chan Kim and Renée Mauborgne, *Harvard Business Review*, July/August 1997.

6 'The hot new medium is ... Email', David S. Bennahum, *Wired*, April 1998.

7 Domino is a Lotus groupware application that transforms Lotus Notes into an Internet application server.

8 'How hardwired is human behavior?', Nigel Nicholson, *Harvard Business Review*, July/August 1998.

Agenda for action: Contribute

The action steps presented in the Agenda for action come from the ideas suggested in this chapter. If you believe that your organization needs to focus on improving the degree to which individuals and teams contribute their insights and information to the organizational knowledge base, this template and its suggested action steps are one way to get started.

The Agenda for action is organized in the same way as this chapter. Each imperative and its accompanying challenges are clustered together. Action steps are suggested for each challenge based on the text and case studies. You decide which action steps make sense for your organization and use the empty space to scribble in any additional ideas that come to mind.

Before you begin, make sure that you have transferred your prioritization ratings for each challenge. The prioritization ratings will remind you whether you believed that the challenge was worth pursuing. The maximum prioritization rating is 16, the minimum is 0.

How you use the prioritization ratings is up to you. For example, depending on the range of prioritization ratings, you may decide to ignore all challenges below a minimum threshold and focus only on those challenges above it. Or you may decide that everything that is not 0 deserves at least some thought. We invite you to use this Agenda for action as a place to start acting on your knowledge management priorities.

Agenda for action

1 Motivation

Members want to contribute their knowledge

Remove barriers to sharing		**A**
		Prioritization rating

Action step	Who should be involved	My first 'to do'
Canvass groups (you can use the Contribution Assessment Guide on page 183) to find out what elements of their worklife reduce the level of knowledge sharing.		
Identify situations where competition for resources (among individuals, teams, groups or businesses) negatively impacts knowledge sharing.		
Assemble a team to assess the costs and benefits of removing barriers to sharing knowledge.		
Other:		

B

Link contribution to opportunity and advancement

Prioritization rating

Action step	Who should be involved	My first 'to do'
Assemble a group of people concerned about knowledge management to discuss how knowledge sharing might be better rewarded in the organization. Brainstorm a list of ways to reward people for knowledge sharing that would be most effective given our culture.		
Meet with members of human resources or others in our organization who determine how performance is evaluated. Discuss ways to incorporate contribution into the evaluation process.		
Compile a list of metrics that will reflect how well people share knowledge and monitor these over time.		
Other:		

C

Withhold benefits from non-contributors

Prioritization rating

Action step	Who should be involved	My first 'to do'
Survey members of my team to determine whether they feel there is any merit to withholding benefits from people who are not contributing or whether they believe such measures would be counterproductive.		
Identify areas where non-contributors could be denied knowledge-sharing benefits (such as access to a database) and define the terms of contribution needed to obtain those benefits.		
Other:		

D

Find points of mutual benefit

Prioritization rating

Action step	Who should be involved	My first 'to do'
Identify groups within our organization that should spend more time sharing information. Recruit representatives from these groups that support the idea of knowledge sharing.		
Convene representatives and brainstorm a list of areas where knowledge exchange would benefit both parties.		
Start small – possibly with face-to-face meetings of the representatives themselves – sharing knowledge in these selected areas. Alternatively, initiate an electronic information exchange or a joint repository where the groups trade reports, papers, etc.		
Other:		

2 Facilitation

Systems and structures support the contribution process

E

Allow employees the time and space to contribute their best work	

Prioritization rating

Action step	Who should be involved	My first 'to do'
Meet with managers of different work groups to discuss the best way to provide employees with contribution time.		
Test the selected approach by piloting it with one or two groups over a specified time period. Make sure to identify evaluation criteria prior to initiating the pilot.		
Meet with members of our information technology group to discuss ways to automate the contribution process.		
Examine work processes, such as budgeting or performance reviews, to determine whether they produce any outputs that can be tweaked to increase knowledge contributions.		
Other:		

Create dedicated roles that support the contribution process

F

Prioritization rating

Action step	Who should be involved	My first 'to do'
Create a list of knowledge management competencies and identify individuals most suited to fulfilling these functions.		
Survey people considered 'experts' to find out what kind of support they need to increase their level of knowledge sharing.		
Assign knowledge support people to selected experts and monitor their ability to assist experts in contributing their knowledge.		
Other:		

G

Prioritization rating

Support transfer of tacit knowledge
Weave an organizational web

Action step	Who should be involved	My first 'to do'
Identify areas where transfer of unarticulated knowledge is most problematic. Determine whether these areas might benefit from either use of professional facilitators or storytelling techniques.		
Pilot storytelling as a method of debriefing teams that have completed important projects.		
Identify knowledge areas in which one-to-one knowledge transfer is critical as possible candidates for mentorship programmes.		
Identify knowledge brokers by asking people who they go to for particular types of information. Look for ways to support the activities of our knowledge brokers.		
Convene a cross-functional team to brainstorm interesting ways of bringing people together to enhance knowledge transfer. Try piloting some of these approaches with people from different parts of the organization.		
Other:		

3 Trust

The organization promotes understanding of and respect for the value of contributed knowledge

H

Support a contract of reciprocity
Create explicit policies on the use of intellectual assets

Prioritization rating

Action step	Who should be involved	My first 'to do'
Informally poll members of the organization to determine whether they believe a contract of reciprocity exists between themselves and the organization and between themselves and other members. Is the contract they describe consistent?		
Examine our groupware systems for opportunities to improve contributor attribution and feedback. Discuss feasibility of these options with technical staff.		
Poll those who contribute frequently to groupware systems as well as those who contribute rarely to determine whether feedback or improved attribution could boost contribution.		
Select a single community as a pilot for some of the options identified.		
Other:		

I

Prioritization rating

Use self-publishing to promote ownership

Action step	Who should be involved	My first 'to do'
Convene groups of people interested in managing their own content and provide necessary technology training.		
Create templates and guidelines that will facilitate the publishing process.		
Monitor whether self-publishing has increased the quantity and quality of knowledge contributions.		
Other:		

J

Prioritization rating

Overlap spans of trust

Action step	Who should be involved	My first 'to do'
Talk with managers about groups in the organization for which they believe a higher degree of knowledge sharing needs to occur. Discuss ways to overlap these communities by selecting key individuals to become members of both groups.		
Experiment with ways that natural groupings of people can be encouraged to increase redundancies in their connections.		
Other:		

7 Assess

> Nothing is secret which shall not be made manifest.
>
> *New Testament*, Luke, viii, 17

When organizations assess how well their knowledge can be leveraged to create value for customers they cross a threshold between the two activity flows of the overall knowledge management process. The process steps that include **Get**, **Use**, **Learn** and **Contribute** lie on the tactical side of the model and become activated by a specific and immediate opportunity or demand. The process steps that are launched with **Assess** and continue with **Build and Sustain** and **Divest** lie on the strategic side of the model and are ongoing in nature. They are not triggered by any one specific event. Instead they are responses to changes in the macroeconomic environment and are manifested by shifts in strategic direction, variations in the speed and intensity of organizational responses to the marketplace, and changes in the level of resource allocations. In contrast to the more democratic spirit of the tactical side of the model which requires everyone to participate and exhibit leadership qualities, the ongoing strategic process is the responsibility of an organization's formally designated leadership.

At a glance . . .

What is new?	Explicit focus on intellectual capital as a generator of value and the move to factor it into the resource allocation process. Assessment based on new types of information that come from a wider range of sources.
What is the problem?	Theory of the organization must be expanded. Reliable metrics have not been developed to measure intangibles.
What is the individual or team objective?	Systematically factor knowledge into the planning process.
What is the organization's responsibility?	Evaluate existing knowledge relative to future needs.

Introduction

In an economy where value and competitive advantage are increasingly derived from the management of intangibles, rather than the ownership of physical or financial capital, organizations are inventing new approaches to understanding and monitoring how well they build the right mix of intellectual capital. Intangible asset balance sheets, models that indicate how new forms of capital interact to create value, and new metrics that seek to guide managers who want to accelerate or redirect how intellectual capital is generated have sprung into existence. Knowledge management is a new enough practice that none of these methods for visualizing, managing or measuring knowledge has taken hold as a standard. But experimentation abounds, and initial results indicate that the organizations committed to using these new metrics have improved their ability to manage the intellectual capital that matters to their stakeholders.

Assessment is not a substitute for strategy. It is a reflection of it and a tool for implementation. Assessment at its best functions like the body's nervous system. It keeps the company attuned to the reality of strategy at the extremities – the points of contact with people who matter – customers, employees, suppliers, regulators and the community. Assessment at its worst becomes an impediment to change because it ceases to provide information about what is really important to the organization. We yearn for an assessment method with the weighty stability of the accounting system which has persisted almost unchanged for 500 years. But as the shape of even the most traditional organizations undergoes permutations undreamed of just ten years ago, the new assessment systems that are added to the traditional financial one follow different, more flexible models.

To assess intellectual capital so that deliberate, constructive initiatives can be strengthened or launched to build, sustain or divest it, organizations must meet the following *imperatives* and *challenges*.

Imperatives and challenges

Perspective	Expand the theory of the organization to capture the impact of knowledge on organizational performance:
	◆ *Identify new forms of organizational capital.*
	◆ *Conceptualize the new tasks of management.*
Integration	Incorporate into the overall management process a new set of frameworks, processes and metrics that evaluate the entire resource base from which the organization generates value:
	◆ *Visualize the underlying structures that guide knowledge management practices.*
	◆ *Experiment with metrics and valuation approaches to evaluate strategic outcomes.*
	◆ *Communicate with key stakeholders.*

1 Perspective

Expand the theory of the organization to capture the impact of knowledge on organizational performance

A theory of the organization is the commonly shared set of facts and beliefs that dictate the way organizations perceive their strategic options. By taking the impact of knowledge into consideration, organizations have the potential to develop a radically different picture of how their businesses work. This, in turn, influences how they view events in the marketplace and, more importantly, whether these events even register on the organizational radar screen.

Traditional financial models and the resulting financial statements represent a common platform for expressing the theory of the organization. Part of what makes these models so compelling is their ubiquity. They are the *lingua franca* of the business world, used by those inside and outside the organization to assess the value of the enterprise as a going concern. The high degree of standardization in financial metrics allows analysts to compare different parts of the organization and different organizations to one another. In addition, the way that the numbers reconcile from financial statement to financial statement creates an integrated picture of how the system has performed under various conditions. *Pro formas* are used to extrapolate how the organization might perform under a different set of circumstances.

While financial ratios and even the compilation of financial statements rely on judgment and opinion, they are almost fully rooted in the tangible – that which can be explicitly counted, measured and monetarily valued. The rise of knowledge management and its emphasis on intangibles has precipitated a contentious dialogue among those who wish to measure the complete resource base of the organization and those who believe it most prudent to stick with the financials. Proponents of measuring intangibles argue that this will allow organizations to expand their view of available strategic options. To accommodate this new perspective about what makes organizations tick, leadership must move toward new ways of thinking by facing these *challenges*.

Challenges

◆ *Identify new forms of organizational capital.*
◆ *Conceptualize the new tasks of management.*

Identify new forms of organizational capital

The current, more open attitude toward intangibles such as knowledge is a counterpoint to the recent enthusiasm that looked to the management of tangibles in reengineering. Even though reengineering is reeling from a wave of criticism advanced from many quarters, it is still the treatment of choice for improving performance among organizations that are perceived as industry laggards. Reengineering bloated organizational processes is not in and of itself a bad idea. However, many practitioners and those upon whom reengineering was practiced acknowledge that something slipped between hoped-for results and those that were achieved. The emerging consensus among those who are beginning to pay attention to knowledge, is that the something that slipped was an understanding of how knowledge flows affected the more tangible process-based activity flows and a way of formally treating those knowledge flows while reengineering. It turns out that many people and activities which appeared superfluous to an organizational process based on the analytic tools of reengineering were actually critical to achieving positive results.

At the same time that the application of reengineering was failing to live up to the theory behind it, thinking from academic institutions on the changing basis of wealth creation was beginning to penetrate business consciousness. In the downsized organization, where the tangibles had been pared to the bone, intangibles began to look like the right substance for regaining muscle without the fat that had been so painfully shed. But how to think about these intangibles in a way that those in the organization would not dismiss as 'too soft' and impossible to connect to action and results? New theories of the organization would have to be created to help people visualize intangibles and factor them explicitly into strategic and operational decision making.

Creating a new theory of the organization that explicitly includes intangibles has been a central focus for knowledge management practitioners. The new theory of the organization owes a deep bow of intellectual thanks to Robert Kaplan and David Norton, the progenitors of the Balanced Scorecard.[1] Their insistence upon a comprehensive view of the organization – one that monitored not only traditional financial performance, but also the activities which gave rise to it, including customer, innovation and learning and internal business perspectives – created a wedge that knowledge management practitioners have proceeded to blast wide open.

A theory of the organization that takes knowledge management into account focuses on how easily and flexibly the organization can convert its knowledge into products and services that will be valuable to customers, now and in the future. The emphasis on knowledge management has elevated the importance of the type and quality of the organization's relationships with its key stakeholders. Knowledge management also promotes a view that looks out into the future to at least the same degree that the organization examines the past and agonizes over the present. These factors play an increasingly significant role in the organization's ability to use its knowledge as a means of creating value for customers. Managing stakeholder relationships to improve the flow of knowledge that can be converted into intellectual assets has become a competence that all organizations must master (see Point of view).

> **POINT OF VIEW** *The new theory of the organization – human, organizational and customer capital*

The Intellectual Capital Model was developed in a collaborative effort that included Leif Edvinsson at Skandia, Hubert St Onge at Clarica, Gordon Petrash at PricewaterhouseCoopers, and Charles Armstrong of Armstrong Industries. It proposes a scenario in which organizations need simultaneously to manage different types of intellectual capital in order to create value (see Figure 7.1).

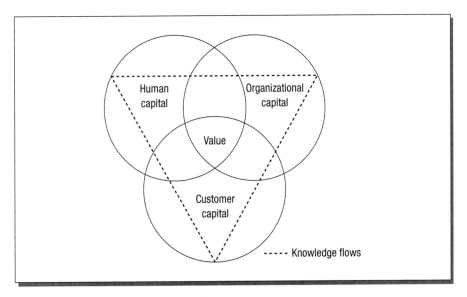

Fig 7.1 ◆ Intellectual Capital Model

To generate value from intellectual capital organizations need to manage knowledge flows between:

◆ **Human capital** – the ability of individuals and teams to apply solutions to customers' needs; competencies; and mind-sets.

◆ **Customer capital** – the strength of the customer relationship; superior customer-perceived value; increasing customization of solutions.

◆ **Organizational capital** – the capabilities of the organization, made up of codified knowledge from all sources – knowledge bases, business processes, the technology infrastructure – the shared culture, values and norms.

◆ **Intellectual capital** – the relationship among human, customer and organizational capital that maximizes the organization's potential to create value.

The dotted lines in Figure 7.1 represent the knowledge flows between the three types of intellectual capital. The better these flows are managed, the more the interrelationships among the three types of capital achieve harmony. As these three types of capital interact in concert, the organization is better positioned to create value. Comparing this way of thinking about intellectual capital with the traditional definition of capital,[2] it is possible to understand intellectual capital as a form of non-material wealth that has the potential to create more wealth. Organizations can destroy the potential for creating wealth if they do not manage the three components of intellectual capital in an integrated fashion. The strong suit of this model is that it explicitly includes customer relationships as a form of intellectual capital, thus broadening the definition of organizational membership beyond the traditional scope of employees.

Think about it!

Take a moment to list the top five sources of each type of capital that would immediately come to mind for others in your organization.

Types of capital

	Human	*Customer*	*Organizational*
1			
2			
3			
4			
5			

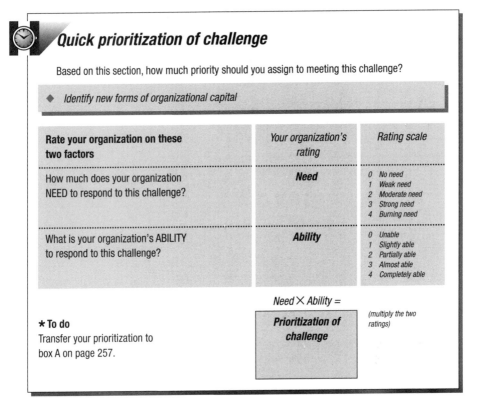

Quick prioritization of challenge

Based on this section, how much priority should you assign to meeting this challenge?

◆ Identify new forms of organizational capital

Rate your organization on these two factors	Your organization's rating	Rating scale
How much does your organization NEED to respond to this challenge?	**Need**	0 No need 1 Weak need 2 Moderate need 3 Strong need 4 Burning need
What is your organization's ABILITY to respond to this challenge?	**Ability**	0 Unable 1 Slightly able 2 Partially able 3 Almost able 4 Completely able

Need × Ability =

★ To do Transfer your prioritization to box A on page 257.	**Prioritization of challenge**	(multiply the two ratings)

Conceptualize the new tasks of management

Championing the development of a different theory of the organization that raises knowledge management to the level of strategy is one of the new tasks of management, especially the chief executive officer or managing director. *The Wall Street Journal* reports: 'Because companies now depend heavily on employees for the creative insights that only the enthusiastic can offer ... CEOs say their top priority is to enhance "intellectual capital" by managing human relationships.'[3] Information technology is now able to provide sophisticated analyses of almost any aspect of the organization CEOs might want to investigate, freeing them to focus their time on dimensions that are not monitored, reported and analyzed. For the most part, the elements of the organization that remain undermanaged consist of its intangibles, paramount of which is knowledge. The challenge of determining how well management is performing these new tasks is keenly felt by those who lend money to knowledge-intensive companies like the Canadian Imperial Bank of Commerce, Knowledge-Based Business Group (see Profile).

Investor pressure also forces senior management to lead the charge of knowledge management at the strategic level. The trend toward shedding non-core assets to improve return ratios and, by extension, value-creating potential of remaining assets has prompted companies to take a long hard look at how to create value going forward. In many instances, companies are determining that these improvements will come mainly from know-how that is no longer imbedded in hard assets. For example, in autumn 1997 Sara Lee Corporation, a leading producer of baked products and other consumer goods, announced that it would shed most of its manufacturing assets and focus growth efforts on leveraging such intellectual assets as trademarks and brand names. To leverage these intellectual assets, Sara Lee must also leverage relationships with the businesses that will now actually manufacture the physical products that will carry its brand name.

Top-level executives must be involved in these efforts to leverage knowledge because it is their involvement which has the greatest influence on whether or not the organization will accept a new way of thinking and acting. In addition, since everyone in the organization must accept and act on the new theory of the organization, a sustained and enterprise-wide educational effort must be launched. Often to ensure that organizational focus does not waver, new jobs such as chief learning or knowledge officer, knowledge manager, director of intangible asset management or intellectual capital controller must be created, and staff must be assigned to execute knowledge-based initiatives. Rarely does anyone other than senior management have the authority to undertake such endeavours.

PROFILE ⟩ *Canadian Imperial Bank of Commerce,*
Knowledge-Based Business Group

Traditional lending models look for a history of profitability, tangible assets and a reasonably predictable business environment. Knowledge-based businesses do not fit this paradigm. Their assets are intangible: the knowledge and expertise of employees, cultures that foster agile responses to market opportunities, collaborative relationships with customers. Traditional lending models cannot be applied successfully to knowledge-based businesses. But the contribution of the high-technology industry to the economy is expanding too rapidly for banks to continue to view knowledge-based businesses in this way.

In 1994 the Canadian Imperial Bank of Commerce (CIBC), the second largest bank in Canada, headquartered in Toronto, launched its Knowledge-Based Business (KBB) financing initiative. Knowledge-based businesses, defined as the high-technology sector of the economy, are projected as a group to sustain annual revenue growth of 15%, and within ten to fifteen years they are expected to constitute 20% of the Canadian economy. These businesses create the technologies which make manufacturers and other industry players 'smart'.

The KBB Group's mission is to break out of the traditional lending paradigm and invent new ways of perceiving value and new methods for valuing early-stage technology businesses that generate wealth from intellectual capital. Doing so means that CIBC can both fuel and benefit from this new force in the Canadian economy. CIBC adopted the term 'knowledge-based' to sharpen its own focus on the 'K Component' of these companies – the central element on which the KBB Group's lending analysis would be based. Not only did the group view clients through this new lens, they took a similar approach to their own organization by mirroring their clients' focus on intangibles and knowledge. The KBB Group would rely on highly specialized and experienced personnel who brought a diverse set of perspectives to the business. The organizational structure would be fluid enough for information to flow easily, without getting snagged on too many protocols or formalities of hierarchy. Innovation would be the order of the day – rigid processes would yield to expediency tempered by wisdom. In sum, the bank's KBB Group would be a knowledge-based business. This was a tall order for any enterprise, but an especially tall one for a conservative, circumspect institution like a bank.

The individual that CIBC tapped to lead the KBB Group, Jo-Anne Raynes, had an unusual background for a banker – one that included chairmanship of an Outward Bound school in Canada. (Outward Bound is an organization that teaches individuals how to connect with their inner strengths as they progress through a team-based wilderness survival experience.) Raynes' challenge was to create a culture of innovation and personal risk taking within the context of a traditional banking operation. If she accomplished her objective, she would unleash the potential for wealth creation not only within the bank, but also within its client organizations. Building on her years of experience leading Outward Bound, she focused first on identifying a set of shared values that would bind together the small group responsible for launching the KBB initiative. She started this process using a new instrument from the consulting firm Values Technology (see Point of View on page 305) that helps people examine the values that are expressed through the choices they have made in their lives. The KBB team learned that they shared a common set of values which included pioneering and innovation. To deepen her team's understanding of one another, the business leader next used the traditional Meyers-Briggs assessment of personality types, styles and behaviours. Building on the common ground of shared values, the Meyers-Briggs information helped the team better interpret individual operating styles. In these ways, the KBB Group developed insight into themselves as individuals and as a team.

Leveraging the strong bonds and improved communications among team members, the KBB Group leader next turned to building a base of knowledge that would be available to all team members. Initially, the knowledge base was developed through face-to-face meetings conducted every three weeks; at least three people had to be involved in the decision-making process for each potential client opportunity. Ultimately, this knowledge base evolved into an enterprise trust, a repository of codified learnings that is available to all KBB team members and their clients.

Extending organizational boundaries to envelope the customer represents a radical change in the way most organizations view 'inside' and 'outside'. Once the customer is 'inside' the organization, the emphasis shifts from offering them solutions to building their capabilities. Financing growth no longer defines the relationship with the client. Instead, the KBB team partners with clients to help them succeed. For example, since many early-stage high-technology companies do not possess deep marketing skills, the KBB team engaged a marketing expert with top-notch credentials to develop a series of interactive workshops based on client case studies. The KBB Group leader's strategic view of her business as a knowledge-based organization is at the heart of this new way of understanding the relationship with the client.

Think about it!

Sketch out your organization's status with respect to elevating knowledge management to a strategic level using the following table. Place an 'x' in the column that best describes timing for these actions in your organization. Tally up the x's in each column to get a rough feel for whether your organization's overall status is current, short term, or long term.

Group	Action	Happens today *Current*	Will happen in the next 2 years *Short term*	Will happen in the next 5 years *Long term*
Investors...	ask us to *discuss* management of intellectual capital.			
	ask us to *provide a formal report* with *a qualitative* analysis of intellectual capital.			
	ask us to *provide a formal report* with *a quantitative* analysis of intellectual capital.			
Senior executives...	*talk* about intellectual capital.			
	manage intellectual capital.			
	qualitatively report on intellectual capital.			
	quantitatively report on intellectual capital.			
The person to whom I report...	*talks about* about intellectual capital.			
	manages intellectual capital.			
	qualitatively reports on intellectual capital.			
	quantitatively reports on intellectual capital.			
I...	*talk* about intellectual capital.			
	manage intellectual capital.			
	qualitatively report on intellectual capital.			
	quantitatively report on intellectual capital.			
	Total			

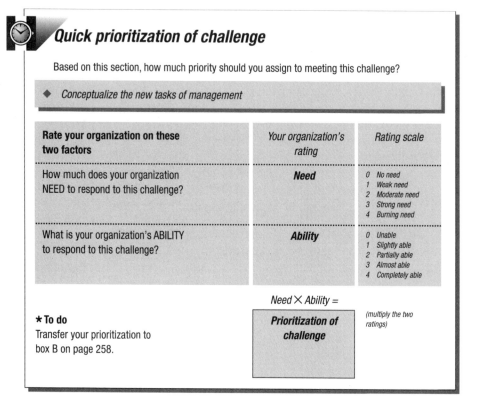

Quick prioritization of challenge

Based on this section, how much priority should you assign to meeting this challenge?

◆ *Conceptualize the new tasks of management*

Rate your organization on these two factors	Your organization's rating	Rating scale
How much does your organization NEED to respond to this challenge?	**Need**	0 No need 1 Weak need 2 Moderate need 3 Strong need 4 Burning need
What is your organization's ABILITY to respond to this challenge?	**Ability**	0 Unable 1 Slightly able 2 Partially able 3 Almost able 4 Completely able

Need ✕ *Ability* =

★ To do
Transfer your prioritization to box B on page 258.

Prioritization of challenge

(multiply the two ratings)

2 Integration

Incorporate into the overall management process a new set of frameworks, processes and metrics that evaluate the entire resource base from which the organization generates value

Many companies find that they have been involved in knowledge management activities for several years before becoming aware that these initiatives constitute 'knowledge management'. For example, Arthur Andersen, the global accounting and management consulting firm, spent at least two years conceiving, building and spreading the use of its Global Best Practices knowledge base before it labelled the project a 'knowledge management' initiative. The Dow Chemical Company's Intellectual Asset and Capital Management group was created out of an inventions management group that was itself a transformation of the patent management group. Companies like Dow and Arthur Andersen began to reflect upon what they were doing and to articulate frameworks, processes and metrics that put their practices into a larger knowledge management context.

If a theory of the organization typically moves from the 'top down', frameworks, processes and metrics by contrast move from what Nonaka and Takeuchi refer to as the 'middle up down'.[4] To evaluate how well the organization uses its knowledge to support strategic objectives, organizations must meet these *challenges*.

Challenges

◆ *Visualize the underlying structures that guide knowledge management practices.*

◆ *Experiment with metrics and valuation approaches to evaluate strategic outcomes.*

◆ *Communicate with key stakeholders.*

Visualize the underlying structures that guide knowledge management practices

Since the mid-1990s, a handful of organizations have been propelled to global prominence based on their ability to uncover and articulate the underlying structures that guide knowledge management practices. Some of them have articulated these structures in what we have called frameworks. Others have articulated them as processes. Frameworks and processes are important because along with the theory of the organization they provide a context for measurement and valuation. Context setting is part of the assessment process because it articulates the set of possibilities that the organization deems 'valid' to act upon.

Knowledge management frameworks

Knowledge management frameworks seek to identify and describe the major strategic levers that can be used to stimulate and manage the creation, flow and storage of knowledge. In this respect, they are guides that point people in the right direction. Most of the frameworks that have become widely known have emerged as organizations recognized that their knowledge management initiatives had far-reaching implications for the entire enterprise. The frameworks they created sought to explain how knowledge management affected every aspect of the organization's drive to achieve its strategic goals by associating knowledge management activities with more generic strategic levers.

Some frameworks like the one used by Skandia are overtly navigational. Skandia's framework, in fact, is appropriately named 'the Navigator'. Celemi, a consultancy that develops learning experiences, uses a framework created by Karl Erik Sveiby that resembles a matrixed score card (see Profiles).

PROFILE ▶ *Skandia*

Skandia is a federation of savings institutions headquartered in Stockholm, Sweden. In 1994 it attracted considerable attention as one of the first organizations to report publicly on its intellectual capital. The company issued an addendum to its annual report that discussed its approach to managing intellectual capital. Central to this effort was an articulation of the dimensions of intellectual capital that were important to the organization and how Skandia intended to manage them. These dimensions and management approach were captured in a framework that the company named the 'Navigator' (see Figure 7.2). Using navigation through uncharted territory as its theme, Skandia portrayed how different business units would use the Navigator Framework to define and manage their intellectual capital.

The core of Skandia's Navigator is its people. Human focus anchors the compass points from which the other forms of intellectual and financial capital flow. Intellectual capital derives from Skandia's focus on its people, customers, processes and renewal and development. Financial capital is expressed as the business result of creating value from intellectual capital. The Navigator also captures a time dimension along an axis of past, present and future. Financial focus looks to the past. Customer, human and process focus are situated in the present. Renewal and development positions the organization for the future. Each business unit within Skandia uses the Navigator as a framework for assembling metrics that create a dynamic view of the business, explaining not only its results, but also how it intends to achieve them through the management of intellectual capital.

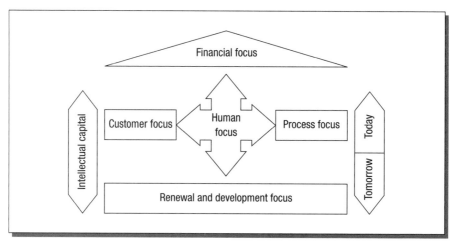

Fig 7.2 ◆ The Skandia Navigator

PROFILE *Celemi*

Celemi, headquartered in Malmö, Sweden, is a rapidly growing global provider of learning experiences through board-based simulations that spread understanding of strategy throughout the organization. In 1995 Celemi included an Intangible Assets Monitor in its annual report as an experimental way of identifying and evaluating assets not considered in the traditional balance sheet. Internally the Monitor is used to set objectives and track performance. Based on the work of Karl Erik Sveiby, one of the leading figures in the measurement of intangibles, the Intangible Assets Monitor[5] organizes Celemi's intellectual capital in three categories and along three dimensions (see Figure 7.3).

External structure, internal structure and competence are the three categories of intellectual capital in Celemi's Monitor. External structure is reflected in Celemi's relationships with customers. Internal structure is the organization minus its people, who go home each night and return on a voluntary basis each day. Competence is brought to the organization by its people. Celemi does not 'own' its external structure or its competence. It must convert each of these intangibles into internal structures that remain with the organization despite the comings and goings of customers and employees. Growth and renewal, efficiency and stability are the dimensions along which Celemi measures its intellectual capital. These add a time dimension to its framework, moving along a continuum from future, through present to past.

The company is also beginning to report a picture of overall value that is derived by combining the growth and renewal, efficiency and stability metrics from all of its intangible as well as its tangible asset categories and calculating a 'monitor value' for each of these dimensions. The resulting graph shows performance relative to plan as the company strives to exceed its targets for creating overall business value.

	Tangible assets	Intangible assets		
	Our financial capital	**Our customers (external structure)**	**Our organization (internal structure)**	**Our people (competence)**
Growth/ renewal	Equity growth Net investment ratio	Revenue growth Image-enhancing customers	Organization-enhancing customers Revenues from new products	Average professional competence, years Competence-enhancing customers Growth in professional competence Experts with post-secondary degrees
Efficiency	Profit margin Net return on equity Profit/Value-added	Revenues per customer	Promotion of administrative staff Revenues per administrative staff	Value-added per expert Value-added per employee
Stability	Liquid reserves Solidity	Repeat orders Five largest customers	Administrative staff turnover Administrative staff seniority, years Rookie ratio	Expert turnover Expert seniority, years Median age all employees, years

Fig 7.3 ◆ Celemi's Intangible Assets Monitor, 1997

Knowledge management processes

Frameworks identify and cluster knowledge management practices around strategic levers; processes are used to organize and harmonize the practices in relation to one another and determine how well they are linked to strategic outcomes. Organizations use processes to create a systemic view of their practices. Knowledge management practices are no different from any others in this regard. To understand whether specific practices fit together and propel the organization toward its strategic objectives, they need to be viewed within a well-articulated context. Processes can be extremely concrete and company specific, such as the one that The Dow Chemical Company uses to manage and evaluate its intellectual asset base (see Profile). The *Fieldbook's* Knowledge Management Process Framework, a generic process that can be adapted by any organization, is another concrete way of linking knowledge management practices to strategic outcomes.

Processes can also be more loosely assembled like the guidelines used by some commercial banks to evaluate the intellectual capital of organizations to which they are contemplating making loans. For example, when Canadian Imperial Bank of Canada's Knowledge-Based Business evaluates potential loan candidates, it has no choice but to focus on the organization's intellectual capital because the typical loan seeker is a start-up high-tech company that has few hard assets. The company's assessment battery ensures that it is able to discern how well the organization's knowledge positions it with respect to its target markets. These knowledge management processes all focus people on specific practices that should result in a particular outcome – replenishing, growing or pruning the knowledge asset base.

▶ PROFILE ▶ *The Dow Chemical Company*

The Dow Chemical Company's Intellectual Asset Management (IAM) process organizes the major activities that the company uses to manage its intellectual assets strategically (see Figure 7.4).

The Dow IAM process has been in use since 1993 when it was launched to improve the company's ability to extract value from its patent portfolio. Its scope has been significantly expanded since then to include trademarks, trade secrets, disclosures of inventions and key technical know-how (process methodology, training manuals, information about critically skilled personnel, etc.). Although the major activities of the process have been labelled and organized sequentially for the purposes of explaining the IAM process, in reality the process is continuous and the steps overlap. The six major initiatives of the process are as follows:

Initiative 1: Portfolio

The Dow Intellectual Asset Portfolio is created by asking each business to articulate its stock of intellectual assets (IAs). These range from patents and trade secrets to technical know-how. This activity ensures that Dow catalogues all existing IAs.

Initiative 2: Classification

Classification organizes IAs in terms of their value or potential value to the business. Although the process that Dow uses to manage its IAs is complex, for the purposes of an overview, it can be simplified into three 'umbrella' value categories that each share two dimensions of use (see chart below). Two of the 'umbrella' value categories represent streams within the Dow organization, while the third represents a stream to an outside party. Information about the IAs is logged into a computer database using common templates and terms to facilitate search and retrieval.

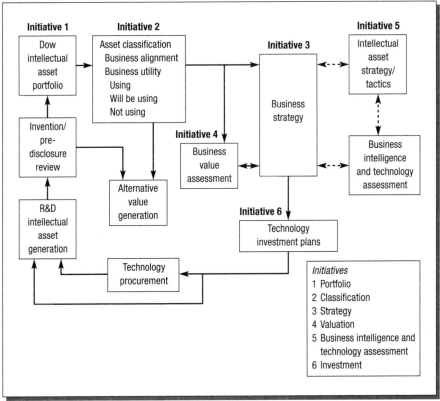

Copyright © The Dow Chemical Company, 1998

Fig 7.4 ◆ The Dow Chemical Company's Intellectual Asset Management (IAM) process

	Umbrella categories for IA classification		
	Dow		*Outside party*
Dimensions of use	Value growth	Value preservation	Alternative value capture
In use			
Will use			

Initiative 3: Strategy

Strategy is the initiative that ensures that the business strategy includes IAs. The process includes analyzing how to leverage full value from existing IAs, and developing plans that close strategic IA gaps and respond to competitive threats. The intellectual asset management tactics are developed to support the business strategy.

235

Initiative 4: Valuation

Valuation approaches at Dow include all standard valuation techniques as well as a methodology developed in partnership with Arthur D. Little called the Technology Factor Method (Technology Factor is a registered trademark of Arthur D. Little). This activity places a monetary value on intellectual assets based on a specific business' plans.

Initiative 5: Business Intelligence and Technology Assessment

IAs are examined in light of what can be gleaned about the competition's business intentions for its IAs – both in terms of the products that the competition plans to bring to market as well as the underlying technologies that support those product offerings. In addition, likely competitive responses to Dow's IA strategy and tactics are considered.

Initiative 6: Investment

Investment fills strategic gaps by assessing outside IAs and/or capabilities and determines whether to acquire or internally develop them.

 Think about it!

The knowledge management frameworks and processes presented in the previous section articulate key strategic dimensions or elements that impact the organization's ability to create, store, share and use knowledge. The process steps of the *Fieldbook's* Knowledge Management Process Framework are listed in the following space alongside a list of strategic dimensions or elements culled from various knowledge management frameworks and processes. As you scan both lists, consider which strategic dimensions your organization should focus on and jot down their letters in the space provided.

Knowledge management process steps	Elements or dimensions I need to consider	Strategic elements or dimensions
Get	....	(a) Technological resources
		(b) Human/people focus
Use	....	(c) Customer focus
		(d) Process/organization and structure focus
Learn	....	(e) Physical resources
		(f) Renewal and development
Contribute	....	(g) Financial focus
		(h) Relationships
Assess	....	(i) Values
		(j) Culture
Build & Sustain	....	(k) Leadership
		(l) Time (past–present–future)
Divest	....	(m) Orientation (internal–external)

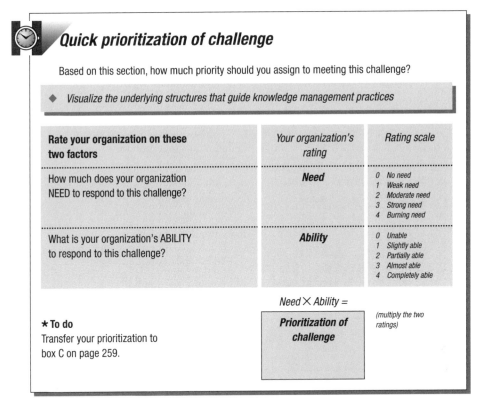

Quick prioritization of challenge

Based on this section, how much priority should you assign to meeting this challenge?

◆ *Visualize the underlying structures that guide knowledge management practices*

Rate your organization on these two factors	Your organization's rating	Rating scale
How much does your organization NEED to respond to this challenge?	*Need*	0 No need 1 Weak need 2 Moderate need 3 Strong need 4 Burning need
What is your organization's ABILITY to respond to this challenge?	*Ability*	0 Unable 1 Slightly able 2 Partially able 3 Almost able 4 Completely able

Need × *Ability* =

★ **To do**
Transfer your prioritization to box C on page 259.

Prioritization of challenge

(multiply the two ratings)

Experiment with metrics and valuation approaches to evaluate strategic outcomes

Knowledge management frameworks and processes help people visualize relationships among key variables that they believe are responsible for producing specific outcomes. Metrics can be embedded in the frameworks and processes to provide the guideposts that let people manage the variables toward these outcomes as they are at Ramboll, a Danish-based engineering and management consultancy (see Profile).

In the knowledge management arena, most metrics are in the experimental stage: here today and gone (or revised) tomorrow. This instability can be disconcerting for measurement traditionalists who want to create a watertight system of metrics that can be compared over time and rolled up, down and across the organization. However, the time is not ripe for this level of precision and consistency in the realm of knowledge management. Not enough is known to propose such a system of measures, but enough is known to share emerging practices from the disciplines of measurement and valuation as they have been applied to knowledge management.

The distinction between measurement and valuation is not well understood by those who approach knowledge management from the human resources or information technology perspective. The same is not true on the other side of the gulf, where the financial analysts, intellectual property attorneys, economists and accountants stand. For this group, measurement monitors activity while valuation places a monetary value on the expected cash flow from an asset or a group of assets that either currently exists or which is expected to exist with some degree of probability (see Points of view).

Measurement covers an entirely different territory. It seeks to describe a particular organizational state by quantifying its inputs and outputs. Measurement has dominated the knowledge management assessment discussion to date, but valuation has begun to influence the direction in which assessment is headed. The influence of valuation has risen as knowledge management has crept onto the radar screen of senior executives, who ultimately need to see how knowledge management translates into financial value. Measurement is good at understanding what is going on and relating activity to operational outcomes such as effectiveness and efficiency. It is not as good at relating effectiveness and efficiency to financial outcomes. For a true science of knowledge management measurement to develop, the fields of valuation and measurement must be combined to create a new discipline.[6]

Knowledge management metrics that are in use today attempt to complete the picture of how well the organization builds, replenishes or depletes its total asset base. Some of the metrics are familiar – percentage of sales from new products, number of college graduates, time to market, employee turnover. Others seek to establish a new way of understanding how well the organization creates and maintains the right knowledge – return on people, 'rookie ratio', loyal customer percentage, number of ideas generated. In addition to metrics that are computed from 'hard' data, an increasing number of 'soft' or qualitative metrics have crept into the repertoire.

The notion of soft metrics has precedent in the customer and employee satisfaction surveys which have become widely accepted measurement tools. The knowledge management movement has extended the use of soft measures into such areas as organizational capability, including innovation potential and knowledge absorption capacity. At the same time, it is pushing the limits of hard metrics to determine the possibility of evaluating areas such as the return on knowledge.

At Avery Dennison, a US-based adhesives and office supply products manufacturer, metrics such as cognitive capability and human capital motivation are being used experimentally to assess the organization's stock of intellectual assets. To communicate these soft metrics, Avery Dennison combines them with 'hard' metrics and presents them visually in spider maps. The spider maps for a particular product development initiative allow the organization to see its strategic shape at a glance (see Figure 7.5). Mapping each project lets the organization create a comprehensive view of its entire development effort, maximizing overall strategic fit and uncovering strengths and weaknesses in its stock of intellectual assets. Whether the metrics themselves are familiar or new, hard or soft, organizations are combining them in ways that create a fresh, more comprehensive view of the business and suggest different ways of managing its value-creating asset base.

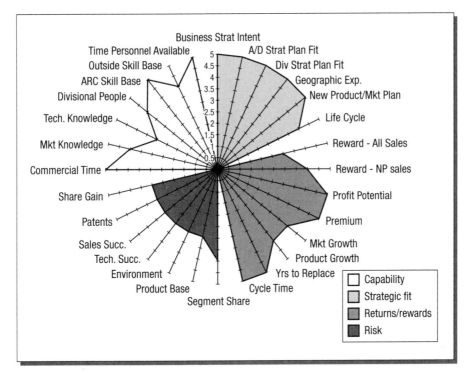

Fig 7.5 ◆ Strategic spider maps at Avery Dennison

PROFILE ▶ *Ramboll*

The world can be viewed from many different angles. Our perspective is clear: See the whole before the detail; see human beings before technology.

from Ramboll website

Ramboll is a consultancy in engineering, management and related fields with about 2,000 employees. The company is based in Denmark and conducts projects in Europe, Africa and Asia. Since the mid-1990s Ramboll has published a set of intellectual capital accounts which it calls the 'Holistic Accounts'. The Holistic Accounts are one way in which the company demonstrates commitment to the Ramboll Philosophy, an expression of the ethical behaviour that the company's leadership strives to embody in all organizational activities.

Ramboll takes a process-based approach to envisioning how the creation and use of knowledge influence financial results (see Figure 7.6). It starts with an articulation of how values and management philosophy affect the way in which human, technological and physical resources are managed to deliver consulting services and ultimately achieve financial results as well as a high level of employee satisfaction and customer satisfaction. Ramboll hooks metrics to each process step as a means of evaluating the company's management of its intellectual capital. Metric information is culled from existing sources since the company does not wish to establish a comprehensive and costly information-gathering system for this purpose alone. Information gathered for other purposes is reused as much as possible. For instance, customer satisfaction and employee satisfaction surveys generate the data required to compute 22 metrics in four categories for customer satisfaction and 76 metrics grouped in nine categories for employee satisfaction. For other process steps, such as technology, the metrics are standard and 'countable'. They include investment in research and development (projects that develop new methodologies within Ramboll), investment in IT platform and percent system failures. All in all, the Ramboll value-creation process contains several hundred metrics. However, only a sub-set of the metrics is actively used in any given year, based on the company's strategic focus.

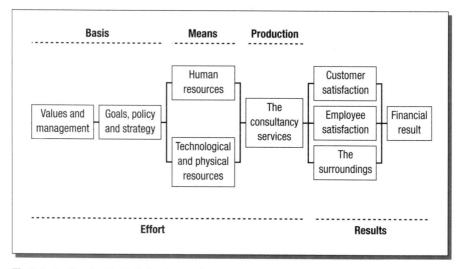

Fig 7.6 ◆ **Ramboll's Holistic Accounts**

The approach that is used to generate the metrics for the Holistic Accounts is as important, if not more important than the metrics themselves. During the formal strategic planning process, every department discusses which metrics would be most valuable for managing its business in the upcoming year. At the same time, the Ramboll Board of Directors meets to establish a set of organization-wide metrics, and the group and unit managers meet to sort out metrics appropriate for their level of management. Bottom-up, top-down and middle-out – the metrics that each level of the organization ultimately uses contain some that are common to all and some that are exclusive to that entity. In this way, Ramboll's metrics create a shared picture of the strategy and the tactics for achieving it without erasing difference and uniqueness. Involving all employees in the process boosts the likelihood that each employee will understand how to use the information provided by the metrics to make better decisions.

At present, the Holistic Accounts are only used in units based in Denmark, where the 'politics' of consumers, employees and the government has had a profound impact on the way in which companies operate. The common culture that Ramboll's Danish employees share makes it easier to promulgate the set of values that undergird the reporting system. As Ramboll thinks about expanding the Holistic Accounts to its non-Danish units, it is grappling with the challenge of promoting a set of values that will be realized in an entirely different way by other cultures. For organizations that operate in many locations around the world, establishing a set of metrics that assesses the strategic fit of intellectual capital will be a challenge on many levels. Creating the metrics may prove to be the least of it.

▶ POINT OF VIEW ▶ *An economist values knowledge*

When you ask yourself what the valuation of knowledge is about, you get the same answer you would have received if you had asked what is economics about – the study of how prices are determined. We have little difficulty understanding what questions to ask or what tools to use when trying to understand how the price of tangibles is determined. For example, if you go to a toy store to buy a board game for your child, you will most likely find your eyes glazing over as you scan a toy shelf loaded with similar board games within a fairly narrow price range. As you try to pick one, you go through a familiar process of determining the value of the game to you. You run through a series of questions such as: How long will my child be interested in this game? How many other members of my family can play this game too? Is this game more interesting than the game next to it? At some point, you decide whether the price is fair given what you will get from the game and you decide to buy it.

Economists ask similar questions, but from a wider perspective. How did the board game get to the shelf in this store? Why did the company choose to produce this board game? Why did other companies choose to compete by offering the other games that are on the shelf? Why does it carry this price? The answers to these questions help economists understand how people make choices. The same type of questions can be asked of companies. Why are some things invented and not others? What makes some things valuable and others not valuable? To answer these questions, economists use tools such as statistical analysis, econometrics (which isolates the impact of specific variables on economic choices), price theory and market definition.

The big difference between asking these questions about board games and asking them about knowledge does not lie in the nature of the questions that are asked or the tools that are used to determine price, but in the degree of creativity that must be applied to find benchmarks. When it comes to the board game in the toy store, it is easy to find benchmarks. If a company invents a computer chip that reduces the cost of electronic computing, however, benchmarks are hard to come by. The market for such an invention is harder to define; comparables are harder to find. If the invention can be patented, then by definition it is unique. However, even the unique invention does not lack precedent. In some cases, the invention replaces something that exists, so you can derive some information from the existing market. If the market is totally new, the tools of forecasting and *pro formas* can be applied. These tools are routinely used in start-up ventures, some of which radically transform markets.

Although companies like IBM make more than US$1 billion each year from licensing, valuing knowledge is important for more than just external transactions. Valuing knowledge that is used within the company has precisely the same benefit. Without this information, it is difficult to evaluate how well management is running the company. How else can we really know if management is generating a return? In the future, organizations will rely on economists to provide them with an assessment of the value of their knowledge in the same way in which they rely on the expertise of other specialists in finance, marketing and human resources. This sort of information will become part of the standard information set that managers use to make everyday business decisions.

Roy Weinstein
Chairman of the Board
Micronomics

> **POINT OF VIEW** *An accountant values intellectual assets*

When the legal, regulatory or tax system gives an intellectual asset such as a copyright, trademark or patent a 'boundary', valuation does not present an insurmountable problem. But in the case of intellectual assets around which the boundaries have not been as well delineated, such as the workforce, company culture or business process know-how, valuation is much more difficult. This is not because we lack valuation techniques. The same ones can be applied to both types of intellectual assets. However, the quality of the input data is vastly inferior when we try to value the ill-defined intellectual asset. For this reason, the results we get using these techniques can be described as 'garbage in, garbage out'.

Improving the quality of the input data is not a simple task. The fact that robust markets for regular trading in some types of intellectual assets do not exist means that we lack a solid foundation for setting their price. For these assets, performance metrics that monitor how management actions affect level, direction and momentum are currently proving to be the best way to understand how these intellectual assets impact business performance. At present, making a definitive link to business performance – the 'value' link – is challenging. Not enough organizations have been collecting sufficient information for long enough, or on a consistent enough basis, to perform rigorous analysis that would determine which measures link to value creation. Right now, different organizations are placing their bets, using different metrics to investigate intellectual assets. At some point in the future, we will be able to see which organizations have been asking the right questions. But for now, we are in a period of large-scale experimentation and there are few definitive answers.

At the same time, existing valuation techniques are not widely understood and as a result, they are underutilized even though they could provide managers with better information about some intellectual assets. There are three basic approaches that can be used to value assets:

1   cost, either historic or replacement

2   market price, the price at which an asset is traded

3   economic benefit, reflecting the revenues, costs and risks associated with commercializing an asset.

These approaches can be used in simple or complex valuation techniques. Traditional cash flow forecasting lies on the simple side of the spectrum. A linear approach, it traces the logical flow of consequences for one scenario of extracting value from an asset. Scenario analysis lies in the middle of the spectrum. It is a branched approach, presenting an array of different scenarios for value extraction and recognizing that a wide range of possible outcomes is possible with intellectual assets. Real option analysis lies on the complex end of the spectrum, and recognizes the reality that management possesses flexibility to exercise judgment. This means that as an investment unfolds, certain scenarios will be modified or ruled out as not profitable. In this way, real option analysis provides a window into the upside of investing in intellectual assets by recognizing that managers will not pursue paths that are possible but unprofitable.

The differences among these three types of valuation techniques are visually depicted in Figure 7.7.

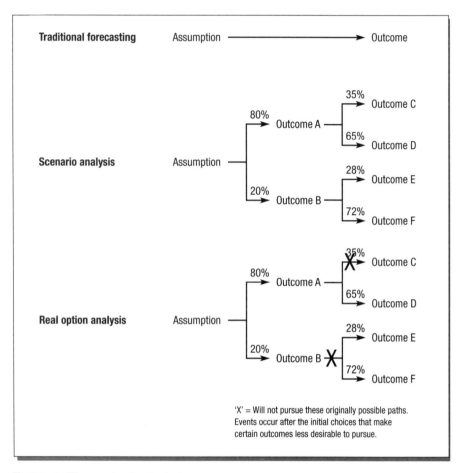

Fig 7.7 ◆ **Three valuation techniques**

Using a variety of analytical tools generates a range of possible prices for an intellectual asset. The reason for using some of the more complex analyses is that traditional valuation techniques tend to disfavour highly speculative investments. For example, if your goal is to send a man to the moon and you wind up inventing Teflon and Velcro, traditional forecasting would not reflect these possibilities. The more complex techniques, in contrast, open up the realm of value creation potential by permitting starts, stops and mid-course corrections in the decision-making process.

Whether managers use valuation techniques or metrics to manage their intellectual assets, ultimately they are faced with the need to perform some type of cost/benefit analysis when considering alternative investments. Regardless of the approach, they must answer the question: 'Can I estimate the improvement that will result from this investment?' Another way of expressing the management challenge is: 'To recoup the investment, how much better does performance need to be?' Valuation techniques and metrics help managers isolate the variables that drive performance and lead to value creation, so that they can make better decisions. This applies to all types of assets, including knowledge.

Mark Bezant
Partner
Arthur Andersen

> POINT OF VIEW *A brand expert values knowledge*

Brands are an increasingly important part of a company's asset base and a vital component of a company's intellectual capital. After all, a brand is not just a name, logo or trademark, but a unique relationship formed between a company and its stakeholders. The relationship or bond is built on a foundation of the perceived – and actual – value of the company's bundle of goods and services, cemented by effective communications such as advertising, promotions, packaging, public relations and word of mouth. The bond is a reflection of the brand owner's relative success in leveraging existing knowledge and capabilities, as well as a competitive advantage that others would find expensive and difficult, if not impossible to replicate. Brands are unique assets, which partly explains why there is no open market for trading them.

Financial valuation of brands is important for drawing linkages between brand performance and its ultimate impact on long-term financial results. Without this information, decision makers responsible for long-term investment in brands are left with unanswered questions about the economic rationale for sustaining brand investment. If the financial value of brands is not understood, it can also impair the ability of brand owners to seek the best value from their brands. For example, a brand may have strong awareness or 'buzz' but may not be value creating for its current owner. If this were confirmed through financial valuation, the brand owner might 'sell' or 'licence' the brand into a different business proposition (for example, through brand extensions). In this way, the brand would create value for the new owner or licensee, and an appropriate price could be charged.

The 'economic benefit' approach to the financial valuation of brands has an important advantage: it offers the brand owner a measurement and ongoing management mechanism for considering the brand on a par with other long-term assets of the business. The approach can also be tailored to incorporate various degrees of complexity, such as the value of strategic options down the road, that might be used to track business performance as a whole.

From a financial perspective, the capital value of any business can be represented as:

$$\begin{bmatrix} \text{Value of capital currently} \\ \text{invested in the business} \end{bmatrix} + \begin{bmatrix} \text{Value creation expected} \\ \text{from the invested capital} \end{bmatrix} = \begin{bmatrix} \text{Capital value} \\ \text{of the business} \end{bmatrix}$$

Value creation expected from invested capital can be thought of as the present value of future expected economic earnings, or the earnings generated above and beyond the 'normal' return expected by investors. The first addend is reported on the balance sheet periodically. The second, despite the best efforts of businesses to communicate their achievements and potential to external audiences, is subject to the vagaries of speculation. Nonetheless, a business that improves its economic earnings over time creates value, and one that does not, destroys it. Brands are part of the 'expected value creation' component. The value of a brand is deemed to be the 'economic benefit' derived by the usage of the brand. As in the case of 'conventional' assets, this economic benefit stems from the expectation of *enhanced* economic earnings, more *secure* economic earnings or both. This is a particularly relevant point when evaluating brands, since they are forward-looking, long-term assets. Historical investment in brands is only relevant insofar as it has created a demonstrably strong foundation for adding value to the brand in the future.

Jakes Srinivasan
Brand Valuation Director
Interbrand Corporation

POINT OF VIEW *A valuation expert values intellectual assets*

Business executives have formally managed hard assets for many years, resulting in substantial realized value. As the basis of competition shifts, however, they must apply some of the same management techniques to less easily visualized asset classes, specifically intellectual assets. A fairly common method for determining the value of an intellectual asset uses appraisal techniques to come up with a hypothetical value. Yet a far more useful approach focuses on the *realized value* of the asset. Realized value is the only value that reflects returns to the suppliers of enterprise capital. If a company does not earn an appropriate risk-adjusted rate of return, it soon finds capital unavailable. Capital is essential for funding development of saleable products embodying intellectual assets.

Intellectual assets have the greatest potential of all asset classes for generating sustainable value. Among the most significant drivers of value within the context of appraisal theory is the ability of assets to create competitive advantage and barriers to entry. Thus assets that are proprietary and possess a high degree of utility embody greater value than easily duplicated commodities. Assets such as patents, copyrights, trade secrets, trademarks, and trade names are proprietary by statute. Intellectual property is legally protected against duplication and use by others in the United States and other countries across the world as a result of agreements such as the *General Agreement on Trade and Tariffs* and the *Patent Cooperation Treaty*. Other intellectual assets are proprietary by nature, such as unique knowledge developed by individuals or collectively by organizations. Assets that are either proprietary by nature or statute tend to be long lived, and thus are a sustainable source of advantage. Barriers to entry effectively create a monopoly within a particular market or technology space, since competitors are unable to offer effective substitutes. This in turn allows owners of these assets to successfully sell products embodying these assets at premium prices. Effective integration of intellectual assets with working capital and fixed assets enables the realization of premium margins, creating sustainable premium returns for owners.

Because they are rarely formally managed, intellectual assets tend to be a greater source of untapped value than traditional assets. For example, intellectual assets are generally not fungible and afford greater variety of combination with other assets. They can be bundled and unbundled into almost infinite combinations, while traditional assets are constrained by their physical nature. Patents present the most vivid example of the ability to bundle and unbundle rights in numerous combinations. Rights embodied in patents may be bundled with marketing and manufacturing assistance, trademarks, technological know-how, or future invention improvements. Rights may also be unbundled to include exclusive or non-exclusive rights within a geography, market or application. Unlike tangible assets, most intellectual assets do not suffer from capacity constraints. Many intellectual assets simultaneously form the basis of multiple licenses, joint ventures, co-marketing programs, and contract development arrangements.

The true value of intellectual assets is their ability to generate sustainable, above-market returns. Managers, however, must take action to exploit more effectively this rich source of potential value. Institutionalizing formal intellectual asset management (IAM) programs provides a framework to focus efforts on extracting the value resident in these assets. Unfortunately, not many companies have such programs, and as a result, much of the value of intellectual assets lies dormant. The adoption of IAM programs can create more efficient markets for the transfer of rights embodied in intellectual assets. This can lead to a decrease in transaction costs and attract more bidders for a given asset, thereby further increasing its value. Companies wishing to succeed in the knowledge economy will create greater value for their owners and attract more capital by focusing on the intellectual asset value-extracting activities available to them rather than computing the hypothetical value of these assets.

Michael Bredahl
Manager, Intellectual Asset Management
PricewaterhouseCoopers

Think about it!

Intellectual capital metric development guidelines

The measurement of knowledge is more of an art than a science at present. The following guidelines can help you think about creating a robust set of metrics for assessing your organization's knowledge.

Principle	Operating tactic	Description
Metrics are multi-dimensional	Value targets and results	'Top and bottom' line metrics, set objectives and measure outcomes.
	Indicators	Predictors of performance, measure focus and momentum, permit adjustment and calibration of action, can be inputs to or influencers of a process.
	Trends	Display of metrics that shows progress over time rather than at a point in time.
	Vectors and velocity	Metrics that show direction toward an objective and the speed with which the objective is being achieved.
Metric set is memorable	Small number of metrics	Basic principle of performance measurement is 'measure the minimum'.
	Easy to act on	Metrics should intuitively link to actions.
	Easy to understand	How metrics are computed should be clear to all, no black box calculations.
Metric development process creates value	Focus inside first	Key internal stakeholders need to participate in the process so that metrics are used for business decision making.
	Focus outside next	Think of stakeholders and pick representatives from each group to participate in the process so that reporting the metrics effectively communicates the organization's management of knowledge.

Intellectual capital assessment metric idea generator

The following metrics have been compiled from organizations that report on their knowledge. The list is not comprehensive, but it is a good base from which you can get started. We have organized the metrics into the three major types of intellectual capital – human, customer and organizational. Use this list to think about metrics that might help your organization to assess its knowledge.

Capital types	Intellectual capital metrics	Proxy for...
Human capital	Percentage of employees with advanced education degrees or average education level of all employees	Capacity for intelligent thinking
	Turnover of experienced personnel	Stability of knowledge base
	Average experience level (number of years with organization, in profession)	Depth of knowledge base
	Percentage of revenues from competence-enhancing customers (serving customers who require employees to develop new skills)	Extent to which customers challenge employees and the organization to innovate, create new knowledge or extend existing knowledge
	Employee satisfaction (developed from a battery of questions on a survey)	Strength of relationship to organization, commitment to sharing knowledge
	Training and education costs per employee	Investment in formal transfer of explicit knowledge
	Value-added per employee	Outcome measure that at least in part derives from leveraging knowledge
Customer capital	Percentage of employees who spend the majority of their time interacting with the customer	Depth and breadth of connection with customers
	Percentage repeat business	Stability of customer relationship
	Percentage business from largest customers	Depth of relationships
	Percentage change in revenues per customer	Depth of relationships and /or breadth of relationships depending on which is strategic objective
	Percentage of revenues from image-enhancing customers (who will make unprompted referrals)	Strength of relationship, ability to leverage it to build new relationships
	Percentage of cooperative arrangements with customers	Extent of knowledge flow and value creation of customer relationships
	Customer satisfaction	Stability of customer relationship
Organizational capital	Percentage of revenues invested in the knowledge management system (or IT system that pertains to knowledge management)	Extent of focus on creating, storing and marketing explicit forms of knowledge available for use
	Percentage of sales from products less than 'x' years old ('x' determined by a standard for 'new' that fits your organization)	Innovation, realization of knowledge creation and use
	Percentage of revenues from organization-enhancing customers (customers for whom the organization must make investments in order to complete work)	Success in building knowledge as customers force the organization to create new processes and/or products that can be leveraged afterward

Capital types	Intellectual capital metrics	Proxy for...
Organizational capital	Percentage of new employees ('new' defined in terms of number of years that it takes for a hire to become productive)	Depth of knowledge base
	Average breakeven time for new product development	Innovation, knowledge sharing and use
	Average response time to customer requests	Ability to gather and use knowledge
	Percentage of sales from proprietary products	Ability to create new knowledge and leverage it into a business result
	Contributions to knowledge base per employee (per year)	Success in building knowledge base
	Usage rates of knowledge base	Potential for leveraging knowledge base

Quick prioritization of challenge

Based on this section, how much priority should you assign to meeting this challenge?

◆ *Experiment with metrics and valuation approaches to evaluate strategic outcomes*

Rate your organization on these two factors	Your organization's rating	Rating scale
How much does your organization NEED to respond to this challenge?	*Need*	0 No need 1 Weak need 2 Moderate need 3 Strong need 4 Burning need
What is your organization's ABILITY to respond to this challenge?	*Ability*	0 Unable 1 Slightly able 2 Partially able 3 Almost able 4 Completely able

Need ✕ *Ability* =

★ To do
Transfer your prioritization to box D on page 260.

Prioritization of challenge

(multiply the two ratings)

Communicate with key stakeholders

Reports on intellectual capital have circulated internally in some organizations since the early 1990s as a way of communicating with employees about the management of knowledge-based assets. In the United States, the possibility that an outside investor could obtain a copy and 'rely' on the information for investment decision making opens the door to potential litigation risk. This has retarded efforts among publicly held US companies to publish these reports, even for internal purposes. However, in Europe, where there are no such legal hassles, organizations are more receptive to issuing reports on the management of knowledge-based assets. A 1998 research study conducted by Arthur Andersen revealed that 42% of a global survey group indicated that their organizations were likely to issue an addendum to the annual report that disclosed how well they managed intangibles in the next five years or less. Almost 25% said that they would report intellectual capital information on the financial balance sheet of their annual reports in the next five years or less. In both categories, a much greater percentage of Europeans indicated that they planned to issue these reports than either North Americans or Asians: 62% of Europeans plan to publish addenda in the next five years and 37% of them believe that intellectual capital information will be reported on the balance sheets of their financial statements in the next five years.[7]

The public reporting trail was blazed by Skandia in 1994 when it began to issue a supplement to its annual reports every six months which provided metrics on the management of intellectual capital. By the year 2000 at least 20 Danish companies will issue intellectual capital reports as a result of efforts by the Danish Ministry of Business and Industry to promulgate guidelines for reporting on intellectual capital (see Profile). Intellectual capital reports may eventually be a way to communicate with capital markets about the value-creating potential of the organization, but initially and for the forseeable future they are mainly a means for communicating inside the organization. They demonstrate a focus on the importance of building, sustaining and divesting knowledge for competitive advantage.

PROFILE ▸ *Danish Ministry of Business and Industry Intellectual Capital Reporting Initiative*

We are … a country that basically only has knowledge as a raw material – plus some agricultural land. So it is important for us to invest in knowledge.
Intellectual Capital Accounts: A New Tool for Companies, a Danish Agency for Trade and Industry, Ministry of Business and Industry publication

In January 1998 the Danish Ministry for Business and Industry launched an Intellectual Capital Accounting initiative to develop guidelines for reporting and managing intellectual capital. Building on an effort initiated by the Danish Agency for Trade and Industry in 1995, this ambitious project seeks to stimulate a worldwide dialogue around the key question: 'What does knowledge mean in a business context?' For the Danish government, this dialogue must take place not only among business organizations, but also among national governments. Ultimately, the meaning of knowledge in business has implications for a nation's standard of living. For this reason, the perspective of governments needs to be factored into the answer. Governments play an increasingly critical role in determining the type of macroenvironment in which organizations try to leverage their knowledge into innovations that generate wealth. The Danish government intends to use its work to spur the creation of international standards for reporting on intellectual capital.

The Intellectual Capital Accounting initiative commenced with a review of the way in which ten Danish and Swedish companies reported and or managed intellectual capital in their organizations.[8] A task force composed of representatives from government, industry and academia issued a memorandum of that review in April 1997 with some preliminary conclusions about the major components of intellectual capital accounts and the context in which they should be reported.

All ten companies studied set the intellectual capital reports in a strategic context in order to integrate the 'new reality' of the company into the current reality. In this respect, the intellectual capital accounts represent an evolution rather than revolution, preserving the way the company understands itself and its environment. To become part of the company's decision-making process, intellectual capital accounts must be woven into the strategic and operational planning and reporting processes. Figure 7.8 shows how the report visually depicted this integration.

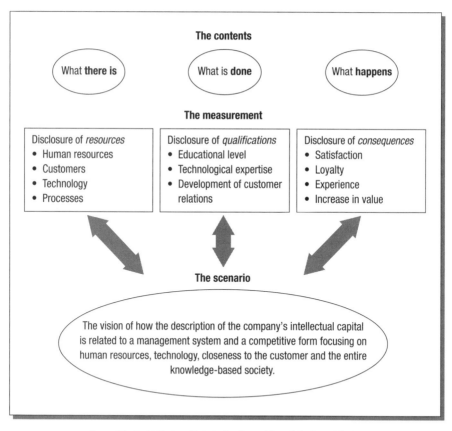

Source: 'The Danish Trade and Industry Development Council, Intellectual Capital Accounts: Reporting and Managing Intellectual Capital', Memorandum, April 1997, Professor Jan Mouritsen, Copenhagen Business School

Fig 7.8 ◆ The concept of intellectual capital accounts

Common elements among the models and methods used by the ten companies under review suggested that intellectual capital accounts should evaluate up to four dimensions of the organization in up to three different ways. The four dimensions are: human resources, customers, technology and business processes. The three different forms of evaluation are: statistical information, internal key figures and effect goals. Statistical information measures 'what is', giving a snapshot of the amount or 'goodness' of various types of intellectual capital. Internal key figures measure 'what is done', providing an assessment of how well the management system builds, sustains and divests intellectual capital. Effect goals measure 'what happens', linking what goes on inside the company to results that come from interactions with its stakeholders.

Table 7.1 is adapted from information in the April 1997 report. It contains examples of the types of measures that could be used in each category taken from the reports of the ten companies whose intellectual capital measures and practices were evaluated for the report. The great range of metrics that appear in the table speaks to the wide variety of perspectives that organizations bring to the challenge of measuring and managing intellectual capital.

Table 7.1 ◆ Examples of measures used to evaluate intellectual capital

Dimension	What is: statistical information	What is done: internal key figures	What happens: effect goals
Human resources	*Size and composition of the employee base* ◆ Seniority ◆ Education levels ◆ Training costs	*Impact of HR administration and policies* ◆ Percentage of employees with a career development plan ◆ Number of training days per employee ◆ Training costs per employee	*Outcomes of HR management* ◆ Employee satisfaction ◆ Turnover ◆ Value-added per employee
Customers	*Size and composition of customer base* ◆ Distribution of turnover on markets and products ◆ Marketing expenses	*Impact of customer relationship practices* ◆ Customers per employee ◆ Marketing expenses as a percentage of sales ◆ Administrative costs as a percentage of sales	*Outcomes of customer relationship management* ◆ Customer satisfaction ◆ Percentage of sales from repeat purchases ◆ Percentage of customers with long-term relationships

Table 7.1 ◆ *(cont)*

Dimension	What is: statistical information	What is done: internal key figures	What happens: effect goals
	Description of IT capacity	*Impact of IT infrastructure*	*Outcomes of IT usage*
Technology	◆ IT expenses ◆ Number of internal and external IT users	◆ PCs per employee ◆ IT expenses per employee	◆ IT literacy
	Description of investment in processes	*Process productivity*	*Outcomes of process management*
Business processes	◆ Costs per process ◆ Human resource distribution by process ◆ Investments in R&D and infrastructure	◆ Lead time ◆ Product development cycle time ◆ Time to market for new products or businesses	◆ Error rates ◆ Quality ◆ Company reputation

Source: 'The Danish Trade and Industry Development Council, Intellectual Capital Accounts: Reporting and Managing Intellectual Capital', Memorandum, April 1997, Professor Jan Mouritsen, Copenhagen Business School

Think about it!

Reporting on knowledge is not a trivial undertaking for an organization. If your organization reported on knowledge, would the various stakeholder groups that are interested in your organization's performance view this information as 'nice' or 'necessary'? Use the following space to think about it by placing a checkmark in the column that reflects the overall response you believe each stakeholder group would have upon receiving information about knowledge.

Stakeholder groups	Nice to know ✓	Need to know ✓
Employees		
Customers		
Suppliers		
Investors		
Regulators		
Communities in which we operate		
Competitors		

Quick prioritization of challenge

Based on this section, how much priority should you assign to meeting this challenge?

◆ *Communicate with key stakeholders*

Rate your organization on these two factors	Your organization's rating	Rating scale
How much does your organization NEED to respond to this challenge?	**Need**	0 No need 1 Weak need 2 Moderate need 3 Strong need 4 Burning need
What is your organization's ABILITY to respond to this challenge?	**Ability**	0 Unable 1 Slightly able 2 Partially able 3 Almost able 4 Completely able

Need ✕ *Ability* =

★ To do
Transfer your prioritization to box E on page 261.

Prioritization of challenge

(multiply the two ratings)

Notes

1 'The balanced scorecard – measures that drive performance', Robert S. Kaplan and David P. Norton, *Harvard Business Review*, January–February 1992, pp. 71–79.

2 Capital is material wealth used or available for use in the production of more wealth. *The American Heritage Dictionary of the English Language* (3rd edn). Houghton Mifflin Company, 1992.

3 'Corporate chiefs have become celebrities', G. Pascal Zachary, *The Wall Street Journal*, September 3 1997, p. A1.

4 Ikujiro Nonaka and HirotakaTakeuchi, *The Knowledge-Creating Company*. Oxford: Oxford University Press, 1995.

5 Celeni's "intangible assets" correspond to our definition of intellectual capital.

6 Insights about knowledge measurement practices tend to come from the measurement camp, since knowledge management has been their bailiwick for longer than it has been for the valuation contingent. A treatment of valuation is beyond the scope of this *Fieldbook*, but two important references are listed in the Bibliography for those who wish to know more about this area.

7 'Knowledge measurement: phase three. Global survey findings report, Asia, North America and Europe', Arthur Andersen, Next Generation Research Group, October 1998.

8 The ten companies whose intellectual reporting accounts and methods were reviewed are: PLS Consult, Ramboll, Skandia, Consultus, Telia, ABB, Sparekassen Nordjylland (SparNord), The Swedish Civil Aviation Administration (SCAA), Sparbanken Sverige and WM Data.

Agenda for action: Assess

The action steps presented in the Agenda for action come from the ideas suggested in this chapter. If you believe that your organization needs to focus on improving how well it assesses knowledge, this template and its suggested action steps are one way to get started.

The Agenda for action is organized in the same way as this chapter. Each imperative and its accompanying challenges are clustered together. Action steps are suggested for each challenge based on the text and case studies. You decide which action steps make sense for your organization and use the empty space to scribble in any additional ideas that come to mind.

Before you begin, make sure that you have transferred your prioritization ratings for each challenge. The prioritization ratings will remind you whether you believed that the challenge was worth pursuing. The maximum prioritization rating is 16, the minimum is 0.

How you use the prioritization ratings is up to you. For example, depending on the range of prioritization ratings, you may decide to ignore all challenges below a minimum threshold and focus only on those challenges above it. Or you may decide that everything that is not 0 deserves at least some thought. We invite you to use this Agenda for action as a place to start acting on your knowledge management priorities.

 **Agenda for action**

1 Perspective

Expand the theory of the organization to capture the impact of knowledge on organizational performance

Identify new forms of organizational capital	A
	Prioritization rating

Action step	Who should be involved	My first 'to do'
Articulate our current 'theory of the organization' – how do we believe that value is created? Contrast this 'theory' with the new theory proposed by the Intellectual Capital Model.		
Use the Intellectual Capital Model as a guide for defining the key types of human, organizational and customer capital that our organization should measure and monitor.		
Initiate a series of dialogues throughout the organization to refine the initial thinking about intellectual capital.		
Promote organization-wide dialogue about the Intellectual Capital Model by establishing an on-line site that is open to everyone in our organization.		
Venture outside the organization and engage key customers and suppliers in discussions about intellectual capital to enlarge our perspective about the forms of intellectual capital that we should monitor and measure.		
Other:		

B

Conceptualize the new tasks of management

Prioritization rating

Action step	Who should be involved	My first 'to do'
Investigate current levels of understanding at senior management, middle management and front-line worker levels to determine the extent to which the organization must be educated about managing knowledge.		
Canvass key investors to determine their level of interest in our ability to measure and monitor knowledge.		
Present the Intellectual Capital Model and an assessment of the degree to which the current decision-making process considers knowledge to our senior executive team and initiate a discussion about their role in the management of knowledge.		
Other:		

2 Integration

Incorporate into the overall management process a new set of frameworks, processes and metrics that evaluate the entire resource base from which the organization generates value

	C
Visualize the underlying structures that guide knowledge management practices	
	Prioritization rating

Action step	Who should be involved	My first 'to do'
Depict our knowledge management process.		
Identify the key enablers that support the knowledge management process.		
Compare our process and enablers to the processes and frameworks presented in this chapter to identify gaps and unique elements of our process.		
Solicit feedback about the depiction of our organization's knowledge management process from key stakeholders to identify gaps and other unique elements.		
Conduct an organization-wide KMD (see Chapter 2 of the *Fieldbook*) to identify 'hot spots' in our knowledge management process where improvement would both be visible and create momentum for additional efforts.		
Other:		

D

Experiment with metrics and valuation approaches to evaluate strategic outcomes

Prioritization rating

Action step	Who should be involved	My first 'to do'
Evaluate the intensity of our organization's current metric environment by identifying how many types of information that are currently tracked on a routine basis.		
Canvass management to learn how they use the information they currently receive to make business decisions.		
Using the intellectual capital metric development guidelines and intellectual capital metric idea generator on page 248, prepare a preliminary set of metrics for monitoring knowledge assets.		
Solicit feedback and input about the preliminary set of metrics from different management groups.		
Team up with a few receptive managers to 'field test' the metrics – focusing on ease of collection and impact on business decision making.		
Other:		

Communicate with key stakeholders

E

Prioritization rating

Action step	Who should be involved	My first 'to do'
Identify key barriers to creating and distributing reports on knowledge. Barriers might include: vulnerability to litigation or theft, future taxation of assets, perceived redundancy with other efforts, costs are clear but benefits are fuzzy, assessing intangibles is perceived role of capital markets rather than organizational management.		
Develop report prototype at business unit and organization-wide levels.		
Partner with key stakeholder groups to prototype reporting process and clarify benefits of sharing this information.		
Collect success stories as first step in documenting benefits. When data is available over several time periods, conduct analysis to link benefits to financial or other strategically critical metric results (e.g., customer retention, public perception of organization, etc.).		
Other:		

8 Build and Sustain

No one is as smart as everyone.

Larry Keely[1]

This step in the knowledge management process, which ensures that future knowledge keeps the organization viable or competitive, requires a fresh look at what it means to manage. Increasingly, organizations will build knowledge through their relationships with employees, suppliers, customers, the communities in which they operate, even competitors. Deriving value from these relationships is what will ultimately force traditional management which emphasizes direct command and control of people to yield to a more facilitative style which emphasizes the management of environments and enablers.

At a glance . . .

What is new?	Allocation of resources to the growth and maintenance of knowledge.
	Emphasis on relationships and collaboration as a source of competitive advantage.
What is the problem?	Difficult to link resource allocation conclusively or directly to specific payback.
	Discomfort with a dramatically different management style and focus.
What is the individual or team objective?	Identify experiments that are risky enough to be recognized as important and sufficiently critical that enough people would like to see them succeed. The result: Momentum for moving forward.
What is the organizational objective?	Craft and implement an action plan for developing and bolstering knowledge that will create competitive advantage going forward.

Introduction

Organizations must do more than get today's job done well. They must also integrate the strategic activities of growth and renewal into the course of everyday work.

When a resource is as volatile as knowledge, strategic activities cannot take a back seat to the exigencies of the moment. If knowledge is allowed to accumulate or dissipate in a strategic management vacuum, leaders will be hard-pressed to determine whether they are creating or destroying it. Knowledge that is not yet part of the organization's resource base but is essential to its future must be developed. Knowledge that is already part of the organization's existing resource base and is critical to the future must be protected and nurtured. Knowledge that serves no current or future purpose must be cleared out to free up and focus resources on achieving the future vision. At the tactical level, the inability to locate and apply knowledge to meet an existing need results in a lost opportunity. At the strategic level, coming up short on the 'right' knowledge delivers a far more serious blow – loss of competitiveness, and ultimately collapse of the enterprise itself.

We have organized the strategic activities for developing knowledge into three major chunks: build, sustain and divest. Building is the favourite among top management. It is the stuff of which empires are made. Divesting is most often triggered by external environmental factors. As a result, organizations frequently operate in crisis rather than strategic mode when divesting. Sustaining is the most overlooked because once a strategic capability has been achieved there is a tendency to rest on one's laurels and take it for granted. While no less important than the other two, sustaining activities are less glitzy and less heroic, so their impact is often underestimated. Building and sustaining are inextricably linked to divesting. They are flip sides of the same strategic management coin. Building and sustaining activities differ more in scope and degree than in kind, so we will discuss them together. We will examine the other side of the coin – divesting – in the next chapter.

In our experience, most people who are responsible for knowledge management today sit close to, but not at, the top executive table. So what are we doing writing about building, sustaining and divesting knowledge if the intended reader of the *Fieldbook* most likely lacks the authority to mandate change by allocating resources? Because what knowledge managers or executives do have, and what the organization wants from them, is an evangelist's passion and conviction that focuses the organization's attention on an important and undermanaged resource. Whether or not you set strategy, you can influence it over time by sending clear messages throughout the organization about developing and supporting the infrastructure and the people that are needed to grow and renew mission-critical knowledge.

To build and sustain knowledge, organizational management must take a fresh look at the following *imperatives* and *challenges*.

Imperatives and challenges

Direction	Resources are channelled in ways that replenish and create knowledge:
	◆ *Subordinate information technology to people.*
	◆ *Structure positions that focus organizational attention on intellectual capital.*
Connection	The organization forms relationships that further its knowledge management objectives:
	◆ *Preach cooperation among internal divisions.*
	◆ *Partner in new ways with other organizations.*
	◆ *Retain the right people.*
Recognition	The organization sees how to extract the value embedded in knowledge:
	◆ *Use knowledge to strengthen the customer relationship.*
	◆ *Disassemble the organizational whole to take a fresh look at its parts.*
Reciprocity	Policies, procedures and cultural norms support a covenant between the organization and its members:
	◆ *Demonstrate that value creation is a values proposition.*
	◆ *Make room for the entire person to show up for work every day.*

1 Direction

Resources are channelled in ways that replenish and create knowledge

Allocating resources is the clearest signal that any senior executive team sends to the organization about what commands attention. Since it has been and still is quite difficult to assess the impact of investing in intangibles, resources have not typically been allocated to them in a straightforward way. When investment does occur, it takes place indirectly or by chance and there is little effort to determine its impact. The assessment practices presented in the previous chapter that are being used to evaluate the impact of managing knowledge on achieving strategic objectives are by no means universally accepted or widely used. Nevertheless, organizations routinely invest resources in ways that build and sustain knowledge. The challenge for those organizations that do not use assessment practices to guide them is knowing whether their investments are in fact building and sustaining or eroding and eradicating mission-critical knowledge.

To build and sustain knowledge through resource allocation decisions, organizations must grow and renew the forms of capital that jointly give rise to intellectual capital. In this section, we will focus on building and sustaining organizational capital, a concept that was introduced and described in Chapter 7 when we discussed the Intellectual Capital Model (p. 223). We present the Intellectual Capital Model again to revisit its key elements (see Figure 8.1).

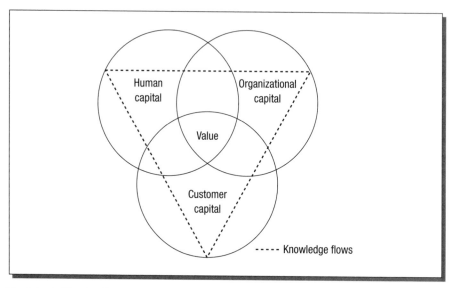

Fig 8.1 ◆ The Intellectual Capital Model

Organizations need to manage the knowledge flows between the different types of capital in order to generate value from intellectual capital:

◆ **Human capital** – the ability of individuals and teams to apply solutions to customers' needs; competencies; and mind-sets.

◆ **Customer capital** – the strength of the customer relationship; superior customer-perceived value; increasing customization of solutions.

◆ **Organizational capital** – the capabilities of the organization, made up of codified knowledge from all sources (knowledge bases, business processes, the technology infrastructure), the shared culture, values and norms.

◆ **Intellectual capital** – the relationship among human, customer and organizational capital that maximizes the organization's potential to create value which is ultimately realized in some form of wealth.

Organizational capital is the intellectual capital that remains in the organization when its members go home. It is the intellectual capital that the organization 'owns' in the traditional sense. Some forms of organizational capital are more concrete than others, for example, intellectual assets such as the information technology infrastructure and operating and management processes. Even though operating and management processes are less tangible than information technology infrastructure, it is clear to most organizations that they can own and control the value extracted from them.

Some industries, such as the service industry, which have traditionally relied more heavily on customer or human capital, are looking for ways to increase and protect their organizational capital. This involves both the conversion of human capital into organizational capital through codification or articulation as well as using forms of legal protection, such as patents and trademarks, to safeguard these newly converted assets. The realization that there may be new ways to extract value from knowledge has inspired organizations like PricewaterhouseCoopers, the professional services giant, to engage in a landmark initiative to identify its intellectual assets and formally manage them.

In later sections of this chapter, we will consider the forms of organizational capital from which value extraction is harder to trace, such as culture, norms and values. We will also discuss forms of human and customer capital which cannot be 'owned', but are better thought of as 'borrowed', 'leased', 'rented' or even more radically, 'volunteered'. The Intellectual Capital Matrix (see Figure 8.2) aligns different types of intellectual capital along two dimensions: ease of managing value extraction and the degree to which it is owned or borrowed. It provides an easy way to visualize differences among the various types of intellectual capital. When organizations succeed in managing them well, the boundaries that separate one form of intellectual capital from the others begin to blur. The blurring is precisely the point of the Intellectual Capital Model, which proposes alignment of the different forms of intellectual capital as the key to achieving the largest possible value creation space from knowledge.

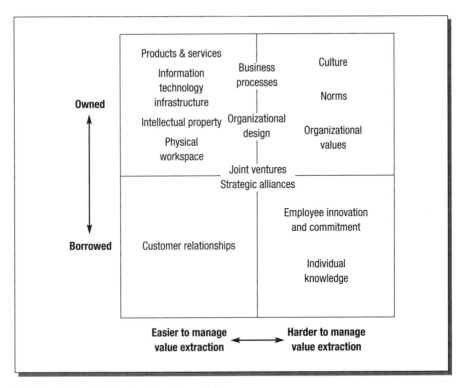

Fig 8.2 ◆ The Intellectual Capital Matrix

To channel resources so that they build and sustain intellectual capital, decision-makers must shift from a 'cost' to an 'investment' perspective. They must face these *challenges*.

Challenges

♦ *Subordinate information technology to people.*
♦ *Structure positions that focus organizational attention on intellectual capital.*

Subordinate information technology to people

One of our favourite Dilbert cartoons shows Dilbert and Wally in conference with The Boss. Before The Boss has a chance to brief them on the problem, the two intrepid engineers have come up with the solution: 'Let's build a database!' Fact: You *will* install an information technology infrastructure to gather, store and share knowledge. But if you think that this is the hardest part of knowledge management – you are in for a rude awakening. It might be the most expensive, but information technology is the least likely to create value if it becomes the centre-piece of your knowledge management strategy.

What do you need to do to make the information technology investment pay off? Subordinate it to the needs of people. Human-centered technology is the phrase that technologists favour to make bits and bytes sound more friendly. If it is more than just a slogan, human-centred technology means that the needs and work practices of people dictate information technology design, not the other way around. In organizations that are strategically focused on building and sustaining knowledge, we do see a shift in the way in which they conceive of their information technology investments. Epitomized by organizations such as the World Bank (see Profile), these companies view technology investment as support for, not replacement of, people. Their use of technology is ultimately aimed at not only improving information flows but also promoting relationships among people.

For global organizations, information technology has helped to lower the barriers of time and geography that impede the flow of information and the formation of relationships. Colossal organizations such as Ford can conduct round-the-clock and round-the-globe product development using technology-supported hand-offs as the workday ends in one part of the world and starts in another. Modest-sized organizations, such as specialty chemicals manufacturer Buckman Laboratories International, can link up sales associates in South Africa, Scotland and Memphis, Tennessee, to discuss the best specialty chemical solution to smooth out a hitch in a customer's chemical production process.

In other instances where 'knowing what we know' is the main barrier, technology can free the flow of information by creating repositories that do not require more than a visit to the personal computer. This is especially significant for large organizations. In smaller companies, where people are more or less known to each other, information flow can be as simple as picking up a phone or walking down the hall. One of the biggest benefits of gathering information in this way is trust.

You know the person from whom the information comes, so you know that you can rely on it. In large organizations, however, more complex technology supports are needed to unstick information and make it trustworthy.

Organizations turn to information technology-based solutions because of the enormous transformation that information technology has wrought on the possibilities for connecting people with other people and with all forms of information. Information technology can be used to form relationships among people who will only rarely, if ever, meet in the physical world. Organizations need to do more than simply support networks that already exist with a technology infrastructure. They need to enable the formation of new networks that would not exist without it. These new technology-enabled networks have given birth to cyber relationships that hold significant value to both individuals and the organization. They are becoming a parallel path through which ideas and information flow and by which knowledge can be created.

> PROFILE *The World Bank*

While it was never the World Bank Knowledge Management team's intention, building a knowledge base and installing the requisite information technology infrastructure to support knowledge storage and sharing initially absorbed most of their time and resources. However, not too far into the process, it was evident that knowledge management practices were more likely to emerge where communities of practice existed than in parts of the Bank where they did not. As a result, the Knowledge Management Program Manager, Stephen Denning, redirected his group's efforts to the social and cultural side of the knowledge management equation.

The World Bank Group, headquartered in Washington DC, has the unique mission of 'reducing global poverty and improving living standards by promoting sustainable economic growth and investments in people'. The Bank has locations in 60 countries around the world, providing advice and knowledge services as it makes loans, $28 billion (US) in fiscal year 1998. The Bank is owned by more than 200 member countries whose views and interests are represented by a board of governors and a Washington-based board of directors. Since 1996 knowledge management has been the strategic thrust of the Bank. By the year 2000 the World Bank Group wants to be the source of best practice and cutting-edge economic development knowledge, an exemplar for internal and external knowledge sharing, the home for a global network of development practitioners and the standard setter for a universal institutional approach to economic development. Knowledge management is the key to making this vision a reality.

'Our clients demanded knowledge management, but our culture didn't easily embrace it. We had a look up, yell down culture,' says Denning. 'When our clients' circumstances were more stable, time was less of an issue. It was difficult to know if the advice we provided was best in the world. It was always sound, but we had no real way to know if it was the best. Now, time and world-class standards of quality are the issue, and our organization has had to radically alter its practices to get our clients the world-class advice they need when they need it.' Meeting these demands has opened up not only the boundaries between the Bank's internal departments, but also between the Bank and its clients.

Examples of knowledge sharing abound at the Bank, but the following is increasingly typical. In the summer of 1998 the government of Pakistan sought advice from the World Bank Group about its plans to remedy the imminent collapse of its highway system with a novel technology. The Bank's recommendation about the technology was needed in two days as the situation was urgent. Formerly, the Bank's people-intensive process would have made such a request out of the question. Gathering and processing the information would have taken 3–6 months at best. Using its new knowledge-sharing system, however, the Bank was able to pose the request to 400 people around the world who were part of a 'road network'. That same day, a Bank task manager sent information about the use of this technology in Jordan. A field office professional in Argentina who was writing a book on the technology also replied with an overview of experiences with the technology in Asia, Australia and Africa – including insights into drawbacks and pitfalls. Of even greater note was the response from outside the Bank, from one of its clients, the head of the South African national roads agency who described significant experience with a closely related technology. The right information was delivered to the Pakistani government, just in time. Afterward, the information was edited and placed in the Bank's knowledge base for future use.

'If you heard this story and thought that the information technology made it possible, you would only be half right,' comments Denning. 'What really made it possible was a change in our organization's culture that has made it okay to say "I don't know" to several hundred people. Such an admission compels the people who do know to respond. Sharing depends on a feeling of community. People identify themselves as part of a group that shares what it knows. Technology is a critical facilitator of this process, but it is only half of the solution. Ultimately, knowledge sharing is a balance of context which technology provides and connection which the community offers.'

Think about it!

How balanced are your organization's expectations about IT and human resources when it comes to knowledge management? Complete each set of statements by entering a percentage figure. Then compare the scores to see how balanced your organization's thinking is today.

People in our organization believe that a *good human resources solution:*

Will take care of ....% of our knowledge management issues

Will boost innovation by ....%

Should be allocated ....% of our knowledge management budget

Will boost knowledge sharing by ....%

Will create ....% more new networks of people

Total your percentages

☐ (HR)

People in our organization believe that a *good information technology solution:*

Will take care of ....% of our knowledge management issues

Will boost innovation by ....%

Should be allocated ....% of our knowledge management budget

Will boost knowledge sharing by ....%

Will create ....% more new networks of people

Total your percentages

☐ (IT)

Divide your HR percentage by your IT percentage and place that value in the blank space to get a rough feel for the balance of your expectations of the benefits that you can derive from these two knowledge management levers.

☐ (HR)
☐ (IT)

.... = ... : 1

Quick prioritization of challenge

Based on this section, how much priority should you assign to meeting this challenge?

◆ *Subordinate information technology to people*

Rate your organization on these two factors	Your organization's rating	Rating scale
How much does your organization NEED to respond to this challenge?	**Need**	0 No need 1 Weak need 2 Moderate need 3 Strong need 4 Burning need
What is your organization's ABILITY to respond to this challenge?	**Ability**	0 Unable 1 Slightly able 2 Partially able 3 Almost able 4 Completely able

Need × Ability =

★ To do

Transfer your prioritization to box A on page 314.

Prioritization of challenge

(multiply the two ratings)

Structure positions that focus organizational attention on intellectual capital

Focusing organizational attention on knowledge is not going to happen just by saying that everyone should share their best thinking. Many organizations will resort to establishing a formal position or group whose job is to evangelize the practice of knowledge management. This means money, a career path, senior executive attention – all of the hallmarks that knowledge management is strategically important to the organization. To ensure that knowledge is built and sustained with an eye on the entire enterprise, some companies are making individuals or staff groups responsible for creating focus and momentum around knowledge-related activities. The staff groups that have become responsible for knowledge management are often a reincarnation of an old function. They are usually in a state of 'becoming' rather than 'being', as they are at The Dow Chemical Company (see Profile).

One of the most visible knowledge management investments in organizational structure is the establishment of the chief knowledge officer as a member of the top management team (see Point of view). The debate about creating this position has polarized the business community. The pro-CKO camp fervently believes that the position raises the strategic visibility of knowledge management by demonstrating that:

◆ it is an ongoing topic of discussion

◆ resources will be devoted to building knowledge

◆ someone is paying attention to whether it happens or not.

The anti-CKO camp is convinced that creating an executive position will effectively remove responsibility for knowledge management from everyone else. They believe that the knowledge turf is one that everyone should be able to claim. They are adamant that it should not become either centralized or bureaucratized.

Both camps express an important point of view and marrying the seemingly opposed positions might offer the best of both worlds. During the initial phase the CKO and staff start as a centralized group that organizes and evangelizes knowledge management practices. Once business value has been successfully demonstrated, the staff transitions over to the business units while retaining dotted-line reporting to the CKO. The staffless CKO maintains a role as primary champion of knowledge-enhancing activities. At some point, however, these activities need to become so embedded in the organization's business processes that the role becomes redundant (see Point of View). It is hard to know if the CKO will really disappear once the position has been created. However, the ultimate dissolution of the CKO role might be the clearest signal that knowledge is everybody's business.

PROFILE ➤ *The Dow Chemical Company's Intellectual Asset Management (IAM) Group*

When organizations decide to implement a knowledge or intellectual asset management strategy, they frequently create a new category of employee whose role is to work closely with the business units to translate the vision of intellectual asset management into a workable reality. If the organization can build from an established base and promote intellectual asset management as an evolution rather than a revolution, the odds of success will be greatly improved. This is the course followed by The Dow Chemical Company's IAM Group which has extended and transformed a legacy founded close to 50 years ago.

In the 1950s huge growth at Dow encouraged top management to organize the company into strategic business units. As they divided the company to spur further growth, top executives realized that they would have to create new groups to ensure that the company maintained a unified and broad perspective about how to fuel future development. One new function that they put into place was responsible for the management of inventions. The Inventions Management group was created, but aside from focusing on inventions, its role was not clearly defined. As a result, the group's activities remained mostly at the tactical level, even though it was staffed with very experienced R&D professionals.

In 1992 a set of factors came into play which forced a change in the role of the Inventions Management group. Patents had become more expensive to acquire and to maintain, R&D expenses across the organization had reached burdensome proportions and several key managers retired from the Inventions Management group. This convergence of events became an opportunity to shift the group's focus from staff to line, to become more proactive with the business units, and to examine not only patents but all intellectual assets. The new IAM group used the 'hook' of reducing R&D and patent expenses to engage the business units. Once they had demonstrated value, they began to teach and institute the practices needed to manage intellectual asset risk, value creation and value preservation as part of the business planning and new product development processes (see Profile on p. 234). Initially part of a central staff group, within two years, most IAM managers were full members of the business units they served.

The IAM group has been instrumental in pushing the businesses to think about IAs in new ways. Their most significant impact within the larger organization has been in stimulating cross-functional discussions within the business units. They are developing new ways to leverage the IAM fishnet structure (see Figure 8.3) which weaves functional expertise together with business strategy expertise to even greater advantage for the company.

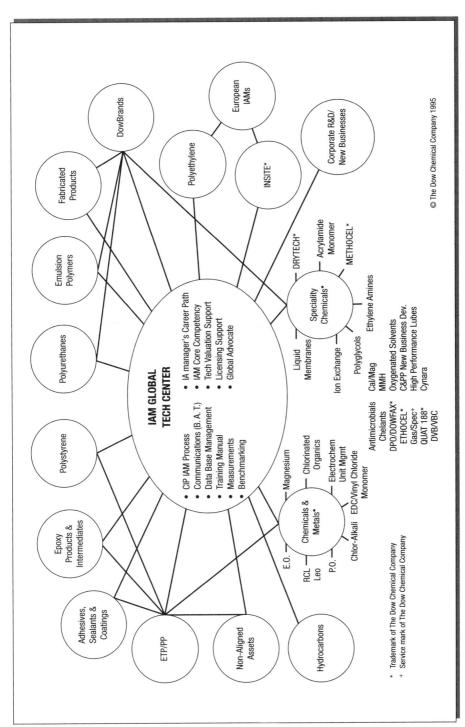

© The Dow Chemical Company 1995

* Trademark of The Dow Chemical Company
+ Service mark of The Dow Chemical Company

Fig 8.3 ◆ **The Dow Chemical Company's Intellectual Asset Management organization fishnet structure**

POINT OF VIEW **The role of the CKO from a research study**

Michael Earl and Ian Scott of the London Business School in association with IBM conducted a survey of CKOs in 1998 to find out who they were, what they did and what they hoped to achieve.

At the time the research was conducted, the researchers estimated that a total of 25 senior executives in North America and Europe met both of the following criteria:

1   The word 'knowledge' was in their title.

2   They were senior executives leading corporate knowledge management initiatives.

The research led the team to conclude that there were three 'generic' goals for a formal knowledge management programme led by a CKO: protection of, maximizing the use of and generating and improving organizational knowledge. Similarly, three 'generic' value targets could be used to assess these programmes: improvement and development of knowledge-based products and services, improvement and redesign of knowledge-based business and management processes, improved decision making in the areas of organizational adaptiveness and responsiveness.

Based on their findings, the researchers constructed a model that captured the complexity of the CKO's job and pictured the 'ideal' CKO profile. That model, slightly adapted, appears in the next Think about it! exercise (page 280). The grey area shows that the ideal CKO is strong in three roles – consultant, entrepreneur and environmentalist – and limited in the fourth – technologist. Earl and Scott also mention two 'operating style' dimensions: managing and leading. Managing by CKOs is principally about distributing ownership of and recognition for knowledge management projects among other members of the organization. Leading by CKOs is principally about being recognized as a seasoned, but still young executive player. Earl and Scott put it nicely: 'The CKO has more future than past, it isn't a sunset job for those nearing retirement.'[2]

POINT OF VIEW **The role of the CKO from a former CKO**

It's a kind of Cheshire Cat. The programme should appear, catalyze, analyze, reorganize and then disappear slowly, with the smile as the last thing to fade.

Victoria Ward

The NatWest Knowledge Management Programme was developed with these risks in mind:

1 **Credibility and position in the enterprise**. The programme is often positioned around human resources, training or technology. It is run and seen as a support function by people without operating experience. The chief executive espouses the cause of knowledge management with passion but does not invest any of his or her own time in it.

2 **Reach, scalability and speed**. It is hard for the knowledge team to reach out from the corporate centre and influence the whole enterprise. Knowledge projects are often isolated, sometimes accidental successes and not rapidly scaleable to impact the whole enterprise or easy to replicate in business areas with very different characteristics.

3 **Short termism**. A knowledge management programme can be a well-meaning, but disconnected strand in a series of activities designed to change the culture in the organization. Cultural change takes 5–10 years to effect in a sustainable way, but knowledge projects are set the task of paying off in months. Not only are they are supposed to pay off in hard benefits, or 'soft' benefits whose hard impact is well understood; they may also be vying for attention with other organizational projects. Short termism also means that the reasons for success or failure in different projects are badly understood because of the urgent need to get 'quick wins' under the belt – with subtle but significant damaging consequences.

4 **Poor knowledge management skills in business heads**. Businesses are managed on a short-term, transactional basis by managers who see the development of effective information strategies as information technology projects, not information system projects. The way a project is initiated and managed at the outset misses key skills and tools which are necessary for success, such as coaching and information science and design skills.

5 **Poor business skills in the knowledge team**. The knowledge team does not run the knowledge programme like a business in its own right. Because there is often little business experience in the knowledge team, there is a lack of hard-edged analysis in the selection of an appropriate portfolio of projects, and at best a partial understanding of risk taking.

6 **Poor branding and communications strategy**. The knowledge programme, given its restricted ability to command and control in almost any enterprise, is forced back onto strategies to influence and create demand, either for the direct services and products of the team, or for knowledge management more generally. Implementation occurs in the business units where understanding of, and commitment to, the programme is likely to be at best fuzzy and at worst non-existent, even hostile.

7 **Organizational baggage**. 'We've already tried that and it didn't work last time.'

The NatWest Knowledge Management Programme was conceived as a two year, three-phase programme (outline follows). We felt strongly that this three-part, investigative, pragmatic, evidence-based approach was right. We also felt that the fake/real, temporary/permanent, field/centralized dynamic needed to be understood.

♦ *Fake/real*: rather than getting caught up in building a sophisticated prototype for an intranet, we slapped together a 'fake' one. It looked fake and it did not really work. By doing this, we could spend our time talking to people about what the real one should look like and do, instead of defending a prototype that we could not possibly get right the first time.

♦ *Temporary/permanent*: all structures in organizations should be temporary, in fact, and that is certainly true for knowledge management structures. We deliberately aimed for a nomadic feel in the first phases.

♦ *Field/centralized*: there is merit in identifying the knowledge management programme as a separate strand where it can have reach, influence and independence. However, there is also merit in hiding it in substantially well-run pieces of the organization. The issue is timing. It can be better to separate the knowledge management programme out when it has some momentum, not at the outset when it is trying to break through. Or a project such as the creation of a directory can be deliberately positioned as a central knowledge project to draw attention to certain issues. Each aspect of the programme should be open for re-integration or separation at every stage. Willingness to see where a knowledge management programme goes based on what happens takes a uniquely unterritorial and highly supported approach. It is not a process for the faint of heart.

Phase one (first six months)

♦ Conduct a couple of small-scale pilots.

♦ Develop at least one broad-based tool such as a series of directories and resource guides to information that was otherwise hard to locate.

♦ Establish the knowledge management team and create an intranet for the team as a clearinghouse, repository and communications vehicle.

♦ Audit all knowledge management-related work in progress.

♦ Create a map to find knowledge 'nodes' and programme cheerleaders.

♦ Commandeer the library as a physical and skills base from which to extend the team's reach.

♦ Attract additional team members.

♦ Manage the growing collection of learnings.

Phase two (middle twelve months)

♦ Conduct a 'wave' of 8–10 pilots building on previous learnings.

♦ Consolidate, iterate and develop the broad-based tools.

◆ Forge common interests among those involved in duplicative or competing projects by creating a 'safe' space in which they can start to share ideas and consider common solutions to common problems.

◆ Consolidate business skills in the team – we envisioned each pilot as a new entity in which we invested venture capital for the entire enterprise. Individual businesses received immediate benefit. The knowledge team captured learnings which it could reinvest in other business areas.

◆ Conduct benchmarking to develop a model for a decentralized knowledge team.

◆ Establish formal links, partnerships and joint ventures with the business areas, other support functions and external suppliers.

Phase three (final six months)

◆ Collate and review all the evidence to determine where to go next. Choices moving forward were:
  - reintegrate the strands into the business
  - pass the programme or individual initiatives over to different groups
  - retain the knowledge management core team and position it as a separate, for-profit, nomadic, enterprise-wide think tank operating as an affinity business.

Victoria Ward, former CKO NatWest Markets Investment Bank (UK),
contributed this section.

Think about it!

We have adopted the Earl and Scott model (see Point of view, p. 276) so that it can be used as a checklist for thinking about the CKO profile in your organization. For each of the four CKO roles we have added infomation extracted from the text of the research report. Based on their study, Earl and Scott believe that the profile of a CKO encompasses four main roles and extends along two operating dimensions. Different organizations tend to stress different aspects of the roles and favour one operating style over another.

Thinking about your organization, consider which qualities or activities would be most important for a CKO in each of the roles and use the checklist to flag them.

Entrepreneur

- Thrives with small staff and limited budget
- Builds from scratch and convinces others to pitch in
- Intuits how the pieces fit together to make the whole greater than sum of its parts

- Demonstrates complete comfort, if not technical proficiency, with information systems and technology
- Binds the knowledge management and information management strategies
- Sponsors the creation of knowledge systems and networks
- Maps, inventories, records, stores and disseminates information

Leading

Environmentalist   *Managing*   **Technologist**

- Exhibits missionary zeal for knowledge management that is infectious
- Lobbies for physical space design that promotes chance encounters
- Designs experiences that shock people out of the ordinary, forcing new perspectives on old situations
- Coordinates events that get people together in a social-professional context improving the quality of conversations

- Relishes the temporary/transitional nature of the role
- Builds consensus with senior executives and operating management
- Collaborates and seeks success through and with others
- Commands authority through persuasion
- Audits knowledge, skills or competence gaps and develops remedies
- Adapts ideals to business realities

Consultant

Quick prioritization of challenge

Based on this section, how much priority should you assign to meeting this challenge?

◆ *Structure positions that focus organizational attention on intellectual capital*

Rate your organization on these two factors	Your organization's rating	Rating scale
How much does your organization NEED to respond to this challenge?	**Need**	0 No need 1 Weak need 2 Moderate need 3 Strong need 4 Burning need
What is your organization's ABILITY to respond to this challenge?	**Ability**	0 Unable 1 Slightly able 2 Partially able 3 Almost able 4 Completely able

Need ✕ *Ability* =

★ **To do**
Transfer your prioritization to box B on page 315.

Prioritization of challenge

(multiply the two ratings)

2 Connection

The organization forms relationships that further its knowledge management objectives

Rethinking the way that resources are channelled to renew and replenish know-ledge not only requires a new way of looking at resources, but also forces organizations into an entirely different position with respect to some of them. Information technology and operating and management processes are owned by the organization. Since these intellectual assets are under the control of the organization, when resources are allocated the 'right way', the organization can count on the returns. But the forms of organizational capital we will now entertain – culture, norms and values – as well as other forms of intellectual capital – human and customer capital – are not owned by the organization. Organizations cannot simply direct resources toward them and be assured of a return. They must engage the hearts and heads of people who are connected to them. They must form connections with people that are unique and enduring.

The importance of relationships in the conduct of business is nothing new. They have always been the shadow 'bottom line' behind the financial 'bottom line'. What has changed and continues to change, however, is the form that relationships take, with whom they are made and the rapidity with which they are consummated and abandoned. The boundaries that demarcate organizational membership are more loosely drawn than ever before, as new models for stimulating value creation through knowledge are tested. Value creation chains are being formed in ways not imagined even five years ago. The focus on core competence has led to a super-specialist mentality, blurring the distinction between suppliers, the company and customers. Who is the company and who is the supplier when the supplier may know more about manufacturing the product than anyone inside the company? Who is the company and who is the customer when Internet advertisers suggest ways to alter the web sites on which their messages appear and the website integrates the advertising message directly into its content?

Experimenting with new forms of connectivity is a gambit that companies hope will help them realize value from exchanging knowledge within and among organizational entities and individuals. The new approaches to forming relationships meet these *challenges*.

Challenges

- Preach cooperation among internal divisions.
- Partner in new ways with other organizations.
- Retain the right people.

Preach cooperation among internal divisions

A famous Pogo comic strip quote proclaims 'We have seen the enemy and they is us!' This sentiment nicely captures the experience of many organizations when they answer the question, 'Why do we find it so hard to form internal alliances?' For years the received wisdom was to encourage unfettered competition among business units. In the early 1980s leading consumer products companies espoused this approach as an insurance policy to guarantee that the company would end up 'winning' in the marketplace. Internal competition condoned the launch of similar products into similar markets. One internal group would experience defeat, but the company as a whole would win. The enemy (competitors) was not only outside the borders of the company, but also within. The view that everyone outside the business unit was an enemy exacerbated the fortified bunker mentality within the business unit. When the business unit was under siege, sharing information with anyone outside it was akin to treason.

Yet, in a 180° turnabout, this is precisely what companies today who are concerned about building knowledge are asking of their people. Loud and strong signals coming straight from the customer have convinced many organizations that knowledge management can help them meet the new market realities. A Grant Thornton 1998 survey reported that 67% of mid-size manufacturers said that their new products were the direct result of customer demands, up from 56% in 1992. Paying attention to how the company's knowledge is used on behalf of the customer elevates the importance of creating internal alliances.

To entertain a discussion about internal alliances, it must be clear that regardless of where it was created and where it resides, knowledge should be available to anyone in the organization who can put it to good use. At Xerox Corporation, policy requires a team of senior executives to make monthly decisions on all uses of intellectual property in the organization (see Point of view). Raising the decision above the boundaries of the individual business units frees this specific type of knowledge from the confines of the home in which it was born to find a home where it can best serve the entire organization. The other tricky piece to master in promoting cooperation is the internal accounting for revenues. When more than one group is responsible for making a 'sale', but the accounting system forces the 'sale' to be sliced into as many pieces as there are groups, it is not easy to cooperate. Letting each group count the full sale on their profit and loss statement for internal purposes is one way to foster collaboration and the pooling of knowledge that is increasingly needed to secure and retain customers.

> **POINT OF VIEW** *Cooperation through healthy competition*

Cooperation among business units is not the opposite of competition, it is one of the results of healthy competition within the organization. Competing stimulates innovation. Healthy competition also factors what is best for the overall organization into the equation.

The push to better understand how resources are used to create value has led many organizations to parse their corporate structures into businesses that can be held accountable for generating a return on a specific set of resources. Understanding how the use of resources leads to a particular revenue stream is a valuable addition to the management toolkit. However, the push toward business unit accountability has frequently meant that the locus of accountability for managing the organization's resources as a whole is unclear. One counterbalancing trend to reconstitute the whole establishes a centralized group, such as the intellectual property groups at Ford, Allied Signal and Xerox, that is accountable for managing some of the organization's resources on an enterprise-wide basis.

When most organizations try to foster cooperation by establishing a centralized group to macromanage a resource like knowledge they run headfirst into the challenge of accounting for the revenues that are generated. In the case of licensing intellectual property, for example, a patent in and of itself frequently has limited value. Often, it is the know-how associated with the patent that creates significant value in the marketplace. While the centralized IP group, which does not have to cope with the task of making and delivering a product or service, may be well-positioned to scope out licensing opportunities, it cannot consummate those agreements without the skills of the business unit, research and development group and the legal department. Only a team effort can deliver the know-how that seals the deal.

When faced with revenue sharing solutions that range from 0–100 to 50–50 to 100–100 (double counting), a basic set of parameters is needed to arrive at a solution that is acceptable to both the centralized group and other members of the team, especially the business unit. When intellectual property is licensed, that set of revenue sharing parameters often includes:

♦ **Relatedness** – How closely does the use of the intellectual property or intellectual asset fit within the core technology or competence of the business unit? The closer the fit, the stronger the argument that the business unit deserves a larger percentage of the revenue stream in exchange for the risk of creating a competitor in the marketplace. Conversely, if the fit is weak, the intellectual property group makes a significant contribution by uncovering new possibilities for generating value and frequently receives a larger share of the revenue split.

♦ **Resource requirements** – What degree of resources will the business unit need to supply in support of the licensing arrangement? The higher the opportunity cost that the business unit must bear, the stronger the argument for a bigger percentage of the revenues.

♦ **Knowledge leverage** – What is the extent to which the business unit will derive future benefits from permitting others to license its technologies? In some instances, broadening the basic technology platform provides huge benefits in the future to a business unit. This is the Microsoft story of network externalities told in terms of any technology.

While never easy, using these and other parameters that are germane to the business' strategic objectives to discuss the revenue-sharing arrangement typically leads to an outcome that both sides feel is reasonable.

Steve Acosta is Intellectual Property Portfolio Manager at the Intellectual Property Business Unit of Xerox Corporation. He has more than 15 years of experience in intellectual property management as a business consultant and a former member of the intellectual property licensing group at Amoco Corporation.

Think about it!

Where are your organization's internal divisions positioned on the spectrum of cooperation to competition with respect to creating and sharing knowledge?

Choose an entity to evaluate such as your entire organization or a segment of it. Break the entity down into major units that you believe need to cooperate around knowledge creation and sharing. These units can be functional units, such as marketing, finance, production, sales etc. or operating units, such as different product or service groups. Use the following space to visualize the extent to which these major units cooperate or compete with one another.

List the units in the boxes. Place an 'x' on the scale to the right of each box to position each unit's overall stance ranging from fully cooperative on knowledge creating and sharing to fully competitive. The unit might be fully cooperative with one other unit, but fully competitive with most others. In this case, the unit's overall stance would be close to fully competitive.

Knowledge creating and sharing across the entity

Units	Fully cooperative	Neutral	Fully competitive

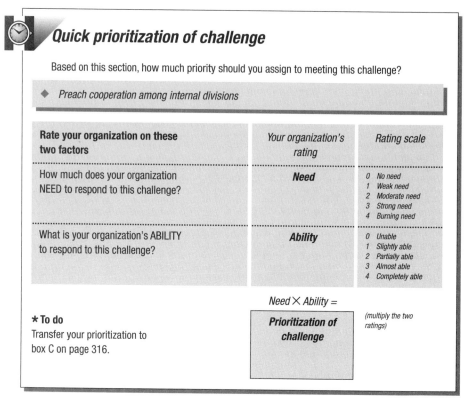

Quick prioritization of challenge

Based on this section, how much priority should you assign to meeting this challenge?

◆ *Preach cooperation among internal divisions*

Rate your organization on these two factors	Your organization's rating	Rating scale
How much does your organization NEED to respond to this challenge?	*Need*	0 No need 1 Weak need 2 Moderate need 3 Strong need 4 Burning need
What is your organization's ABILITY to respond to this challenge?	*Ability*	0 Unable 1 Slightly able 2 Partially able 3 Almost able 4 Completely able

Need ✕ Ability =

★ **To do**

Transfer your prioritization to box C on page 316.

| *Prioritization of challenge* | (multiply the two ratings) |

Partner in new ways with other organizations

The terms 'networking' and 'strategic partnerships' have entered the corporate vocabulary to describe the new ways in which value is created. The terms create a mental image of what happens when relationships are formed. Conduits are established that permit the bi-directional flow of value in the form of ideas, information, parts, products, cash – you name it; if it has value, it flows through networks. Information technology has allowed these networks to expand into cyberspace, as intranets become extranets, bringing suppliers and customers into the organizational fold to share ideas and collaborate on new products and services.

Both networks and strategic partnerships are less formal than alliances, joint ventures or mergers. In some instances they are the precursor for these more formal relationships. In others, they never move beyond the informal stage because value creation is highest when the entities are more loosely tethered. The picture is not all rosy, of course. Looser relationships might offer more flexibility, but they carry ambiguity and its accompanying anxieties. Trust must be very high and carefully tended for these relationships to work.

Many niche consultancies are networked organizations that pull together resources from a large pool of talent to service clients. The teams that show up at the client's door are frequently a coterie of consultants from small practices who band together to provide the expertise needed to fulfill a contract secured by one member of the group. Strategic partnerships bump the conduits up a notch to open new markets or transform existing ones for complementary services or products with companies that might previously have been competitors or a vertically integrated single organization. ProGroup, a workplace diversity consulting firm, uses both approaches to deliver services to its clients (see Profile).

The idea of collaborating with other organizations to open a new market rather than amassing all of the resources within one organization challenges the idea of organization and the existing models for creating value. For example, Daimler-Benz AG (now DaimlerChrysler) debuted its new Smart car in the autumn of 1998. The super-efficient European city car was the result of a joint venture called Micro Compact Car or MCC. MCC partners Daimler-Benz with Société Suisse de Micro-électronique et d'Horologèrie SA, the home of the Swatchwatch. The Smart car represents a radical departure from other small urban automobiles currently on the market, not only in terms of design, but also in the way in which it is being brought to market. More than fifteen different organizations are responsible for building the Smart car. The manufacturer, MCC, owns only some of the knowledge needed to bring the product to market, and that knowledge is worthless without the full cooperation and commitment of the thirteen other organizations with whom it has partnered.[3]

▰▰▰ PROFILE ▰▰▰ *ProGroup*

When business partnerships seek to build mutual knowledge, a shared set of core values is the linchpin of the relationship.

ProGroup, headquartered in Minneapolis, Minnesota, is a consulting firm that specializes in workplace diversity. A niche player in a rapidly growing segment of the consulting industry, the 30-person organization relies on its network of 65 external consultants and an expanding array of relationships with other organizations to serve its customers. Relationships with other organizations run the gamut from formal to informal, close to loose and contractual to handshake. The way its president, Myrna Marofsky, sees it, the less formal the relationship, the greater the potential for exponential growth on the part of both parties. 'Our informal relationships that rely on shared understanding result in both companies getting smarter,' reflects Marofsky. 'The more formal relationships really seem to be about ProGroup getting smarter. Our partner's "intelligence" is much less of an issue. We are buying their expertise, not working together to boost both of our knowledge bases.'

For informal relationships to work, it is essential that the companies share a set of core values and a common reason for being (see ProGroup's core values that follow). 'As idealistic as it sounds, ProGroup's purpose is to change the world,' says Marofsky. 'Our relationship with Domino Consulting works because that is their reason for being as well.' ProGroup and Domino Consulting, a similarly focused consultancy based in the United Kingdom, started to share ideas and codevelop publications in 1994. Until 1998 there was no financial exchange between the organizations. In fact, one of their projects was a financial success for Domino but a failure for ProGroup. 'These relationships only succeed if you take the long view. We could have called it quits when the project failed for us. But we believe that our two organizations together can do more to grow our industry than either organization can independently. In the long run, that benefits both of us, whether we ultimately merge or remain separate entities,' states Marofsky.

At the same time, there are strong business reasons for entering into more formal arrangements that are designed to access knowledge through products rather than through relationships. ProGroup purchases learning tools and guidebooks that have been developed by others to extend and deepen their product line. These arrangements typically start with licensing agreements and end with ProGroup negotiating ownership of the other organization's intellectual property. 'These relationships build our knowledge base, but not the knowledge base of the organization with whom we have the relationship. Accessing knowledge by acquiring products is as valid a path to pursue as accessing knowledge by building relationships. However, it is clear to us that the former contributes only to our competitiveness, not the viability of our entire industry. We have to be competitive, but it will be a worthless competence if there is no industry in which to compete. In the final analysis, we want to play a part in making sure that our industry remains relevant and, perhaps, helping it to some day change the world,' concludes Marofsky.

ProGroup's core values:

◆ We are committed to the success of ProGroup and each other.

◆ We will speak well of our colleagues and clients.

◆ We hold ourselves responsible for our well-being, as well as our behaviours and decisions.

◆ We will listen with respect to each other and to our clients and will be clear and honest in all communications.

◆ We are a living laboratory and will continually grow and learn through research, education and experience.

◆ We will partner with clients and do our best to identify and address their needs.

◆ Once we make a commitment to a client, we will meet or exceed it.

◆ We recognize the diversity of ProGroup as a strength to be accepted and appreciated.

◆ Good intent is assumed and we act in ways that build trust.

◆ Although we are doing serious work, our workplace will be a positive place where we can laugh and have fun.

Think about it!

Think about the way in which your organization partners with other organizations using networked relationships and strategic partnerships or alliances. Think of one partnering effort that you felt was successful and another one that was less so. Circle the words that best describe each of those relationships. When you have completed the table, see if any patterns emerge that seem to distinguish your successful partnering effort from the one that was less successful.

	Successful partnering effort		Unsuccessful partnering effort	
Operating style was...	Formal	Informal	Formal	Informal
People generally said they felt...	Uncomfortable	Comfortable	Uncomfortable	Comfortable
Integration of work processes was...	Tight	Loose	Tight	Loose
Norms about knowledge sharing were...	Explicit	Implicit	Explicit	Implicit
Knowledge-based growth favoured...	One partner	Both partners	One partner	Both partners
Values were...	Different	Similar	Different	Similar
Partners were...	Colocated	Linked virtually	Colocated	Linked virtually
Agreement was...	Typical	Unique	Typical	Unique

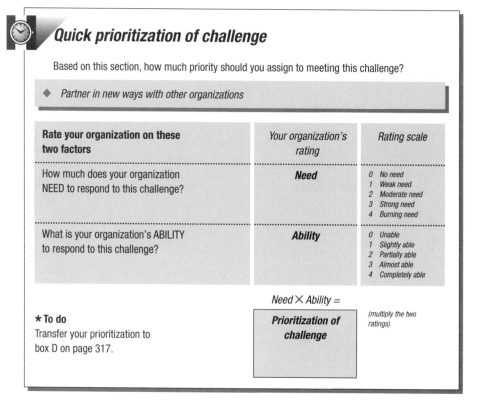

Quick prioritization of challenge

Based on this section, how much priority should you assign to meeting this challenge?

◆ Partner in new ways with other organizations

Rate your organization on these two factors	Your organization's rating	Rating scale
How much does your organization NEED to respond to this challenge?	**Need**	0 No need 1 Weak need 2 Moderate need 3 Strong need 4 Burning need
What is your organization's ABILITY to respond to this challenge?	**Ability**	0 Unable 1 Slightly able 2 Partially able 3 Almost able 4 Completely able

Need × Ability =

★ To do
Transfer your prioritization to box D on page 317.

Prioritization of challenge

(multiply the two ratings)

Retain the right people

Charity begins at home. If organizations can form unique and enduring relationships with those closest to them – their own employees – they stand a better chance of forming these relationships among internal units, with other organizations and with customers. To retain the right people, organizations often use more stick than carrot. Non-compete agreements are becoming standard issue in employment contracts, spelling out the penalties for taking expertise that the organization considers proprietary into the marketplace. According to Pearl Meyer, a New York compensation consultant, 20% to 25% of middle managers joining a new company now sign employment agreements, up from 5% or less in the late 1980s.[4] Non-compete agreements are used to make it more difficult for the individual employee to take know-how and shop it around. In the United States, these agreements are often difficult to enforce, rendering them less effective than most companies would like them to be.

However, organizations are going to greater lengths to protect their intellectual property than ever before. In part this is because as information flows more freely within organizations, heedless of hierarchical position, more people have access to mission-critical, and often sensitive knowledge. For example, in April 1997 The Dow Chemical Company sued General Electric Company for hiring fourteen former employees of its plastics division, an act that was characterized as stealing trade secrets. One of the former Dow Chemical employees was a 32-year-old engineer, hardly the kind of employee who is typically thought to possess critical corporate knowledge. Yet a state court judge in Michigan ordered that GE transfer the engineer to a job in a different area to ensure that the knowledge he acquired at Dow could not be used in the same way at GE.[5]

The problem with the stick approach is that it can lead to a siege mentality among employees. If you share more than you have to, people will know everything that you know. Once the knowledge is visible, the organization can protect it and restrict your using it as you see fit. When individual and organizational agendas diverge, the problems mount. While the stick is a necessary evil that organizations must use to protect their intellectual capital, it only extends to that which is legally recognized. There is much other knowledge that cannot be legally protected and organizations need to know how to safeguard it as well. That is where the carrot approach comes in. First of all, organizations need to know which people possess mission-critical skills. Human resources systems are now available that can help an organization keep track of and easily zero in on employees with important skills so that retention strategies can be planned and implemented (see Point of view). At SmithKline Beecham, an organization-wide system stores information about individual competencies, accomplishments and career objectives. The system is used by managers to make sure that people with leadership potential are not barred from career development moves that would benefit both them and the organization.

But this of course begs the question – what are mission-critical skills? Clearly those that pertain to the core competence of the organization belong in the basket. However, in knowledge-based organizations, skills such as innovative thinking and knowledge-sharing ability are also being tossed into the mix. In organizations that recognize the importance of building and sustaining knowledge, a new set of attributes is being recognized as valuable and explicitly incorporated into the employee retention strategy.

▶ POINT OF VIEW ▶ *Monitoring the development of mission-critical knowledge*

Organizations recognize that they need an enterprise-wide plan for identifying and developing employees whose skill sets are critical to the future. A new class of enterprise-wide skills management tools helps organizations achieve this objective in a systematic, proactive way.

Resumix provides advanced automated staffing and skills management solutions that help organizations source and identify the most qualified people to accomplish strategic corporate objectives. The company uses a combination of integrated artificial intelligence technology, image processing, client/server architecture and database technology to incorporate both hard and soft information about applicants or employees in its analysis of skill sets. 'Most organizations use the system to manage a very specific slice of knowledge management. They have a position that needs to be filled and want to find the best person to fill it,' says Dr Kathy Brush, Vice President of Marketing. 'However, we are beginning to see some organizations wake up to the power of using the system across the full spectrum of knowledge management which includes aligning the human resource retention strategy with the overall business strategy.'

For the Resumix approach to function properly, employees must maintain a current version of their resumé on the system. 'We find that employees who are interested in being considered for growth positions – the ones who possess the behavioural characteristics most organizations seek – are motivated to keep their resumes up to date,' remarks Brush. The Resumix system scans all resumés in the database. Its artificial intelligence application reads the words in context, using 140,000 grammar rules to determine the precise type of skills that any one person possesses. Once all resumés have been analyzed, the system then applies a set of algorithms to match skills to a specific set of job requirements. The same analysis can be compiled at the aggregate level to conduct a gap analysis of the overall organization's skill base compared with its strategic requirements.

Retention systems such as this are increasingly important for large or rapidly growing organizations that are unable to keep track of resident skill sets. 'Individuals can use the system to track their own development plans against the needs of the organization,' says Brush. 'This kind of system offers employees a tool for career management that fills in some of the hollowness of "employability". It is a win–win for the employee and the organization.' On the drawing board is a new suite of workforce planning products that will explicitly incorporate behavioural characteristics into the system using an instrument such as the Meyers Briggs Personality Indicator. In addition, information about employee career objectives, performance evaluations and employee availability will be part of the new system. 'We want to help organizations do a better job visualizing their human resource knowledge base along multiple dimensions so that they can explicitly manage these resources to meet strategic objectives,' concludes Brush.

Think about it!

Think about how well your organization retains its mission-critical knowledge. In the left-hand column, list what most people in your organization or group would say are the top five types of mission-critical knowledge. Then think about how well positioned you are to retain it by circling 'yes' or 'no' in response to the questions in the columns to the right.

Top five types of mission-critical knowledge	Do you know which group or individuals possess it?	Do you have a system or process in place to ensure that you retain these people?
1	Yes No	Yes No
2	Yes No	Yes No
3	Yes No	Yes No
4	Yes No	Yes No
5	Yes No	Yes No

Quick prioritization of challenge

Based on this section, how much priority should you assign to meeting this challenge?

◆ *Retain the right people*

Rate your organization on these two factors	Your organization's rating	Rating scale
How much does your organization NEED to respond to this challenge?	*Need*	0 No need 1 Weak need 2 Moderate need 3 Strong need 4 Burning need
What is your organization's ABILITY to respond to this challenges	*Ability*	0 Unable 1 Slightly able 2 Partially able 3 Almost able 4 Completely able

Need × *Ability* =

★ **To do**	*Prioritization of challenge*
Transfer your prioritization to box E on page 318.	*(multiply the two ratings)*

293

3 Recognition

The organization sees how to extract the value embedded in knowledge

Information technology has blasted apart the tangible world, yielding entirely new ways of creating value. Knowledge that was previously buried suddenly floats to the surface or the technology itself creates entirely new types of knowledge. The challenge for well-established organizations is to set aside the blinders of bias and habit that come from experience in order to see how to extract value from new and newly uncovered knowledge.

Organizations that are trying to peer into this new world of value creation must face these *challenges*.

Challenges

◆ *Use knowledge to strengthen the customer relationship.*

◆ *Disassemble the organizational whole to take a fresh look at its parts.*

Use knowledge to strengthen the customer relationship

The simple exchange of money for a product or service is being transformed into an incredibly complex relationship with the realization that information is part of the swap. Organizations recognize that information itself is value in an unrealized state. The widespread use of sophisticated means for extracting, storing and combining information has raised the stakes for organizations that want to claim and protect their market position. As a result, organizations are working hard to open channels between themselves and customers that promote the flow of information. At the most basic level, they want to know demographic information, past purchasing patterns and intentions to purchase in the future. However, to sustain competitive advantage, companies want customers to participate in product development and refinement decisions. They want to get to know them intimately so that the relationship becomes a long-term proposition.

The availability of sophisticated information technologies not only makes it possible to share customer information across an enterprise, it has also created the expectation among customers that this information *will* be shared. Why should a customer have to supply the same information to four different departments of the same company? Guests at The Ritz Carlton already pay a premium for the level of service and the quality of its rooms and facilities. Using information technology the organization is now able to leverage the relationship one property might have with a customer across the entire organization. A guest who frequents The Ritz Carlton in Boston is no longer surprised when her personal preferences are known on a first visit to The Ritz Carlton in Kansas City (see Profile).

Gathering customer information is generally burdensome to customers when they are required to offer it. This is one reason why Ritz Carlton chooses to collect its guest preference information solely through observation. For organizations that continue to gather customer data the old-fashioned way – by asking – there may soon be a price to pay. Internet-based companies already use information provided by the customers who visit their sites to funnel a specialized set of related information and services back to them. The Internet site functions as a broker, ensuring that the customer base (known as a community) only receives information or services that match their needs. Companies wanting to reach this community vie for the right and pay the site operator for access. At some point in the future, it is conceivable that the brokering role may disappear altogether. Customers may charge companies an access fee or demand some other form of concession for the right to advertise to them. Labelled 'reverse markets' by Internet trend spotters, this is not truly a new phenomenon. Producers and distributors of grocery items have long extracted concessions from grocery stores in the form of valuable shelf positioning in exchange for receiving special pricing and particular products. Purchasing groups are not new either. Small companies have banded together to form large groups that muscle price concessions out of those who wish to sell to them in exchange for volume purchasing.

What is new about the economic model that is developing on the Internet is its explicit valuing of information, its future orientation (the information obtained by web sites embodies the potential to create value at some future date) and its direct link to the end-user of the service or product. The raw potential of customer information for conversion into future value turns up the volume on the importance of building and maintaining strong relationships with key customer groups.

> PROFILE *The Ritz Carlton Hotel Company*

Many organizations in the hospitality industry are relentless about asking their customers for feedback so that they can improve service. At The Ritz Carlton Hotel Company, the burden of gathering feedback does not fall on the customer. Instead Ritz Carlton employees, trained in the fine art of detecting customer preferences, unobtrusively read between the lines, gathering detailed information about what their guests do and do not like so that each subsequent visit to a Ritz Carlton property becomes an increasingly personalized experience.

Despite the legendary heritage of its name, The Ritz Carlton Hotel Company LLC is relatively new. Founded in 1983 when William B. Johnson bought The Ritz Carlton Hotel in Boston and the rights to the Ritz Carlton name, the company has used the standard of service established by the Boston landmark as its benchmark. The original Ritz Carlton revolutionized the concept of hospitality in the United States, catering to the very wealthy in a luxury setting by taking an extremely personalized approach to caring for its privileged guests.

The company quickly grew from a single hotel to 30 within ten years. From the outset, management realized that to preserve its legacy of pampering guests and creating 'a home away from home', attention to their personal preferences could not falter. As President and Chief Operating Officer, Horst Schulze noted when the company was in its infancy, what customers ultimately want is recognition. The challenge was how to take the level of recognition that is possible in a single hotel and achieve it across the enterprise, so that one-time guests who found themselves in a city with a Ritz Carlton would make it their first choice.

The core insight that guests value recognition and personal attention has led The Ritz Carlton to eschew traditional industry approaches to customer relations. The company refuses to participate in frequent flyer programmes that give customers mileage points in exchange for patronage – they consider this purchasing loyalty rather than earning it. They are also committed to gathering customer information in a subtle and unobtrusive fashion. While customers can fill out the brief surveys left in rooms, they are never badgered for feedback with questionnaires shoved under their doors or presented to them at checkout. The Ritz Carlton has taken a different route. A critical part of the job description of every employee – from housemaid to bellhop to reservations clerk to restaurant manager – is to collect information on guest preferences. Everyone is issued a 'preference pad' which is used to note anything they observe about a guest that might help the company offer better, more personalized service during future stays. All employees receive intensive training in how to observe and gather useful customer preference information.

'We began by just collecting preference data on so-called VIPs,' explains Dan Collins, Vice President, Marketing, Revenue Management and Distribution Support. 'But now as soon as any guest comes to us, we initiate a guest profile. Of course we gather basics, such as the type of bed customers choose, or whether they prefer smoking or non-smoking rooms. But we also look for the less obvious – What did the customer use from the minibar? Did they select apples or bananas from the complementary fruit basket? Do they like to be near an elevator or an ice machine? Did they request extra towels or pillows?'

This information is reviewed by a guest recognition coordinator who determines which of it is actionable. It is then entered into a company-wide database. Information technology has enabled The Ritz Carlton to leverage its customer knowledge across the entire organization, which now consists of 35 hotels and resorts worldwide. The most recent development has been customized software, which Ritz Carlton considers a work in progress, to capture and share this customer knowledge. Standard records ensure that basic information is always collected, from name and address to preferences for payment, how the customer likes to be addressed and language spoken. These templates also make it easier to input, organize and access customer data. The database interfaces with the property management system, and there is now direct communication between all properties in the company.

Says Collins, 'The system puts a lot of information at our fingertips so we don't have to spend time on the phone with a customer gathering information about their preferences. Most companies would chalk that saved time up to greater efficiency and shorten the reservations process. But we take a different approach. We stay on the phone those extra twenty seconds to see whether there is one more thing we can find out about guests that we can use to make their stays more enjoyable.' It all adds up to a level of service that The Ritz Carlton views as its hallmark and which its customers have come to expect.

Think about it!

Use the following space to consider your organization's current status in building strong relationships with key customer groups that possess information critical to sustaining competitive advantage. List the top five customer groups whose opinions and ideas about your products and services are critical to your organization's future. Place an 'x' on the scale to the right of each box to estimate the strength of your organization's relationship with these groups.

Strength of relationship

Customer group	Strong	Neutral	Weak
	◆------------------┼------------------◆		
	◆------------------┼------------------◆		
	◆------------------┼------------------◆		
	◆------------------┼------------------◆		
	◆------------------┼------------------◆		

Quick prioritization of challenge

Based on this section, how much priority should you assign to meeting this challenge?

◆ *Use knowledge to strengthen the customer relationship*

Rate your organization on these two factors	Your organization's rating	Rating scale
How much does your organization NEED to respond to this challenge?	**Need**	0 No need 1 Weak need 2 Moderate need 3 Strong need 4 Burning need
What is your organization's ABILITY to respond to this challenge?	**Ability**	0 Unable 1 Slightly able 2 Partially able 3 Almost able 4 Completely able

Need × Ability =

★ To do
Transfer your prioritization to box F on page 319.

Prioritization of challenge

(multiply the two ratings)

Disassemble the organizational whole to take a fresh look at its parts

To understand the value-creating potential of knowledge, organizations need to condone the disaggregation of the whole in order to reexamine the nature of the parts. In an era of holistic and systems thinking, it might seem counterintuitive to suggest that organizations should actively take themselves apart to find new ways of creating value. But the type of disaggregation that is proposed here differs from the mechanistic approach that has dominated reengineering in which the whole is disassembled to look for ways of making it cheaper, faster and better.

In this case, the whole is taken apart in order to create something new, rather than improve something that already exists. The term 're-purposing' has been coined as a way of describing how organizations take a product, process or other know-how and place it in a new context to create a different value proposition. In many instances it is difficult to recognize that the parts which mesh seamlessly to make the whole can be 're-purposed'. For example, when organizations develop an expertise in a support function, it can be very difficult to overcome the feeling that a competitive advantage is being 'given away' by re-purposing that expertise as a consulting service. The same concern prevents organizations from considering how their technology systems and the information in them have the potential to not only improve existing processes and their outputs, but also to serve as the raw material for products or services themselves. However, when organizations overcome these biases, the results can reinvent an industry as they have at Massey Ferguson, an agricultural equipment manufacturer (see Profile).

Information technology has profoundly altered the landscape of possibilities for commerce and how companies perceive their products and services. Rayport and Sviokla, in two *Harvard Business Review* articles,[6] introduced the concepts of the 'marketspace' and the virtual value chain to describe a radically new environment for conceiving, developing and selling products and services. The market*space* is a cyber-analogue to the traditional marketplace. Each day that another person establishes an Internet account, more of us become more comfortable with this new marketspace. Purchasing an airline ticket over the Internet is one way to enter the marketspace. The ticket agent and the ticket itself – once staples of the value-creation process fully located in the physical realm – are gone. In their place is an interaction with a computer, creating a set of digital information that secures a seat on an airplane. The content – the ticket – is gone, replaced by a set of digital information that secures the right to a seat. The context in which the ticket was purchased – an interaction with a travel agent – has been transformed into an electronic interaction. The infrastructure – the airplane and airport – are still intact, but only until we, like members of the starship Enterprise, can ask Scotty to 'beam us up'.

This transformation of content, context and infrastructure defines the marketspace. The virtual value chain comes into existence as a direct result of recognizing and manipulating the information that is created or freed up as a result of transacting business in the marketspace. Amazon.com, the on-line bookseller, exploits the value embedded in its virtual value chain when customers engage in on-line dialogues about the books they have purchased. These on-line dialogues generate interest among other potential purchasers at very little cost to Amazon. They are a form of almost free advertising that is perceived as highly credible by customers because it comes from readers, not publishers, of books. Moving the transaction of purchasing a book to a virtual environment permits Amazon.com to exploit a virtual value chain that would not be possible in the physical world.

Conversely, the unbundling of skills needed to develop and sell products and services in the market*space*, has forced many organizations to reexamine their portfolios to see how their products and services might be unbundled and re-purposed to create value in the market*place*. The relentless advent of new technologies has disturbed our notions of how tightly certain types of knowledge are bound to their hosts. New technologies have been able to embed highly sophisticated knowledge directly into products. Seeds that can detect and ward off certain pests, tyres that sense when they are not operating correctly and communicate to the driver via a dashboard warning device, automobile directional systems that can produce a map indicating the most direct route to a destination – all are ways in which knowledge has been unbundled to create value. Technology has raised the stakes for organizations and made it increasingly important to willingly and aggressively examine all expressions of know-how from every angle to ensure that all possible value combinations are explored before a competitor detects them.

PROFILE ▶ *Massey Ferguson*

Massey Ferguson, owned by Atlanta-based AGCO, one of the worldwide market leaders in agricultural equipment, is at the vanguard of creating 'smart' equipment that embeds the expertise of the skilled farmer directly into the tractors and harvesters used to sow and reap crops.

While great advances have been made in farming equipment throughout the decades, information and communications technologies transformed the industry in the late 1980s. Before then, it was difficult, if not impossible, to determine precisely the productivity of many agricultural activities. Farmers had detailed information about the inputs they used to grow crops – nutrients, fertilizers, pesticides, seeds, etc. But determining the output – yield – was tricky, and farming equipment did not contribute to an understanding of agricultural productivity. It was big, heavy and stupid!

The traditional method of calculating yields called for placing crops in a trailer, hauling them to a weigh bridge and subtracting the weight of the trailer. Then the size of the field from which the trailerload had come was approximated so that the crop weight over the field size could be used to determine average yields. Yield measurement improved when a mechanism was developed for the combine harvester that calculated and displayed cumulative and spot yield rates. But the breakthrough idea that led to being able to precisely plot the yields of the entire field at virtually any spot came from an engineer who sat in a field with other engineers and farmers and idly wondered about uplinking the harvesters to satellites.

What if information from the harvesters could be relayed to satellites that sent back information about the exact point on the earth on which the harvester was working? What if a map could be created from that data? As it happened, that satellite system did exist. The United States Defense Department had just opened access to its Global Positioning System. Between the harvester and the satellites, a complete topographical colour-coded map of a field's yield per yard could be generated. Massey Ferguson dubbed this system Fieldstar™, its Precision Farming system. Once yields were known, investment decision making could be improved.

Going forward, Massey Ferguson anticipates embedding even more intelligence into its equipment that will not only provide retrospective information (how much did you get?), but also prospective information (how should you plant?). Yield information along with other data about soil conditions can be used to set parameters in the sowing equipment to specify precise levels of inputs for virtually each square yard of a field. Managing inputs and measuring outputs will give farmers the ability to improve profit margins and farm in a more environmentally friendly way.

In 1998 Massey Ferguson and Norsk Hydro, the largest fertilizer manufacturer in Europe, collaborated on a pilot project for a smart tractor. The tractor can 'ask' a growing crop how much nitrogen it needs as it approaches a particular spot and then deliver exactly the right amount from the rear of the tractor as it passes over it. Knowledge that was inseparable from engineers and farmers has been extracted, captured, organized, converted and embedded in smart machines, leaving the engineers and farmers time and space to ask more 'what if?' questions.

 Think about it!

Unbundling knowledge from products and services to determine if it can be used differently, as well as thinking about information that feeds into decision-making processes as stand-alone sources of value, is a new practice for most organizations.

Use the following space to play around with how knowledge can be re-purposed. Take three of your organization's products, services or types of information and list their knowledge components. Then, let your imagination run wild as you ruminate on ways to re-purpose them. For example, consulting firms can package some of their analysis in software applications or paper-based diagnostic tools. Companies like Saturn, the General Motors manufacturing unit, take expertise in team building and sell it as a consulting service.

Product, service or information	Knowledge components	Re-purposed as what type of new product or service? (individually or collectively)
1	a	
	b	
	c	
2	a	
	b	
	c	
3	a	
	b	
	c	

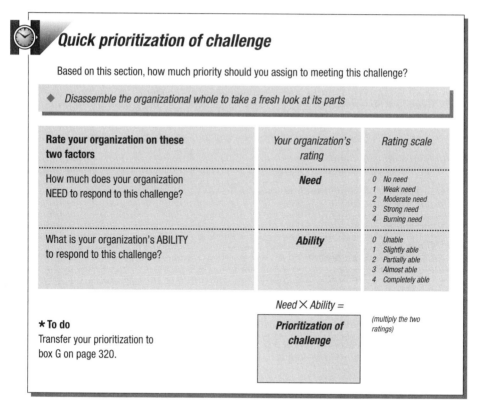

Quick prioritization of challenge

Based on this section, how much priority should you assign to meeting this challenge?

◆ *Disassemble the organizational whole to take a fresh look at its parts*

Rate your organization on these two factors	Your organization's rating	Rating scale
How much does your organization NEED to respond to this challenge?	*Need*	0 No need 1 Weak need 2 Moderate need 3 Strong need 4 Burning need
What is your organization's ABILITY to respond to this challenge?	*Ability*	0 Unable 1 Slightly able 2 Partially able 3 Almost able 4 Completely able

Need $\times$ Ability =

★ To do
Transfer your prioritization to box G on page 320.

Prioritization of challenge

(multiply the two ratings)

4 Reciprocity

Policies, procedures and cultural norms support a covenant between the organization and its members

Values embodied in policies, procedures and cultural norms are the way an organization invites individual members to participate in its growth and development. Policies and procedures are the espoused norms of the organization. Typically few people know what they are or where to find them. The operating norms are what people instinctively recognize as the real rules for determining conduct and assigning accountability. Operating norms provide answers to the basic questions of engagement with the organization: What is the obligation of the organization to its stakeholders? What is the obligation of the member to the organization? When operating and espoused norms converge, the result is a high-trust environment. People in high-trust environments feel confident that what is said will be done.

To ensure the give and take that will build and sustain knowledge, the organization must rise to these *challenges*.

Challenges

◆ *Demonstrate that value creation is a values proposition.*

◆ *Make room for the entire person to show up for work every day.*

Demonstrate that value creation is a values proposition

The most important insight of process reengineering – that every link in the value creation chain counts – acquires even greater significance when organizations turn to knowledge management. There, the focus widens to include the entire organizational system and the entire human being. Knowledge management also widens the perspective of value creation beyond the customer to many stakeholders. Its central tenet is that if value is to be created for customers, then value must also be created for all stakeholders. This can be seen in the set of metrics that are used to assess knowledge management performance – most of which include some method of tracking performance vis-à-vis key stakeholder groups.

At present, it might be possible to sustain competitive advantage by being very good at one type of value creation (e.g., shareholder, customer, employee, community, etc.). Over time, however, the competitive bar tends to rise in all industries and laggards learn how to mimic the leader's strengths. Value creation can no longer be visualized as a pyramid with shareholder or customer value at the apogee. Instead, the new image is a web of stakeholder value creation with all points interconnected and interdependent. When organizational values such as those at the Mutual Group (see Profile) support a view of the organization's knowledge management objectives as fashioning and sustaining a web of stakeholder value creation, they support a source of competitive advantage that is difficult to copy. This is where value creation and the set of values that frame the organization's agenda meet. Unless people within the organization can be relied upon to act in an ethical and consistent fashion, it is next to impossible to sustain a web of stakeholder value creation (see Point of view). The organization's espoused and operating norms guide individual behaviour toward collective purpose. They form the threads that string together the web of stakeholder value creation.

▶ PROFILE ▶ *Clarica*

Installing a learning platform was one way that leadership expressed its commitment to Clarica's values, providing the mechanism for information to flow freely and become available to all so that the values could be realized.

Clarica, a financial products and services organization headquartered in Waterloo, Ontario, launched its initiative to articulate the company's core values in the summer of 1997. In the not-too-distant future, Clarica's executives knew that they would subject the organization to severe stress as they put into place a plan to dramatically reshape the organization into a more dynamic, fast-paced and larger entity. Clarica would place the customer at the centre of the organization with the clear purpose of providing superior customer-perceived value. As customers' needs changed, the organization would immediately sense the shift and respond. To reach the size required to effectively compete in its markets, Clarica would acquire MetLife, integrating a new set of employees into the enlarged organization. Clarica would also demutualize. It would no longer be owned by its customers; it would now have investor-owners. These sweeping structural changes demanded that something remain constant. Clarica needed a beacon by which to navigate through turbulent times. Its values became that beacon.

Clarica leadership believed that the only way to truly articulate its values would be to include virtually everyone in the organization in the process. Without full acceptance, the values could not be an honest reflection of the organization. To gather the information needed to glean these underlying values, Clarica used the Values Technology methodology (see Point of view). All Canadian and US employees as well as all Canadian agents – about 5,500 people – were surveyed about the current level of practice with respect to values. In addition, transcripts of customer focus group sessions and documents that described the company's history were analyzed. Interviews with retirees surfaced forgotten details of the company's past. Workshops to discuss future values were conducted with Clarica's 125 senior-level managers and executives. The process culminated in the articulation of three core values for Clarica that drew on its past and illuminated the way to the future (see Figure 8.4).

While the process of articulating values was underway, Clarica's Senior Vice President of Strategic Capability, Hubert St Onge, was also implementing the information technology infrastructure needed to support the values. 'The values and the information technology complement each other,' says St Onge. 'Neither amounts to much without the other for Clarica. Without our learning platform which links us all together and to our organization's knowledge base, we would not be able to make good on our values. Both the values and the information technology helped us move away from the subcultures and divergent leadership styles that characterized our organization, toward a community of practice and a collaborative approach that we knew was necessary to thrive in the future.'

Fig 8.4 ◆ Clarica's core values

POINT OF VIEW *Understanding how values lead to value creation*

Values Technology was founded in 1992 by Dr Brian Hall whose 30 years of research on the subject has led him to conclude that human behaviour is based on 125 values.

Values are the priorities by which we live our lives. They are very basic to our lives, underpinning all of our behaviour. Behind the 125 values, we have identified 4,000 synonyms and 5,000 skills. Each person functions on about six values priorities at any given moment. Productive relationships are based on the values that two or more persons hold in common. Knowledge creation and new ideas occur out of special relationships that form when values are commonly held.

Values measurement makes an organization's values explicit and highlights where there are productive and creative or conflicted and non-productive relationships. Relationships are the channels through which an organization transforms and delivers its knowledge. The organization's management processes and business practices are an expression of these relationships and they are fuelled by common values expressed as corporate beliefs. When the values of employees are aligned with the organization's beliefs, the result is an energized, almost magical experience that is felt by the customer as well.

The reason that individuals choose certain values priorities, and the reason these choices are so important is that values give life meaning. Abraham Maslow put it another way when he noted that 'values are our motivation system'. Values underpin the very meaning of life precisely because they are connected to the two basic hinges of day-to-day existence: relationships and knowledge. Being successful in life and business has always meant having special knowledge and developing relationships – it is that simple. The success of any business is based on what the people within it know. However, knowledge must be connected to relationships. Traditional management relationships are task focused and top down. They limit creative interactions by limiting knowledge transfer and development. Today, a firm's management and team structures need to be collaborative so that business processes and customer service flow from a base of trust formed in high-quality relationships. Values priorities are the glue that holds these relationships and knowledge together. All relationships, personal and team, are based on a minimal set of commonly held values priorities.

Dr Brian Hall
Values Technology

Think about it!

Use the following space to think about how your organization's values support building knowledge that allows you to create value for key stakeholders. List your values, the impact that each value has on your organization's ability to build and sustain knowledge and the stakeholder groups most affected by these values in the spaces provided.

For example, a value embracing diversity might be extremely important in terms of achieving innovative solutions. When organizations are able to work with different perspectives, this often leads to breakthroughs in thinking (impact on knowledge). This type of knowledge would be very important to customers who need unique solutions.

	Values	Impact on knowledge	Stakeholder groups
1			
2			
3			
4			
5			
6			
7			

Quick prioritization of challenge

Based on this section, how much priority should you assign to meeting this challenge?

◆ *Demonstrate that value creation is a values proposition*

Rate your organization on these two factors	Your organization's rating	Rating scale
How much does your organization NEED to respond to this challenge?	*Need*	0 No need 1 Weak need 2 Moderate need 3 Strong need 4 Burning need
What is your organization's ABILITY to respond to this challenge?	*Ability*	0 Unable 1 Slightly able 2 Partially able 3 Almost able 4 Completely able

Need × Ability =

★ **To do**
Transfer your prioritization to box H on page 321.

Prioritization of challenge

(multiply the two ratings)

Make room for the entire person to show up for work every day

The well-known story of how 3M's Post-It® Notes were invented seems a little shopworn, but it is worth mentioning because in addition to the many other truths that it contains is one about the entire person showing up for work every day. One of the inventors of Post-It® Notes was not only a research chemist, he was also an active member of his church's choir. Every Sunday the choir needed to mark the hymnal with the songs for that week's service. Each week the songs changed, so the markers could not be permanent. The research chemist got tired of the markers falling out of the hymnal when he flipped from one page to the next. He knew about a 10-year-old adhesive with interesting physical properties that seemed to be either too weak or too strong for any known application. Affixing this adhesive to paper and then using the treated papers as markers was the perfect solution to the hymnal problem. Would Post-It® Notes have been invented without the inspiration of the church hymnals? Maybe, but maybe not.

Each company has its own stories of the product or service that might not have been if someone had not been inspired by a weird and wacky source that had ostensibly had absolutely nothing to do with their work life. Chinaberry, a mail order book service, has numerous stories of how its employees' personal interests have led to business innovations (see Profile). If the interests of home and work life are comingled, the possibilities for mutual enrichment are high. For example, at The Mining Company (recently renamed About.com), an Internet company that hosts communities of interest, employees are encouraged to use their interests and backgrounds to help evaluate subject material. As a result an individual with an interest in sports and a professional background as an investment banker became the editor in charge of the business and sports 'hubs'. A woman who was a native of Russia was asked to evaluate people who wanted to serve as web site guides for Russian literature, even though this was unrelated to her job.

Building and sustaining knowledge requires the organization to take a holistic view of the employee and recognize that beyond the immediate skills the employee brings to his or her tasks there is a range of interests and abilities that are potentially valuable to the enterprise. Somehow the organization must take care not to cordon off these extra-curricular talents even if their applicability is not always apparent. These talents combine with work-specific skills to form the web of associations that translate into creative insight. They are a rich source of emotional enthusiasm that organizations are ill-advised to keep out of the work environment.

Skandia, an insurance organization headquartered in Sweden, has added a novel twist to the idea of making room for the whole person to show up for work every day. In 1997 the company introduced the idea of involving its three generations of employees in the strategic planning process. Five Future Teams were established with members ranging in age from their early 20s to their 60s. These teams engaged in structured encounters designed to stimulate multi-generational dialogue about the company's future. Their work was ultimately presented to Skandia's leadership in a highly unconventional format – for example, in one case, a group of professional actors was engaged to perform a play written by a member of the Future Team. The Future Teams project created a model for thinking differently not only about the big picture at Skandia, but also about the tactics that are used to realize the vision. The need to develop leaders who can listen to and incorporate ideas from different generations has influenced the way the organization thinks about its management development programs. In 1999 it launched a programme for its Nordic team that explicitly sought to develop a competence in making room for all three generations to contribute to Skandia's future.[7]

In our workplaces, we often treat people as if one tiny little corner of their minds is all we want them to bring to the workplace. In the case of 'knowledge workers' the problem is that this tiny little corner of the mind may not be the place from which inspiration arises. More often than not, inspiration is a happy confluence of the entire mind and body. If inspiration and innovation are sought-after ideals, the entire person is going to have to show up for work every day.

PROFILE ▶ *Chinaberry Book Service*

'Everybody here has a voice, and everyone is encouraged to contribute,' says Chinaberry's first employee, Mary Arter. Contribution often takes the form of some personal passion or commitment that has its origins outside the workplace.

Chinaberry Book Service is a mail order catalogue company which sells books and other items targeted to children, parents and families. The company began as an exercise in self-expression. Founder Ann Ruethling, a homemaker who had begun a personal quest to find positive, non-violent and non-sexist literature to read to her toddler daughter, decided that others could benefit from her extensive research. The book service started, not as a business, but as a way to communicate with like-minded parents who were concerned about the kinds of books their children were exposed to. 'The only reason we started selling the books I'd discovered was because we didn't want people to read about them and then not be able to get hold of them,' notes Ruethling.

As the company grew beyond the confines of her home and family, Ruethling began to think about creating a work environment that would reflect the same values that guided her choice of books, particularly a belief in the importance of the individual. The company now employs between 20 and 30 full- and part-time people, taking on an additional 30 or 40 during the Christmas holiday season. This is also the time of year that Chinaberry 'thanks' its employees by featuring their pictures and a brief description of them in the holiday catalogue, giving customers a glimpse of the people who make up this very personal company.

Mary Arter tells the story of a former chef who joined Chinaberry, a woman who also had a particular knack for connecting with customers. 'She loved the image of our customers getting together, and one day she had the idea of creating a cookbook made up of recipes from Chinaberry customers. She was so enthusiastic about the concept that she said she'd put it together on her own time. And she very nearly did!' Today, *The Chinaberry Cookbook* is a consistent seller.

Ruethling points to other examples of how employees with deep concerns about community and the environment have changed the way work is being done at Chinaberry. 'The woman who is in charge of our returns to publishers couldn't stand the fact that the publishers were simply ripping off the covers of slightly damaged books and tossing them. So she decided to initiate partnerships with publishers to donate books to worthy causes.' Another person in the Chinaberry warehouse has taken it upon herself to set up a recycling centre. Employees who have no service near their homes can bring in their recyclables. The company also recycles packing materials to use on outgoing packages whenever possible.

'Work is a microcosm of life,' says Ruethling. 'We learn many valuable things about life in the workplace.' But the organization's commitment to embracing its employees as individuals has meant the business has benefited from what people bring to it from their everyday lives.

Think about it!

How much do you know about the passions and outside interests of the people who work for or with you? Pick a work team that you either manage or of which you are a member. List the members of that team and their extra-curricular activities or interests in the spaces provided in the following table. Have you or could you use their passions to further work-related goals?

Work team members	Their passions or outside interests
1	
2	
3	
4	
5	
6	

Quick prioritization of challenge

Based on this section, how much priority should you assign to meeting this challenge?

◆ *Make room for the entire person to show up for work every day*

Rate your organization on these two factors	Your organization's rating	Rating scale	
How much does your organization NEED to respond to this challenge?	*Need*	0 No need 1 Weak need 2 Moderate need 3 Strong need 4 Burning need	
What is your organization's ABILITY to respond to this challenge?	*Ability*	0 Unable 1 Slightly able 2 Partially able 3 Almost able 4 Completely able	

Need × Ability =

★ To do
Transfer your prioritization to box I on page 322.

Prioritization of challenge

(multiply the two ratings)

311

Notes

1 *New Rules for the New Economy*, Kevin Kelly, Penguin Putnam, New York, 1998.

2 You can read more about this study in 'The chief knowledge officer: a new corporate role', M.J. Earl and I.A. Scott, *Sloan Management Review*, Winter 1999.

3 'Can Daimler's tiny "Swatchmobile" sweep Europe?', Brandon Mitchener, *The Wall Street Journal*, October 2 1998, p. B1.

4 'More managers have trouble jumping ship', Ann Davis and Joann S. Lublin, op. cit..

5 Op. cit.

6 'Managing in the marketspace', Jeffrey F. Rayport and John J. Sviokla, *Harvard Business Review*, November–December 1994. 'Exploiting the virtual value chain', Jeffrey F. Rayport and John J. Sviokla, *Harvard Business Review*, November–December 1995.

7 Interview with Anita Schedin, Skandia, and 'How Skandia generates its future faster', Polly LaBarre, *Fast Company*, December/January 1997.

Agenda for action: Build and Sustain

The action steps presented in the Agenda for action come from the ideas suggested in this chapter. If you believe that your organization needs to focus on improving how well it builds and sustains knowledge, this template and its suggested action steps are one way to get started.

The Agenda for action is organized in the same way as the chapter. Each imperative and its accompanying challenges are clustered together. Action steps are suggested for each challenge based on the text and case studies. You decide which action steps make sense for your organization and use the empty space to scribble in any additional ideas that come to mind.

Before you begin, make sure that you have transferred your prioritization ratings for each challenge. The prioritization ratings will remind you whether you believed that the challenge was worth pursuing. The maximum prioritization rating is 16, the minimum is 0.

How you use the prioritization ratings is up to you. For example, depending on the range of prioritization ratings, you may decide to ignore all challenges below a minimum threshold and focus only on those challenges above it. Or you may decide that everything that is not 0 deserves at least some thought. We invite you to use this Agenda for action as a place to start acting on your knowledge management priorities.

Agenda for action

1 Direction

Resources are channelled in ways that replenish and create knowledge

A

Subordinate information technology to people

Prioritization rating

Action step	Who should be involved	My first 'to do'
Canvass groups that rely heavily on the information technology system to find out: 1) how well it provides them with the knowledge they need to get their work done and 2) what they would like to keep and change about the current system to better meet their needs.		
Compare information about what works and what does not work vis-à-vis the IT system across groups to identify similarities and differences in IT-supported knowledge needs.		
Open up the discussion to customers and suppliers. If they use the system, include them in the first action step. If they do not use the system, find out how access to it might improve not only their operations, but also ours.		
Determine the extent to which our IT system promotes the formation of new networks of people and find stories of how these new relationships affected our ability to improve business processes and/or performance.		
Other:		

B

Structure positions that focus organizational attention on intellectual capital

Prioritization rating

Action step	Who should be involved	My first 'to do'
Convene a small team from among the areas of the organization most concerned about knowledge management to sketch out the business case for a knowledge management executive and/or central knowledge management group in our organization.		
Describe the roles and responsibilities of a knowledge management group and/or a knowledge management executive.		
Consider existing people within the organization who might step into knowledge management roles and discuss the possibility with them.		
Consider existing groups within the organization that might be transitioned into a knowledge management role.		
Collect information about what both our competitors and some leading knowledge management organizations are doing in this area.		
Other:		

2 Connection

The organization forms relationships that further its knowledge management objectives

C

Preach cooperation among internal divisions

Prioritization rating

Action step	Who should be involved	My first 'to do'
Scan across our business segments to identify knowledge or technology that is currently used by more than one segment.		
Determine how our policies support or hinder cross-segment cooperation to develop knowledge or technologies.		
Collect information about what our competitors are doing in this area.		
Convene a cross-business segment group to map current and anticipated customer needs to existing and future knowledge and technologies. Discuss how to increase sharing knowledge and technologies across the segments.		
Other:		

D

Partner in new ways with other organizations

Prioritization rating

Action step	Who should be involved	My first 'to do'
Create a matrix that displays each business or unit and the type of relationships they have with other organizations.		
Canvass our suppliers and customers to see how they partner with other organizations.		
Collect information about what our competitors are doing in this area.		
Identify the business groups or units most suited to these new forms of partnership and discuss the possibility of launching pilots to experiment with them.		
Other:		

E

Retain the right people

Action step	Who should be involved	My first 'to do'
Collect turnover statistics. Try to determine: 1) planned vs. unplanned turnover, 2) types of skills and know-how that were lost when people left or were let go, 3) lag time until people find new jobs, 4) % salary difference paid in new position, 5) time and cost to reestablish optimum operating levels etc.		
Compare retention practices in the operating units with formal human resources policies.		
Determine what policies are in place to safeguard know-how and intellectual property.		
Convene a group of different operating units to identify mission-critical skills and know-how that are specific to each unit and those that are common across the units. Discuss ways to improve retention of people who possess these skills and know-how.		
Other:		

3 Recognition

The organization sees how to extract the value embedded in knowledge

F

Use knowledge to strengthen the customer relationship

Prioritization rating

Action step	Who should be involved	My first 'to do'
Identify types of information that are routinely extracted from customers as part of the standard sales transaction or post-sale customer service interactions.		
Determine if information is purchased from other sources that is currently used or might be used to strengthen existing customer relationships or develop new products and services.		
Discuss with the operating units and post-sale customer service groups how both types of information described above are used to strengthen the customer relationship and develop new products or services.		
Convene a small group of different business units to examine how existing customer information could be put to better use and what additional information should be collected going forward to improve customer relationships and develop new products and services. Also consider new ways to collect it electronically.		
Collect information about what competitors are doing.		
Other:		

G

Disassemble the organizational whole to take a fresh look at its parts

Prioritization rating

Action step	Who should be involved	My first 'to do'
Identify business units or groups that have launched a new service or product based on knowledge that was considered a byproduct of their core business.		
Interview some or all of these groups to find out how they uncovered the new service or product possibility and developed it. Specifically identify the knowledge components that were leveraged into the new product or service.		
Compare processes from these groups to detect similarities and differences.		
Determine the extent to which advances in information technology or other technologies do or might affect our organization's products or services.		
Other:		

4 Reciprocity

Policies, procedures and cultural norms support a covenant between the organization and its members

Demonstrate that value creation is a values proposition	H
	Prioritization rating

Action step	Who should be involved	My first 'to do'
Obtain the organization's espoused values. Canvass key operating unit managers to determine how clearly they link the organization's values to their unit's ability to create and share mission-critical knowledge and ultimately to serve key stakeholders.		
Contact representatives from external stakeholder groups and determine how easily they can identify our values. Discuss the impact these values have on their willingness to share information with us.		
Host a roundtable with front-line employees, managers, executives and key stakeholders to discuss findings from these efforts and to think about how we can improve our commitment to these values.		
Other:		

Make room for the entire person to show up for work every day

Prioritization rating

Action step	Who should be involved	My first 'to do'
Document stories of how people's outside interests and passions have contributed to our business – serving customers or suppliers, creating new products or services, improving organizational processes – anything!		
Find out if we formally track people's outside interests and passions or if there is an informal system, such as bulletin boards (electronic or cork board) that bring this information to the attention of others.		
Discuss with key operating managers how the organization might make better use of these interests to both build loyalty and improve organizational performance.		
Consider how these interests might help us engage some of our customers more fully with the organization.		
Other:		

9 Divest

> The greatest difficulty lies not in persuading people to accept new ideas, but in persuading them to abandon old ones.

> **John Maynard Keynes**

Organizations tend to hold on to knowledge that they have developed, even if it is no longer providing any direct competitive advantage. In fact, some forms of knowledge can be more profitable if they are used by parties outside the organization. Organizations that examine their knowledge base in terms of both opportunity costs – resources spent maintaining assets that could be better spent elsewhere – and alternative sources of value creation will realize the benefits of divestiture.

At a glance . . .

What is new?	Understanding of why, when, where and how to formally divest parts of the knowledge base.
What is the problem?	Psychological, political and measurement hurdles must be overcome for organizations to let go of knowledge because people are highly invested in owning it and the cost of maintaining it is not well understood.
What is the individual or team objective?	Incorporate opportunity cost analysis of retaining knowledge into standard management practice.
What is the organizational objective?	Understand which parts of the knowledge base will be unnecessary for sustaining competitive advantage and industry viability.

Introduction

Just as most people tend to be pack rats, so, too, organizations find it hard to shed activities and resources that at one time produced valuable outcomes. Individuals and groups are highly invested in the management of these resources and activities so the political problems involved in relocating them, often outside the organization, are thorny to negotiate. However, organizations can realize significant benefits by divesting themselves of knowledge that no longer meets their strategic objectives. Divesting non-critical knowledge frees up time and resources for growth and maintenance of knowledge that is strategically important.

Knowledge, like tangible assets, requires resources to maintain its value, and, like tangible assets, it may provide diminishing returns to the organization as the economic environment changes and new opportunities are pursued. Traditional divestiture decisions that relate to knowledge and include:

- selling, licensing or donating a patent

- spinning off or selling an unaligned business

- outsourcing a function or operating process

- terminating a training programme

- retraining, relocating or firing individuals with obsolete or ill-fitted skills

- replacing or upgrading information technology systems

- terminating partnerships, alliances and contracts.

Not many organizations undertake this step of the knowledge management process with a clear picture of their knowledge base or insight into how they are divesting parts of it. However, a growing number of organizations are beginning to develop divestiture practices for their intellectual property – a narrowly defined class of intellectual assets that is the easiest to understand because it represents the most concrete of all intellectual assets. In fact, the inspiration for adding Divest to our knowledge management framework came from the activities taking place in intellectual property (IP) management groups that are following the trend-setting lead of The Dow Chemical Company's Intellectual Asset Management Group (refer to Profiles of this group on pages 234 and 273.)

One of the most significant and under-appreciated contributions of these IP groups is the notion of divesting intellectual assets as a planned, purposeful activity. It inspired us to explore what divesting knowledge might look like as companies think strategically about knowledge management. The divest process step takes us furthest into the speculative future compared with all of the other knowledge management process steps. We are ad-libbing to some extent, because we do not really know of many companies that divest what they explicitly recognize as knowledge in a deliberate way. A more frequent scenario occurs when companies unwittingly divest knowledge, jettisoning it along with tangible assets, sometimes with a troubling sense that they are divesting more than they can account for.

To divest knowledge without sliding into organizational anorexia, leadership must be able to envision a continuous flow of knowledge into, through and out of the organization. Focus cannot be directed toward any one place in the flow, but must scan the entire stream. While considering whether or not to acquire and whether or not to dispossess, companies must master the art of the following *imperatives* and *challenges*.

Imperatives and challenges

Forbearance	Unnecessary knowledge is not acquired in the first place:
	◆ *Discriminate between forms of knowledge that can be leveraged and those that are limited.*
	◆ *Find alternatives to direct acquisition in order to experiment with knowledge.*
Conversion	Knowledge that is a drain on resources is converted into sources of value:
	◆ *Recognize and dispense with true resource drains.*
	◆ *Avoid throwing out the baby with the bathwater.*

1 Forbearance

Unnecessary knowledge is not acquired in the first place

To explore fully what divesting knowledge might look like, we want to add an unexpected 'twist' to the idea of divest: *the idea of not acquiring in the first place*. Divesting in our framework is not only about 'ridding' the organization of the tendency to hoard the unnecessary. It is also about having the strategic discipline not to acquire, not to blast ahead just because everybody else is doing it, or give in to the knee-jerk response of adding a capability because the competition is moving in that direction. This 'not acquiring' complements building and sustaining as does getting rid of non-strategic knowledge. For that reason, both fit our idea of divesting.

Forbearance might seem like a strange concept to introduce into the world of organizational strategy. Strategy brings to mind images of athletic activity: forging fearlessly into new markets or cutting through the sloth that drags down growth in existing ones. Forbearance evokes a more contemplative state of mind and a more nuanced approach to action. It is the strategic analogue of the 'learning' process step of the Knowledge Management Process Framework. Neither one is a passive state. However, both process steps seem more eastern than western in their emphasis on alert watchfulness and an economical, almost chaste intervention style.

In this way, forbearance is a new frontier for the knowledge management process. Not acquiring or creating knowledge in the first place forces organizations to conceive of new ways to pursue strategic objectives. Forbearance demands that organizations wrestle with these *challenges*.

Challenges

◆ *Discriminate between forms of knowledge that can be leveraged and those that are limited.*
◆ *Find alternatives to direct acquisition in order to experiment with knowledge.*

Discriminate between forms of knowledge that can be leveraged and those that are limited

If the competition is sinking millions into a new technology, it seems to make sense to 'wake up and smell the coffee!' After all, the competition is smart or it would not be the competition – those companies whose actions keep executives, managers and, today even the rank and file up at night worrying about the viability of their own enterprise. Shouldn't the response be to execute a quick change order to the budget and allocate at least a comparable amount of resources toward a similar effort? This is the very real dilemma that presents itself almost daily to organizations of all sizes in all industries.

The notion of discriminating between forms of knowledge that can be leveraged and those that are limited is a kissing cousin to the ideas of 'stick to your knitting' and 'focus on your core competence' espoused respectively by Tom Peters and Gary Hamel and C.K. Prahalad. The directive to focus on leveragable forms of knowledge suggests that organizations need to understand how value is created and used, and that they need to stick close to the source when venturing into new territories. This is especially true for research-intensive organizations such as Monsanto Company (see Profile) which face the daunting prospect of placing huge bets on an uncertain future and have to know when to cut their losses.

At Celemi, a rapidly growing professional services organization based in Malmö, Sweden, customers are sought out, not only for revenues, but also for their potential to stretch the knowledge base of the organization (see Profile on page 232). In the company's Intangible Assets Monitor (issued within its annual report), this intellectual capital is tracked as 'organization-enhancing customers'. On the flip side, some customers are turned away because meeting their demands will not result in knowledge that can be leveraged for growth beyond the limited purpose for which it was developed. All organizations take on or decline work that is beyond their existing capabilities, but few do it with as clear an understanding of what they are accepting or rejecting in terms of the creation of knowledge as Celemi. For Celemi, the *way* in which it grows is as important as the absolute level of growth itself. Pursuing customers at least partly based on which knowledge can be leveraged for future value creation helps this small, rapidly growing company build the knowledge base it needs in an efficient way. Celemi is able to manage the inherent tension of sustainable growth which is fuelled by both accepting and rejecting work.

Operating in this way is not limited to consulting firms where knowledge is clearly the stock in trade. DPR Construction, a Redwood, California-based company that has grown from 12 to 2,000 people since its inception in 1990, has been so successful in its knowledge-based approach to the construction industy that it has begun to turn away projects in which it cannot fully participate. Serving primarily clients in business sectors such as biotechnology, high tech, pharmaceuticals and entertainment, DPR has adopted many of the techniques and processes that are more familiar to its fast-paced clients. Not the least of these is the manner in which the company approaches learning. If DPR cannot be involved in working with clients at the beginning of a project to articulate their needs, and cannot continue to partner with them through to project completion, then DPR's own learning capacity is diminished. The company chooses to turn these projects down, pursuing others instead.[1]

Few organizations have been able to resist the allure of information technology as the ultimate lever for generating value from knowledge. IT systems are supposed to deliver friction-free conduits through which information can travel, and provide smart storage tanks that literally learn who needs what information when. However, many organizations are finding that comprehensive, fully integrated IT systems cannot deliver the leverage they had hoped for. For example, Pacific Gas & Electric Co. (PG&E),[2] a US West Coast utility company, scrapped its back-office system after two years of development when market deregulation moved much faster than the system designers could manage.

The way in which information technology applications are developed is notoriously linear. A change downstream can cause millions of lines of code to be rewritten and thousands of new glitches to appear. Yet, markets are moving quickly these days, especially those that were once regulated. Software applications that convert complex business processes to a new information system are ill-equipped to deal with the changing demands placed on them by the marketplace. PG&E revised its plans and kept a 30-year-old first-generation computer system to which it made slight modifications. At Chrysler Financial, a highly sophisticated system was scrapped in favour of a plain vanilla standard augmented by people on phones. The lesson learned by these companies: in a fast-changing environment, it may be better to resist investing in the 'latest' technology if it compromises the organization's ability to sense and respond. Information technology is not the silver bullet that transforms information into highly leveragable knowledge.

In the high-technology business, the phrase 'three dogs barking' has been used to characterize the frenzy that is whipped up every time a promising new technology breaks onto the scene. One dog begins barking, and if two more join, soon the whole kennel is a yapping zoo. Of course, the first dog could have been barking at a leaf blowing in the wind, but by the time the entire kennel is howling, no one can tell any longer. It is not easy to discriminate between forms of knowledge that can be leveraged and those that are limited, especially if your entire industry is barking after the moon. However, knowing the difference will become an increasingly important means of reducing risk and expanding the potential for growth, as organizations place bets on the future.

PROFILE ▶ *Monsanto*

The research and development centres of major corporations are a natural home for knowledge-building activities. When strategy changes and resource allocations shift within these centres, this also opens the door to divestment of knowledge. The challenge lies in strategically managing R&D to ensure that it provides the highest leverage for future value creation.

Monsanto Company, a large Life Sciences organization headquartered in St Louis, Missouri, focuses its forays into new technologies by setting its sights firmly on the future. For many years the company supported a diversified R&D programme that covered a wide range of chemical, pharmaceutical and agricultural technologies. But about 10 years ago Monsanto's senior management charted what was at the time a uniquely conceived path to become a life sciences company focused on food, health and wellness for people. 'Monsanto is close to 100 years old,' reflects Jane Rady, Vice President of Prospecting for Knowledge Management. 'In the space of about 20 years we have gone from a company that thought in terms of producing chemicals shipped in tank cars to one that thinks in terms of innovating chemicals that are shipped in test tubes. We used to serve a small number of customers who bought a commodity product in bulk. Now we serve a diverse group of customers who purchase tiny amounts of uniquely designed products. The base of knowledge that is required to be a life sciences company is profoundly different from the one we relied on to be a basic chemicals company.'

To become this new type of company, Monsanto directed its R&D activities into biotechnologies that supported advances in agriculture, nutrition and pharmaceuticals and out of its core business of basic chemicals. 'Our investment in building this knowledge base represents a huge amount of future value,' says Susan Welsh, Vice President of Knowledge Management. 'We will not realize the full impact of this knowledge in the marketplace for the next 8–15 years. However, given macroeconomic and global demographic trends, we are reasonably confident that focusing our efforts in these three areas will lead to higher leverage than if we continued to maintain a broadly diversified programme.' Narrowing the R&D focus by deepening knowledge in three core areas does not mean that Monsanto has forsaken looking in the 'white spaces' among them for innovative ideas.

Rady talks about the deliberate choice to build knowledge in areas that are the most amenable to lateral flows and lateral connections. 'When we looked down the road,' she says, 'we could not see these knowledge flows moving between our basic chemicals business and our life sciences business. That is why we spun off the basic chemicals business two years ago. It is also why our life sciences business operates as one group. Many of our competitors have imitated our focus on life sciences, but they do not integrate their businesses as we do. Building a base of knowledge that can be leveraged on behalf of the total business is central to our efforts, and our organizational structure reflects it.' This approach supports Monsanto's strategy, which views the product, not as the end point, but as a mode for delivering information and know-how. For example, Monsanto's New Leaf Superior potato has been genetically engineered to destroy its most pernicious pest, the Colorado Beetle. When a company has made the conceptual leap to think of its products as mechanisms for leveraging knowledge, it is clear that they know how to determine which elements of their knowledge base can be leveraged and which are limited.

Think about it!

To what extent can you leverage the forms of knowledge that you extract from relationships with your customers and suppliers, and the business practices related to your processes and products? For each of the categories, think in terms of specific examples. For instance, pick your top customers or your best-selling products and consider them along two dimensions of leverage – stretching your capabilities and building your knowledge base.

Category	Two specific examples	Stretch our capabilities?	Build our knowledge base?
Customer	1.	Yes No	Yes No
	2.	Yes No	Yes No
Suppliers	3.	Yes No	Yes No
	4.	Yes No	Yes No
Processes	5.	Yes No	Yes No
	6.	Yes No	Yes No
Products	7.	Yes No	Yes No
	8.	Yes No	Yes No

Quick prioritization of challenge

Based on this section, how much priority should you assign to meeting this challenge?

◆ *Discriminate between forms of knowledge that can be leveraged and those that are limited*

Rate your organization on these two factors	Your organization's rating	Rating scale
How much does your organization NEED to respond to this challenge?	*Need*	0 No need 1 Weak need 2 Moderate need 3 Strong need 4 Burning need
What is your organization's ABILITY to respond to this challenge?	*Ability*	0 Unable 1 Slightly able 2 Partially able 3 Almost able 4 Completely able

Need $\times$ *Ability =*

Prioritization of challenge

(multiply the two ratings)

★ **To do**
Transfer your prioritization to box A on page 349.

Find alternatives to direct acquisition to experiment with knowledge

To meet the uncertain and risky future head on, organizations also need to find ways of experimenting with knowledge that they might need. This can be accomplished by pursuing non-acquisition strategies such as making do with what you already have or borrowing someone else's stuff. Making do with what you already have is not only the purview of the small, resource-constrained organization. It is also the strategic choice of organizations that could otherwise make significant investments in direct acquisition such as professional services giant, Ernst & Young (see Profile). Creating the opportunity to get feedback from the market and to calibrate the forms and extent of knowledge that will be required to support market demand before making a direct acquisition is one of the strongest reasons for making do with what you already have. In Ernst & Young's case, this need was buttressed by an equally strong drive to be first to market with an innovative solution.

The most common way to borrow someone else's stuff in the business world is to enter into a strategic alliance. We discussed strategic alliances in Chapter 8 as a way of forcing more slack into organizational relationships to discover new ways of creating value. Strategic alliances are also a way to experiment with forms of knowledge without having to acquire them directly. Alliances range from informal agreements to explicit and detailed contractual relationships. For example, an organization may apprentice a technical expert to a supplier organization to determine whether certain skills should be developed. Or organizations may work through a third party, such as a research consortium, to pool knowledge from a group of companies so that the collective knowledge base can be used to reinvent or revitalize an industry. Finally, organizations can form a close working partnership short of merging that allows them to leverage knowledge to make a combined market offering. For example, The Dow Chemical Company and Du Pont, competitive rivals in most markets, formed an alliance to develop and market elastomer technology-based products such as Neoprene which is used in such consumer products as ski pants to make them water resistant. Dow provided the technology and Du Pont provided the manufacturing and marketing expertise. Each company possessed knowledge whose value was higher when combined, but neither wished to invest in building that knowledge independently.

In many instances, the cultures or organizational structures needed to successfully develop and market a form of knowledge may be so different that they cannot be sustained in a merged organization. In other instances, it does not make economic sense to acquire the hard assets that are tied to the desired knowledge. When strategic alliances work, knowledge thrives in both the separate and combined spaces. World-class levels of performance are achieved without the pain of calibrating the size of the workforce in response to the vagaries of the marketplace. Forbearance in this sense is a strategic discipline that promotes broader marketplace efficiency.

Another way to tap into an organization's knowledge base that falls short of out-and-out borrowing is to consciously locate in a specific geographic area. Michael Porter has written about a new economic form that he calls the 'cluster'.[3] Clusters are industry-focused groups that form in specific localities, drawn there by a concentration of skills and talent. The cluster becomes self-sustaining when it not only attracts newcomers, but also retains old-timers. The blend of new and old blood provides a rich base of knowledge that enhances all of the cluster's participants. For example, in Hollywood, California, the entertainment cluster includes companies involved in all aspects of the business – from technicians to talent to dealmakers. Porter describes the importance of bumping into people at social gatherings and events or attending the same civic and professional associations as one reason why clusters are firmly tethered to place. These casual encounters provide a context of trust for the exchange of ideas. Simply being in a specific place may offer opportunities to experiment with forms of knowledge without acquiring them.

Forbearance is an act of organizational self-control in the face of enormous pressures to meet competing investments head on. However, to navigate the treacherous shoals of fast-paced global markets, organizations must know how to steer around some opportunities and how to reconnoitre others to assess when, if and how to acquire knowledge.

PROFILE ▶ *Ernst & Young*

The development of Ernie, Ernst & Young's Internet service for its customers, epitomizes the 'make do with what you have and let the market be your teacher' strategy that characterizes forbearance.

When Ernst & Young, one of the Big Five professional services companies, launched its on-line service, Ernie, in May 1996, it was venturing into the then unknown medium and market of the Internet. E&Y did not create a huge new business unit or invest in a colossal infrastructure to support this new venture, but cobbled it together and got it to market quickly. 'We went from concept to first connection in 90 days with three full-time people,' recalls Bob McIlhattan, Vice Chairman of US Consulting Services. 'Two strategic decisions at the outset made this speed to market possible. First, we stuck to our knitting. E&Y delivers solutions, not products. Ernie is a solution, not a product. Second, we focused on adding value to the client relationship with an innovative approach that met untapped needs of both our traditional client base and companies for whom our traditional services were priced out of reach.'

Several other factors also contributed to E&Y's ability to rapidly deploy Ernie. The company viewed Ernie as a marketing rather than a technology challenge. Speed to market dominated the service development process, not technology. Most critical of all, E&Y reversed the prevailing wisdom of the Internet at the time and opted for a pull rather than a push model for Ernie. Rather than amass a large database of information and push it to customers, they engineered a channel through which customers could ask E&Y questions and get a response from an expert. 'We used the market to improve Ernie,' recounts Chuck Benson, National Director for Connected Consulting. 'Our overriding goal was to improve learning – not just for the client, but also for E&Y. We needed the market to provide continuous input and feedback to help us develop Ernie in ways that truly delivered value.' Market input and feedback led E&Y to evolve Ernie into a self-service model from its original 'you ask–we answer' roots. Over time, the company has placed more and more of its analytical tools on Ernie, giving clients direct access to its consulting methodologies.

These changes in Ernie have contributed to and reflected changes in the way that E&Y views its relationship with all clients, not just the small, rapidly growing companies that were Ernie's original target market. For the small, rapidly growing company, Ernie provided a way to start building a relationship with clients for whom E&Y's consulting services had previously been priced out of reach. However, even for the multi-billion dollar organization, Ernie provided a connection to E&Y during phases of its relationship with the company where previously there had been no point of connection. 'We realized that at different times in our relationship with clients, they are information seekers, not solution seekers. Our traditional mode of delivering service – a professional in the field – cannot cost-effectively deliver information. Ernie lets our clients connect to us for information in a way that we can deliver at a price point that makes sense,' says McIlhattan.

Ernie has also changed the way that E&Y thinks about its traditional consulting services. For example, the company has almost completely shifted its delivery of software selection services to Ernie from its field consulting practice. 'We got so many questions from Ernie customers asking what software should they choose for a financial system or for enterprise resource planning, that we knew it should be the first self-service tool we put on Ernie,' offers Benson. 'The biggest challenge for our clients is not really the selection of software, it is the implementation, and that is where our field consulting practice offers the highest value. By putting the software selection tool on Ernie and offering software vendors access to 14,000 potential customers if they kept their data current, we can focus our efforts where we add the most value and still deliver a total solution to our customers.' Experimenting in partnerships with its clients has helped E&Y make better decisions about how to direct its knowledge-building efforts. Including clients in the service development process lets E&Y borrow their know-how to shape the way the company builds its own.

Think about it!

What knowledge does your organization need to experiment with in ways that fall short of direct acquisition? Consider the most pressing demands of the most important segment of your customer base. What will you need to know or know how to do in order to continue to serve these customers? List these types of knowledge and jot down ways in which you might experiment with them.

		Non-acquisition options for experimentation		
Knowledge we need to experiment with	Make do *with what people, processes, products etc. we already have?*	Borrow from		
		Consortium	*Partnership or alliance*	*Geographic location*
1				
2				
3				
4				
5				

Quick prioritization of challenge

Based on this section, how much priority should you assign to meeting this challenge?

◆ *Find alternatives to direct acquisition in order to experiment with knowledge*

Rate your organization on these two factors	Your organization's rating	Rating scale
How much does your organization NEED to respond to this challenges?	*Need*	0 No need 1 Weak need 2 Moderate need 3 Strong need 4 Burning need
What is your organization's ABILITY to respond to this challenges?	*Ability*	0 Unable 1 Slightly able 2 Partially able 3 Almost able 4 Completely able

Need ✕ *Ability* =

★ To do
Transfer your prioritization to box B on page 350.

Prioritization of challenge

(multiply the two ratings)

2 Conversion

Knowledge that is a drain on resources is converted into sources of value

Converting knowledge is our preferred way of thinking about the second dimension of divesting. Typically divesting simply means getting rid of. What happens after things and people are gone rarely enters the picture. Conversion understood only as 'getting rid of' is an activity that is hard to snuggle up to. Picture Al Dunlap, former CEO of Scott Paper Company and Sunbeam Corporation, and his axe-wielding swings through struggling corporations or the reflexive response of publicly held companies that cut loose entire classes of employees to appease investors' need for a strong quarterly showing. We are lobbying for a more comprehensive way of looking at divesting knowledge that includes not only forbearance (not acquiring in the first place), but also redirecting knowledge once its usefulness in the original context has sunk below a desired threshold.

Even when the conversion is planned for, it is almost always a painful process because it involves the dislocation of people. First, resources that have been pumped into the development or maintenance of knowledge flagged for conversion must be withdrawn. Then the knowledge must be redeployed. This can be somewhere inside the organization or outside its boundaries. If converting knowledge is not a routine activity in the organization or the industry, the pain and shock of withdrawal hit with overwhelming force.

Converting knowledge requires that organizations possess x-ray vision to peer beneath the obvious to its true potential for creating value. Sometimes knowledge has little potential to create value within the organization and needs to be shifted outside its boundaries. At other times, knowledge has only been partially utilized, and unexploited aspects can be brought to the fore, making retention possible through redeployment. At all times, the human dimension of converting knowledge must be considered.

To effectively convert knowledge so that it continues to generate value, organizations must grapple with these *challenges*.

Challenges

◆ *Recognize and dispense with the true resource drains.*

◆ *Avoid throwing out the baby with the bathwater.*

Recognize and dispense with true resource drains

The outtake valve that releases unaligned knowledge appears to be painfully stuck for most organizations until some outside event knocks it open. In part, this occurs because the cost of retention is an opportunity cost. Organizations are notoriously bad at paying attention to what they are *not* doing because they are overwhelmed by what they *are* doing. Knowledge that generates no appreciable value can be a drain solely because it requires resources to retain it. However, recognizing that it is a drain requires the subtle art of reading weak signals. Typically, the volume must be cranked up before the signals register. This can happen when the economics of an industry undergo change.

For example, the impetus for a more dynamic form of intellectual asset management in the intellectual property (IP) function occurred about a decade ago, pioneered by such innovators as Gordon Petrash, now at PricewaterhouseCoopers. The 'ah-ha' typically started with a look at the company's patents. For many businesses, patents are a source of pride. Racking up high patent counts quantified the results of innovation. The higher the count the better. However, keeping patents in force costs money. Patents that are in use deliver a revenue stream against that cost. If there is a reasonable expection that a particular patent will be used, future revenue streams can be estimated, if somewhat crudely. However, the IP group discovered that many patents were maintained without a clear connection to a current or expected business use. They represented innovations that could not be leveraged into a revenue stream for the business or any other part of the organization. It was a 'no brainer' that this stock of intellectual property needed a different management approach. First, the IP group determined that no part of the organization had an expectation of ever using these patents. Then, it began to explore other ways to derive revenues from the them – licensing, selling and even donating them. This same exercise was extended to trademarks and brands. At some point, it dawned on the IP group that the management of all of the company's intellectual assets could be evaluated in this way. Exploring this virgin territory of know-how and the least concrete forms of knowledge is the next frontier of the IP function.

Furthermore, the ability to sell products directly over the Internet has forced a reevaluation of the relationships that salespeople create and maintain – a recognizable form of intellectual capital. In the winter of 1998, Estee Lauder, a beauty products manufacturer and marketer, quietly embarked on a direct-to-the-consumer web site for one of its lines that bypassed the traditional retailer channel which utilized salespeople.[4] When a salesforce is the only way a company forges customer relationships, it is hard to see the salesforce as a resource drain. Yet using a salesforce might actually cause the organization to forgo exploring other, less resource-intensive ways of forming customer relationships. In the case of Estée Lauder, establishing a relationship with the end-user opens up the possibility of direct communication that could lead to an improved and highly refined understanding of current as well as future product preferences. Instead of trying to intuit customer preferences from such market research staples as focus groups, surveys and salesforce debriefs, the company could directly engage in an on-line one-to-one dialogue with its customers. Looking at knowledge (such as how customer relationships are formed) in terms of opportunity costs or the cost of passing up other avenues for value creation, can lead to more informed decisions about divestment.

In industries as diverse as food products and high technology, when leaders sustain their position over time, developing strong brand recognition in the marketplace, they invariably come to a crossroads. They can continue to invest in the development, production and marketing of their goods, or they can outsource various parts of the process – effectively divesting themselves of parts of their knowledge base that are not the best bets for the future. Sara Lee, a diversified consumer products company based in the United States, with an especially strong brand of snack cakes and pies, decided to exit manufacturing altogether and focus exclusively on marketing, sales and new product development. Maintaining excellence in product manufacturing would have been a drain on resources – an investment that could not provide the same return as one made in the company's solid base of marketing skills. Hewlett-Packard, the high-technology company headquartered in the United States, has reached much the same conclusion, outsourcing an increasing amount of its production to others while more intensively focusing on research and development and building its brand recognition as a way to beef up distribution channel dominance.

Another organization that has recently begun to resist the urge to do everything on its own is the US Government's Department of Defense. The DOD's notorious need for control has taken it so far afield that it has even created design specs for baking chocolate chip cookies. But since the Gulf War, when military satellites became so overloaded that the air force was reduced to flying hard copies of attack plans to waiting carriers, the Pentagon has turned to commercial sources to meet some of its needs. In a massive cultural shift, the DOD has in some cases formed joint ventures with civilian organizations to develop 'dual use' technologies for both military and commercial applications. They have even purchased simulations, such as Mäk Technologies' Spearhead, which are sold to the general public. As the DOD increases its purchase of off-the-shelf technology, it can increasingly reserve development dollars for technologies that really need to be proprietary to the military.[5]

When an organization outsources a particular function, it is in effect deciding that certain forms of knowledge, while necessary, are not significant contributors to its mission-critical knowledge base. Nevertheless, choosing an appropriate outsource partner can be critical. For example, organizations cannot afford to be cavalier about who manufactures their products. If the manufacturers they select do not achieve world-class levels of performance, their brand strength is compromised. Most companies develop very close relationships with those to whom they outsource in order to keep tabs on performance. Not being able adequately to evaluate how well knowledge is put to use can be serious, even tragic. Airlines have come under intense criticism in past years for their outsourcing practices. Some airlines outsourced important safety processes to contractors. Undetected policy and procedure differences between the outsource partners and the airlines resulted in catastrophic system failures – passenger planes exploding because inaccurately marked cargo was permitted in the hold.

Being able to see that maintaining certain parts of the knowledge base drains the organization's resources without promising a reasonable return is no easy task, as demonstrated by Kodak's Reloadable Camera Division (see Profile). However, as the globalization of markets and relentless introduction of new technologies force rapid changes in the economics of industries, it is a skill that more organizations will need to possess.

▶ PROFILE *Kodak*

Divesting knowledge that is a drain on resources clears both psychic and financial space to invest seriously in the capabilities that deliver value to customers. It blazes a clear path to long-term viability, but in the short term, raising and answering questions about value creation can be a painful process. Early in 1999, Kodak's Reloadable Camera Division completed a significant redefinition of its business following an 18-month process of asking uncomfortable questions and acting on the equally uncomfortable answers.

Facing the same challenge as many other large, engineering-intensive, branded product organizations, the leadership of Kodak's Reloadable Camera Division elected to make a 180° shift from a technology-push to a consumer-pull business. 'We compete in an industry that is fiercely competitive. Although we possessed high brand equity, expertise in optics and photosystem technologies, and sound development and manufacturing skills, we needed to find our competitive cut-through in the market,' says Karen Smith-Pilkington, General Manager, Cameras and Batteries, and Vice President, Eastman Kodak Company. 'Some of our skills and related investments did not provide visible differentiation to the consumer. Identifying where we really added value in the consumer's eyes was critical ... and it was painful. We had to rationalize our investment stream, capabilities and assets in order to align them with those of two strategic partners before we could develop and deliver improved products.'

The Reloadable Camera Division used market-based surveys, benchmarking and the House of Quality to identify consumer wants and desires. The market-based surveys asked consumers, retailers and after-sales support organizations in eight countries about the division's product portfolio, programmes and support. Benchmarking provided a view of the competitor landscape. These approaches produced irrefutable facts about what customers valued and what they did not. The House of Quality initiative gathered input from every area of the business. It analyzed the organization's value-creation chain starting with the voice of the consumer and ending with the knowledge base of the organization. The process helped the division determine which knowledge and capabilities they needed to retain and invest in and which ones they would obtain through partnering. 'The feedback was brutal and necessary,' recalls Smith-Pilkington. 'It helped us double up our investments and skills in the areas where we could really add value rather than diffusing them.'

The ruthless self-examination concluded with the Reloadable Camera Division determining that it could become a stronger player in the camera industry if it devoted resources to maintaining and extending a base of knowledge that included:

◆ optics innovation

◆ optimized feature configuration

◆ design for efficient manufacturing

◆ a deep understanding of the customer to define the product category.

'This decision helped us determine what knowledge had to remain in the business and what could be sourced from a partner,' says Mark Schneider, Director of Research, Development and Manufacturing. 'At the same time, we believed it was essential to retain some knowledge of all aspects of the camera business inside the division or we would not be well-positioned to select strong partners and bring value to our side of the relationship.' The Engineering Knowledge Database which contains key notes on design points and general business-related information is one way in which the division holds onto some of the knowledge that it needs to evaluate and support partners. Identifying and proactively mentoring a new type of engineer for future design and commercialization leadership positions is another. 'In the past, we promoted individuals who over time had become experts in a specific technology or group of technologies,' remarks Schneider. 'Now we are structuring assignments to develop people who understand how the interrelationships among camera technologies create value for consumers. This calls for systems integration expertise – a coupling of broad technology skills and an understanding of consumer market fundamentals. The result is a new type of engineer who is much better suited to working effectively with our partners.'

Think about it!

Few organizations spend much time thinking about what they are not doing. Fewer still have thought this way about organizational knowledge. Get yourself started down the road of exploring opportunity costs related to the way your organization maintains or builds its knowledge base.

Start by listing what most people in your organization would say are five forms of non-critical knowledge that your organization currently supports. To help you identify these forms of knowledge, think about what your organization absolutely has to know how to do and know about to serve customers. Then, recall activities the people in your work group complain about as taking time away from their real work. For example, salespeople often complain about having to provide information about prospecting that never goes anywhere. If it really does not, then maintaining this knowledge is non-critical. Finally, jot down the major ways in which your organization supports the development and maintenance of this non-critical knowledge and how involvement in these activities precludes other options.

	Options taken and not taken	
Top five forms of non-critical knowledge that we currently support	*What we do currently to maintain this form of knowledge*	*Paths we are unable to pursue because of our current activities*
1		
2		
3		
4		
5		

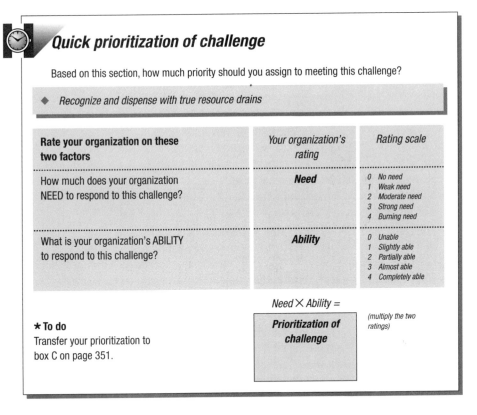

★ To do
Transfer your prioritization to box C on page 351.

Avoid throwing out the baby with the bathwater

Certainly some knowledge should be shown the door. But sometimes knowledge reaches the door precipitously, before its full value to the organization has been ascertained. By the time the organization realizes that valuable knowledge has been let go – usually in the form of people with particular expertise, tacit knowledge, relationships or understanding of internal processes – it is too late to do anything about it. Getting the horse before the cart is a challenge given today's highly mobile workforce, but organizations such as Harvard Pilgrim Health Care are finding novel approaches to retain mission-critical knowledge (see Profile).

Not too long ago, people could count on lifetime employment when they joined an organization. In return for their loyalty, commitment and contribution, they were virtually guaranteed a job that would pay them a living wage or better. Regardless of the changes that the organization might undergo – launching or exiting businesses, opening new locations and closing others, expanding or contracting its position in the value chain – employees could take their talents and skills and put them to use somewhere in the organization.

Oddly enough, with the increasing emphasis on knowledge, some organizations are once again offering something close to this traditional arrangement. At the Rover Group, a manufacturer of cars and off-road vehicles based in the United Kingdom and part of the BMW Group since 1994, employees who commit to a career with the organization can count on a corresponding commitment from the organization to help them develop it. Having retrenched from a workforce of almost 200,000 to about 40,000 in the early 1990s, Rover Group leadership believed that to succeed the organization would have to boost the level of employee contribution to organizational performance. Recognizing that employees who had just lived through seeing 160,000 of their colleagues let go would need evidence of the company's good faith, Rover Group cast a wide net over the entire group of employees. Rather than focusing on specific task-related skills to determine who receives career support, everyone who binds themselves to Rover Group with a commitment to self-development can expect the organization to go the distance on their behalf. Almost a decade later, that commitment still stands. Today, Rover Group is poised to leverage the goodwill and dedication of its employees to achieve levels of technical excellence and flexibility demanded by its affiliation with the BMW Group.

Canadian Imperial Bank of Commerce's Employment Continuity Policy uses a similar approach for dealing with employees who are impacted by changes in the bank's strategic direction. This policy is firmly grounded in the practical. Like many banking institutions, CIBC had been reconfigured several times in response to major structural changes in the financial services industry. Rethinking strategic direction led to divesting certain segments of the business and the people who worked in them. The bank tracked its impacted workers and discovered that a very high percentage of them found jobs quickly at a significantly higher salary level. Talent, experience and history were walking out the door and going on to create value for other organizations. CIBC lacked the tools to capture and consolidate this base of knowledge and redeploy it within the bank. This inability to peer beneath the surface of current work to core capabilities troubled the bank. The Employment Continuity Policy was enacted to fill this void. Canadian regulations specify that displaced workers must be given three months' notice before their employment is terminated or be paid the equivalent in severance. CIBC created a unique entitlement for all employees with satisfactory performance evaluations. They are entitled to an additional period of up to six months' paid employment during which their full-time job is to find a new job elsewhere in the bank. Their manager provides them space, phones and a computer while CIBC offers workshops in resumé writing, interviewing and job search techniques. The Employment Continuity Policy gives CIBC the first crack at these highly valuable employees before they shop themselves around to other markets. In fiscal year 1998 a period of non-stop changes in the banking industry, CIBC maintained a 50% redeployment rate for its impacted employees.

Rover Group and CIBC base their decisions to redeploy employees internally on the general principle that committed employees are a source of competitive advantage. Other organizations focus on a more narrowly defined business case to redeploy an employee whose original role no longer exists. The business case can be made from the top down or it can come from the outside in. At McKinsey & Co., a premier consulting firm headquartered in the United States, there was a long-standing 'up or out' policy that made no room for those who, despite their valuable knowledge, could not commit to the lifestyle required to climb the ladder towards the gold ring of partnership. But the firm began to realize that it was haemorrhaging potentially committed people who delivered significant value to the firm and it developed alternative career paths for some of these individuals. At the same time, as clients began demanding that the consultants who served them had access to the entire knowledge base of the organization, it became essential to develop a group that could meet this need. These two trends converged, resulting in the Rapid Response Network, a special unit of senior consultants who helped connect field professionals with the information they needed (see Profile on page 37). Members of the Rapid Response Network were not on a partner track and might eventually have left the firm. Creating positions for them meant that McKinsey was able to retain experienced professionals with both content expertise and the expertise to access the firm's knowledge base.

A similar story exists at Motorola, the technology giant based in Schaumburg, Illinois, where the finance group is renowned for its two-day close of the corporate books and its increasing reliance on business self-audits. If the finance group is not spending all of its time closing the books and conducting audits, why not reduce its numbers? The company did not jump to this obvious response. Instead, Motorola has been able to tap its finance group as strategic business partners rather than as 'number crunchers'.

The ramifications of wiping out a class of employee are far reaching and have come back to haunt just about every organization that has gone this route. To fully enter the managed care market, Aetna Inc., a major health insurer in the United States, acquired an aggressive health maintenance organization, US Healthcare, in the summer of 1996. The new entity, Aetna/US Healthcare, found meshing business processes and cultures difficult for many reasons. However, at the heart of many problems was a lack of understanding about how people mattered to the company. The CEO, Richard Huber, was quoted as saying: 'I am the first one to admit it: We had some serious service degradation. We suffered more pain than we expected, and some of it was self-inflicted. ... In cutting loose so many skilled people so soon... we screwed up.'[6] Trying to coax savings from the claims-processing system, the company installed a new technology system while reducing medical management offices from 57 to 11 and claims-processing centres from 44 to 25. More than 4,000 long-term Aetna employees were let go as a result of these efforts. The remaining claims-processing employees were mostly newcomers who could handle only 3–5 claims per hour compared with the dismissed veterans who processed up to 17 per hour using the old system. At the medical management offices, relationships that had sped up decision making were reduced to transactions, many more of which were needed to reach closure.

Some of the most important types of knowledge are embedded in people. When knowledge that is inseparable from people is converted without regard to morale, a chilling message is sent to those who remain: We are capable of treating you in exactly the same way. As Joe Cothrel, Vice President of Research at

Participate.com has observed: 'Businesspeople would universally view opening a window and tossing out a $6,000 PC as an unacceptable waste of corporate assets, but they cut loose employees in whom they have invested much more with very little consideration and almost no horror at the waste of it.' When knowledge is converted taking full measure of the impact on people, however, the gains can be astronomical. Planning ahead about people means that companies will truly have to understand what resources they have before tossing what at first glance might seem like dirty bathwater.

PROFILE ▶ *Harvard Pilgrim Health Care*

'Conventional wisdom says work hard to retain people,' muses Debra Speight, CIO at Harvard Pilgrim Health Care. 'But our industry turns conventional wisdom upside down. Average industry turnover is 15–20%. Despite our ongoing efforts to maintain an attractive organizational culture, we face the challenge of being a not-for-profit in an industry where large sums of money are regularly thrown at talent. It hit me one day that if I couldn't do any more to retain people, I at least needed to retain their knowledge.'

Harvard Pilgrim Health Care (HPHC) is a 4,800-employee health maintenance organization that serves 1.3 million members with 20,000 medical services providers throughout New England. Together with its sister organization, Harvard Vanguard, a group of wholly owned medical practices staffed by 4,300 employees, HPHC generates revenues of $3 billion US. Not surprisingly, its information technology group numbers a healthy 500 people. The group manages all of the information flows between the two organizations, as well as among members and providers. HPHC's IT group has gained notice for an unusual programme launched in 1998 by its CIO, Debra Speight: it pays 'knowledge bounties' to departing employees. When employees decide to leave, they are asked to fill out detailed questionnaires about what knowledge they needed to do their jobs and what procedures or tricks of the trade they used most often. Exiting employees then present their responses to a panel, made up of their peers as well as senior executives, which judges what the knowledge is worth. Employees can win awards of between $1,000 and $5,000. The point is to demonstrate to employees that the company wants to know what they know.

As the knowledge bounties programme develops, HPHC continues to refine its understanding of what knowledge is truly valuable. Speight has come to believe that what HPHC most needs to learn from departing employees are the stories they tell about how work gets done in their groups. When a director reporting to Speight announced his departure, she personally spent time listening to his views about the workstyles and habits of key individuals in his department. She probed deeply into the politics and interpersonal dynamics of the team and made sure that his successor also heard these stories. 'In the past, we might have paid a knowledge bounty to have a departing employee untangle the spaghetti of our code,' reflects Speight. 'But the Y2K problem has had the positive side effect of forcing us to straighten out all of our confusing code, not just the code pertaining to the year 2000. It also helped us see that knowledge about such mechanics is not what really hurts when we lose people. What hurts is the loss of the insight they bring to management that coaxes the best performance out of others.'

While some may baulk at the idea of paying a bonus to employees whose intention is leaving the company, Speight believes that this is a knee-jerk reaction that changes upon reflection. From her perspective, knowledge bounties are just another form of recognition awards. While acknowledging that a fine line separates knowledge bounties as recognition awards from knowledge bounties as an entitlement, Speight is a pragmatist. 'We pay to retain people,' she asserts. 'If we can't retain the individual, why do we shrink from the idea of paying for their knowledge?'

Think about it!

Redeployment of people is one of the best ways to avoid throwing out the baby with the bathwater. Use the following table to think about the conversion potential of groups or forms of knowledge that you are planning to divest. Consider whether they possess untapped value for your organization and should receive a second look. Place a checkmark in the box of the most likely redeployment possibility for each group or form of knowledge and jot down a few notes about how to redeploy them in the space provided.

Groups or forms of knowledge that we are planning to divest	Redeployment possibilities				Notes about how to redeploy
	Some individuals but not as a group	All individuals but not as a group	Sub-set of the group	Entire group	
1	☐	☐	☐	☐	
2	☐	☐	☐	☐	
3	☐	☐	☐	☐	
4	☐	☐	☐	☐	
5	☐	☐	☐	☐	

Quick prioritization of challenge

Based on this section, how much priority should you assign to meeting this challenge?

◆ *Avoid throwing out the baby with the bathwater*

Rate your organization on these two factors	Your organization's rating	Rating scale
How much does your organization NEED to respond to this challenge?	**Need**	0 No need 1 Weak need 2 Moderate need 3 Strong need 4 Burning need
What is your organization's ABILITY to respond to this challenge?	**Ability**	0 Unable 1 Slightly able 2 Partially able 3 Almost able 4 Completely able

Need × Ability =

★ To do

Transfer your prioritization to box D on page 352.

Prioritization of challenge

(multiply the two ratings)

Notes

1   'Building the new economy', Eric Randsell, *Fast Company*, December 1998.

2   'Pulling the plug', Bernard Wysocki, Jr., *The Wall Street Journal*, April 30 1998, p. A1.

3   'Clusters and the new economics of competition', Michael Porter, *Harvard Business Review*, November–December 1998.

4   'Clinique solves web dilemma with quiet ads', Tara Parker-Pope, *The Wall Street Journal*, November 12 1998, p. B1.

5   'The Pentagon finally learns how to shop', Edward Robinson, *Fortune*, December 21 1998.

6   'Old line Aetna adopts managed-care tactics and stirs a backlash', Lucette Lagnado, *The Wall Street Journal*, July 29 1998, p. A1.

Agenda for action: Divest

The action steps presented in the Agenda for action come from the ideas suggested in this chapter. If you believe that your organization needs to focus on improving how well it formally divests knowledge, this template and its suggested action steps are one way to get started.

The Agenda for action is organized in the same way as this chapter. Each imperative and its accompanying challenges are clustered together. Action steps are suggested for each challenge based on the text and case studies. You decide which action steps make sense for your organization and use the empty space to scribble in any additional ideas that come to mind.

Before you begin, make sure that you have transferred your prioritization ratings for each challenge. The prioritization ratings will remind you whether you believed that the challenge was worth pursuing. The maximum prioritization rating is 16, the minimum is 0.

How you use the prioritization ratings is up to you. For example, depending on the range of prioritization ratings, you may decide to ignore all challenges below a minimum threshold and focus only on those challenges above it. Or you may decide that everything that is not 0 deserves at least some thought. We invite you to use this Agenda for action as a place to start acting on your knowledge management priorities.

Agenda for action

1 Forbearance

Unnecessary knowledge is not acquired in the first place

A

Disciminate between forms of knowledge that can be leveraged and those that are limited

Prioritization rating

Action step	Who should be involved	My first 'to do'
Gather information about our previous investment and divestment decisions over a specific time frame. Interview the person or teams who participated in these decisions to see what factors were important in making these decisions and whether, with hindsight, they believe that the decisions were sound.		
Catalogue our mission-critical knowledge, thinking in terms of important elements of our knowledge base. Use the Think about it! exercise for this challenge as a template. Keep the list business based so that operating management understands it. Circulate the list to obtain consensus and clarify language.		
Recirculate the list compiled in step 2 asking a cross-section of managers in the organization to separate the knowledge types into two categories – limited and leverageable – where the latter refers to knowledge that stretches our capabilities or builds our knowledge base. Ask them to describe their rationale for assigning each knowledge type to these categories.		
Identify an interested operating unit and experiment with this process in an upcoming business planning cycle to determine its usefulness in resource allocation decisions.		
Other:		

B

Find alternatives to direct acquisition in order to experiment with knowledge

Prioritization rating

Action step	Who should be involved	My first 'to do'
Gather information on past acquisitions and analyze them based on our need to add skills or know-how for the overall business or some segment of it. Determine whether we explored other alternatives for acquiring this knowledge and the rationale for the decisions.		
Canvass managers to find out how they make acquisition decisions. Compare decision-making criteria to look for patterns. Find out if we have an organizational policy. If so, compare current practices to the policy. Document gaps, especially those where practice improves upon policy.		
Find out what acquisitions we are currently considering, which ones we have abandoned and why. To what extent are we exploring non-acquisition options to gain needed knowledge?		
Find out how we currently experiment with knowledge using alternatives to direct acquisitions: a) apprenticeships outside the organization, b) alliances, c) membership in industry research consortia, trade associations, etc.		
Identify an interested operating unit and explicitly incorporate the non-direct acquisition approach into the upcoming planning cycle.		
Other:		

2 Conversion

Knowledge that is a drain on resources is converted into sources of value

Recognize and dispense with true resource drains

C

Prioritization rating

Action step	Who should be involved	My first 'to do'
Use the Think about it! exercise for this challenge to develop a list of non-critical knowledge that the organization routinely maintains. Circulate the list to obtain additional information and achieve consensus.		
Convene a group from different businesses and customer segments to discuss how current approaches for maintaining this non-critical knowledge precludes taking action in different ways (i.e. conduct opportunity cost analysis). Consider whether any of the options not being pursued should be experimented with in the future.		
Other:		

D

Avoid throwing out the baby with the bathwater

Prioritization rating

Action step	Who should be involved	My first 'to do'
Review current policies for terminating employees and groups to determine the extent of our concern with the impact on remaining personnel and on the ex-employee. Review past decisions involving terminations to see if they included an attempt to transition the employee or group elsewhere.		
Canvass managers to learn about actual practice and their awareness of policies. Document gaps, especially those where practice improves upon policy.		
Convene a group from different businesses, functions and processes to use information from the review to discuss how existing groups could fill knowledge gaps if their roles were altered or transformed. Document the business case for redeployment.		
Other:		

10 Looking ahead: management through a knowledge lens

Once you start down the knowledge management path, it is easy to get mesmerized, focusing on the process for its own sake, drawing a line between those who get it and those who do not. But the bottom line is that the goals of knowledge management are the same as those of management: long-term organizational viability through the consistent generation of stakeholder value. Knowledge management provides a new lens through which the organization and the management process itself can be viewed. It brings into focus different aspects of the organization which in turn impact both *what* gets managed and *how* it gets managed.

Taking a look through a knowledge lens, what do we see?

The role of the leader shifts from being the source of knowledge to managing the process through which people use knowledge

The complexity of today's organizations has revolutionized the role of the leader. In simpler times it made sense to direct organizational knowledge flows upwards, because up was where decisions were made. In this model, the leader was the expert. Unfortunately, the traditional model has failed to deliver consistent results. In today's organizations, expertise is highly specialized and more likely to reside in the front-line worker who operates at the point at which customer meets company.

Where does this leave those who sit at the top of today's organizations? Some have argued that in the knowledge-driven era, these leaders should no longer sit at the top of the organization, but rather in the centre. Regardless of how you envision organizational design, the role of the leader has definitely changed. From a knowledge perspective, true leadership hinges on an ability to grasp the value-creating potential of the organization's knowledge base. The leader must not only set strategy, but also communicate it in a compelling fashion. Neither setting strategy nor communicating it is possible without managing knowledge flows.

The shift from *being* the source of all knowledge flows to *managing* the network of knowledge flows lies at the heart of new leadership. Today's leaders must pay attention to environments rather than rules; coach rather than tell; ask the right questions rather than provide the right answers. The result is a more distributed decision-making system, in which all members can and must participate. Leadership through a knowledge lens has far more to do with sharing the burden than it does with playing Atlas and carrying the weight of the world on one's shoulders.

Employees look like customers and customers look like employees

It used to be that employees were recruited to join companies for the long haul, often for life. It used to be that when a company developed a new product or service, development took place inside the company. It used to be that training was an investment companies made in their employees. Customers, on the other hand, although the source of organizational sustenance, were clearly outside the enterprise. They could offer feedback and the organization would be happy to take it under advisement. While it was important to keep them happy, if they left, others would take their place. Through a knowledge lens, the landscape of employees and customers looks quite different. The most noticeable change is that the language used to describe employees and customers has become almost interchangeable. Employees must evaluate switching costs when considering new jobs and companies now actively recruit their customers.

Faced with the high cost of pushing new employees up the learning curve, organizations are offering a bevy of attractive incentives to retain their best employees – those who are besieged by offers from others on a regular basis. Perks ranging from on-site day care to flextime are used to attract and retain desirable employees in the same way that airlines grant special privileges to their frequent flying customers. Access to the organization's knowledge base as a means of boosting individual performance levels has been added to the mix of employee benefits. These perks and benefits become switching costs that employees must factor into their plans to change jobs, just as customers must factor these costs into changing suppliers.

Customers look very different through a knowledge lens as well. Companies selectively recruit customers with whom they can enter into long-term relationships. They evaluate customers on the basis of whether a long-term relationship will stretch the organization and grow its knowledge base. They even enter into partnerships with customers to cocreate products or services, effectively extending organizational boundaries to bring the customers inside.

These trends reflect a new understanding that the right questions are not 'Who is the customer?' or 'Who is the employee?' but 'How do we attract and cultivate knowledge that will create long-term value for this organization?'

Freedom of choice characterizes the relationship between the organization and its members

Just as employers have begun to view the task of recruiting employees through a knowledge lens, so have employees begun to take a similar look at the organizations for which they choose to work. For those who make their bread by virtue of their brains – and that is getting to be quite a large percentage of the working population—organizations are the place both to improve and strut one's stuff.

Organizations offer a variety of resources that help individuals increase their knowledge equity: training, challenging projects, access to other knowledge workers, databases, networks and libraries. They also offer employees something that is difficult to get as an outsider: a stage. The organizational stage (or the organizational brand) determines the audience before whom knowledge workers can perform. The better the stage, the better the audience. Access to both resources and audience increasingly influences the decision of where to work. In return for access, workers contribute individual know-how that generates value on behalf of the organization.

Clearly it is in the organization's best interest to support this virtuous cycle. As intellectual capital becomes a larger and larger percentage of the base from which value is created, organizations own less and less of what sustains them. If the best knowledge workers can pick and choose their employers, they become similar to volunteers who decide where to expend their discretionary energy. Envisioning employees as volunteers dramatically alters the traditional employer–employee relationship. Pay and benefits become simply the cost of competing for talent. Organizations need to look beyond these to the intangibles that attract and retain volunteers: environment, community and values.

The boundaries of the organization have begun to blur

Despite the fact that two of the major objectives of knowledge management are customer value creation and sustaining competitive advantage, when organizations first adopt knowledge management practices, they typically choose to start with activities that fall far short of achieving these goals. Most initiatives focus on internal transfer of best practices in an effort to minimize reinventing the wheel – the low-hanging fruit of the knowledge management tree. The benefits are obvious, measurable and consistent with current process improvement practices. Internal knowledge sharing may positively impact customers through reduced costs and increased speed to market, but customers have little to no direct influence over how this is done. They are still on the outside, waiting for benefits to pass through to them. Internal knowledge sharing may also open a window of competitive opportunity, but the window does not stay open very long. The kinds of improvements that result from internal knowledge sharing are easily copied by competitors in a relatively short period of time.

However, when organizations take the leap and include not only customers, but also competitors in their knowledge management framework by bringing them inside the boundaries of the organization, the possibilities for true breakthroughs are enhanced. True knowledge sharing transcends the endless recycling of what the organization already knows and forms what Nonaka and Takeuchi called a self-sustaining spiral of value creation. When customers are welcomed into the organizational system, true competitive advantage can be forged by weaving together the basis for long-term relationships that are difficult to unravel with a single price concession from another organization. Bringing customers inside the organizational boundary may cause some slight discomfort, but bringing competitors in triggers a case of the hives for most companies. Yet, it is increasingly the case that industry viability is best sustained by collectively joining forces in the pre-competitive space. Competition is an empty promise if the industry itself lacks a future. The knowledge management lens blurs the edges of the organization to find new ways to create and sustain value.

Measurement and valuation emerge from the black box

Most people in organizations view measurement as the unpleasant last hoop through which good ideas are made to jump before getting the go ahead. Unpleasant though it may be, most people in organizations are familiar with organizational performance measurement. Input and output metrics are part of the corporate vocabulary. But the fact that valuation is not the same as measurement comes as news to many and what exactly valuation might be is unclear. When arguing for a knowledge management programme, people are tempted to throw up their hands and insist that leadership take it on faith because measurement is out of the question. Valuation does not even enter the argument.

Get ready for change as measurement and valuation emerge from black box economic theories to become standard management tools, spurred by the need to measure and value the costs and benefits of managing knowledge. Organizational performance measurement is fast becoming the land of leading indicators, as organizations invent new ways to predict financial outcomes. Vectors and velocity have taken their place alongside point-in-time, and pictures in the form of strange new graphs like spider charts are replacing columns of numbers as organizations seek ways to envision how they are extracting value from their complete resource base. The formerly obscure science of valuation is moving out of the realm of economics and intellectual property management to become part of the basic organizational decision-making process as managers are challenged to place a monetary value on the benefits of investing in knowledge. Knowledge management is forcing the tools of measurement and valuation into the hands of the operating manager who must come to grips with making investments in and extracting value from knowledge.

Meaning making is a high art form

Access to information is only a small part of the knowledge management equation, and it can be worse than useless if people either do not understand what they get or cannot find what they need. On the information technology side, demand will continue to skyrocket for applications that help users sift through and organize information as well as add value to it. Some expert systems are already smart enough to create maps of the knowledge that people *might* want to access based on the knowledge that they are aware they need to seek. Intelligent agents help people shop for the best deals the Internet has to offer. Sophisticated data-mining techniques can ferret out trends and connections based on masses of facts and figures that it would be impossible for the human mind to process.

Yet making sense of this infoglut, some of which is straightforward, some of which is heavily nuanced or context dependent, is still beyond the reach of most technology. The growing focus on knowledge as a source of value will be accompanied by a corresponding demand for 'infomediaries' – people who are not necessarily content experts but who can do much of the initial sorting, organizing, summarizing, notifying and connecting of people to information. These human filters – the librarians, the knowledge managers, the researchers and the writers – will help control the information floodgates so that organizations are not cast adrift in a meaningless sea.

Middle managers look like a good idea after all

Now that the dust has settled on the whirlwind housecleanings of the late 1980s and early 1990s, quite a few organizations have found some gaping holes. In cases where skilled surgery might have been the better alternative, many organizations took an axe to what looked like bloated bureaucracies. With the hindsight of a knowledge lens, however, middle management was not always a useless layer that kept the front line from talking to the executives. Quite often it was the communications link that connected the two. With their expertise in project management, understanding of how the organization really worked, and preservation of institutional memory, many middle managers are sorely missed. Just witness the number of former employees companies have hired back as independent contractors.

As organizations begin to restore some of these positions, they will do so with a revitalized view of the role of middle managers as orchestrators of knowledge flows. In addition to the top-down, bottom-up and inside-outside task of translating strategy into action and action into meaningful information that impacts strategy, middle managers will increasingly be asked to look *across* the organization. Their success will hinge on the ability to facilitate communication across traditional and process silos, leverage resources, transfer best practices, identify synergies and encourage knowledge reuse.

Trust is a valuable currency

One result of freer information flows is that more people have access to what was once considered proprietary and only available to the organizational elite. When a company bares its soul to workers – whether through open book management, frank discussions of strategy or a sharing of trade secrets – trust is essential. Paradoxically, the very act of treating people as trustworthy engenders trust.

Trust plays an important role from the perspective of employees as well. Knowledge management practices have created a tension between organizations, which are seeking to get people to 'contribute what they know', and workers, who know that 'what they know' keeps them employed. Unless employees can trust that knowledge sharing actually increases rather than decreases their value to the organization, the best laid knowledge management plans will fail. Organizations that view their employees through a knowledge lens understand that dealing with people openly and honestly is the best route to gaining access to what they can never truly own – individual knowledge.

IT systems are a context for connection

When the first computer network was invented more than two decades ago, it was intended for remote access and manipulation of data. Few people predicted the true killer app – E-mail, the ability to communicate with other people virtually. Knowledge bases and rapid Internet access aside, from a knowledge perspective, technology triumphs in its ability to connect more people in more ways than ever before. E-mail, intranets, discussion forums, chat rooms – they all make the truly networked organization possible. Not only can an engineer from Sweden communicate freely with her counterpart in Venezuela, but all customers, suppliers and outside parties can be brought into the tent with relative ease.

Leveraging knowledge across the organization is one way in which people choose to describe the goal of knowledge management. But simply making information available through electronic networks hardly amounts to leveraging it. Leveraging comes from conversation, the back and forth questioning, the easier access to expertise and the broadened sense of membership in different communities that virtual communication makes possible.

Opposites blend and are the better for it

Knowledge management today has a decidedly schizophrenic character. It caroms from the hard-edged bits and bytes of information technology to the softly shaped contours of interpersonal dynamics. People naturally gravitate toward one pole or the other. It is hard to tell that they are talking about the same thing. It is even harder for them to see that they are. To help knowledge management practitioners back up far enough to see that they are all on the same playing field, a new way of talking about the organizational system has been advanced: the concept of organizational ecology.

When the organization is understood as an ecological system, it becomes possible to hold a both/and rather than an either/or position with respect to knowledge management. Information technology modifies human behaviour at the same time that human behaviour modifies information technology. Failures fertilize success. Trust and measurement both contribute to system success, each one is ascendant at different times. Rationality and leaps of faith are not mutually exclusive options. Peering through a knowledge lens at the brave new organization we will see the social anthropologist join hands with the software application analyst.

Every lens provides a different perspective. We believe that the knowledge lens is a useful addition for organizations as they strive to make sense of the world we live in today.

Selected bibliography

The bibliography that follows is a highly unscientific sampling of the books that sit on our shelves and the shelves of colleagues who have contributed to the thinking in this *Fieldbook*. Taken together, these books create a picture of the wide range of disciplines that are brought to bear on the emerging field of knowledge management.

Foundation books

Drucker, Peter. *Post Capitalist Society*. New York: HarperCollins, 1993.

Nonaka, Ikujiro and Takeuchi, Hirotaka. *The Knowledge-Creating Company: How Japanese Companies Create the Dynamics of Innovation*. Oxford: Oxford University Press, 1995.

Polyani, Michael. *The Tacit Dimension*. London: Routledge & Kegan Paul, 1966.

Information management

Davenport, Thomas H. *Information Ecology: Mastering the Information and Knowledge Environment*. Oxford: Oxford University Press, 1997.

Tufte, Edward R. *The Visual Display of Quantitative Information*. Chesire, Connecticut: Graphics Press, 1983.

Tufte, Edward Rolfe. *Envisioning Information*. Chesire, Connecticut: Graphics Press, 1990.

Knowledge management

Allee, Verna. *The Knowledge Evolution: Expanding Organizational Intelligence*. Boston: Butterworth-Heinemann, 1997.

Amidon, Debra M. *Innovation Strategy for the Knowledge Economy: The Ken Awakening*. Boston: Butterworth-Heinemann, 1997.

Davenport, Thomas H. and Prusak, Laurence. *Working Knowledge: How Organizations Manage What They Know*. Boston: Harvard Business School Press, 1998.

O'Dell, Carla, Grayson, C. Jackson, Jr. and Essaides, Nilly. *If We Only Knew What We Know: The Transfer of Internal Knowledge and Best Practice*. New York: Free Press, 1998.

Stewart, Thomas. *Intellectual Capital: The New Wealth of Organizations*. New York: Currency/Doubleday, 1997.

Learning

Senge, Peter M. *The Fifth Discipline: The Art and Practice of the Learning Organization*. New York: Bantam Doubleday Dell Publishing Group, 1990.

Senge, Peter M., Kleiner, Art, Roberts, Charlotte, Ross, Richard B. and Smith, Brian J. *The Fifth Discipline Fieldbook: Strategies and Tools for Building a Learning Organization*. New York: Bantam Doubleday Dell Publishing Group, 1994.

Measurement

Edvinsson, Leif and Malone, Michael. *Intellectual Capital: Realizing Your Company's True Value by Finding its Hidden Brainpower*. New York: HarperCollins, 1997.

Sveiby, Karl Erik. *The New Organizational Wealth: Managing and Measuring Knowledge-Based Assets*. San Francisco: Berrett-Koehler Publishers, 1997.

Organizational structure

Handy, Charles. *The Age of Unreason*. Boston: Harvard Business School Press, 1989.

Quinn, James Brian. *The Intelligent Enterprise: A Knowledge and Service-Based Paradigm for Industry*. New York: Free Press, 1992.

Wheatley, Margaret J. *Leadership and the New Science: Learning about Organization from an Orderly Universe*. San Francisco: Berrett-Koehler Publishers, 1992.

Stakeholder relationships

Hall, Brian. *Values Shift*. Rockport, Massachusetts: Twin Lights Publishers, 1995.

Savage, Charles. *Fifth Generation Management: Co-creating through Virtual Enterprising, Dynamic Teaming and Knowledge Networking* (rev. edn). Boston: Butterworth-Heinemann, 1996.

Valuation

Sullivan, Patrick H. *Profiting from Intellectual Capital: Extracting Value from Innovation*. New York: John Wiley & Sons, 1998.

Smith, Gordon V. and Parr, Russell L. *Valuation of Intellectual Property and Intangible Assets* (2nd edn, 1998 supplement). New York: John Wiley & Sons, 1998.

Index